The European Heritage in Economics and the Social Sciences

Jürgen Georg Backhaus

For other titles published in this series, go to
www.springer.com/series/5902

Jürgen Georg Backhaus
Editor

The State as Utopia

Continental Approaches

Springer

Editor
Prof.Dr. Jürgen Georg Backhaus
Universität Erfurt
Fak. Staatswissenschaften Lehrst.
Finanzwissenschaft/Finanzsoziologie
Nordhäuser Str. 63
99089 Erfurt Thüringen
Germany
juergen.backhaus@uni-erfurt.de

ISBN 978-1-4419-7499-0 e-ISBN 978-1-4419-7500-3
DOI 10.1007/978-1-4419-7500-3
Springer New York Dordrecht Heidelberg London

Printed on acid-free paper

Springer is part of Springer Science+Business Media (www.springer.com)

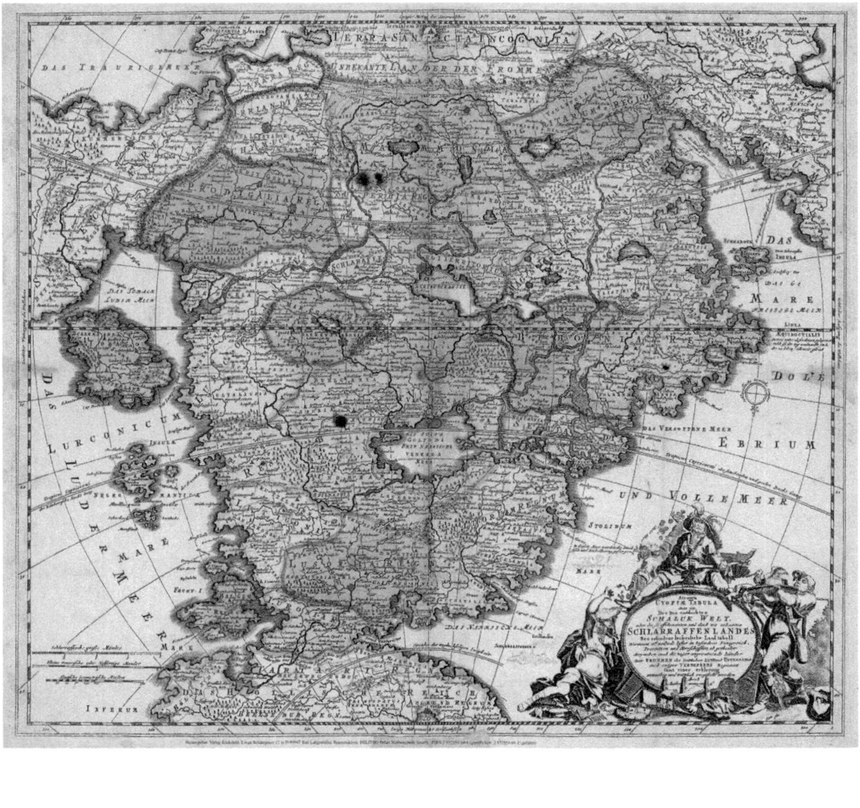

TERRA SANCTA INCOGNITA
DAS TRAURIGE MEER
PRODIGALIA REG
DAS
MARE
LINEA
AEQUINOCTIALIS
DO L'E
DAS VERSOFFENE MEER
EBRIUM
UND VOLLE MEER
STOLIDUM
LURCONICUM
DAS
LUDER MARE
MEER
INFERUS
UTOPIÆ TABULA
SCHALCK WELT.
SCHLARRAFFENLANDES

Contents

Introduction 1
Jürgen Georg Backhaus

A Demand-Revealing Utopia 3
Nicolaus Tideman

Economic, City Planning and Environmental Proposals by Plato in the City of Atlantis and of the Laws 7
Christos P. Baloglou

Property in a Utopian State, Informed by Ideas of Pufendorf and Locke 11
Nicolaus Tideman

John Stuart Mill and the Utopian Tradition 19
Michael R. Montgomery

The State as Utopia: Some Thoughts on Theocracy 35
Gerrit Meijer

Justi's Concrete Utopia 41
Hartmuth Becker

The Kingdom of Ophir – A "Realistic Utopia" 57
Günther Chaloupek

Is Montaigne a Utopian? 67
Marcel van Meerhaeghe

Labour in Utopian Socialism 77
Hans Frambach

Iambulus' "Sun State" and T. Campanella's "Civitas Solis": Some Comparative Parallels and Links of Two Utopias 89
Christos P. Baloglou

Developing Society According to Man's Development 115
Arno Mong Daastøl and Johannes Michael Hanel

The Utopian Element in the Formation of Doctrines on the State in German "Staatswissenschaften" 161
Karl-Heinz Schmidt

Utopia: Johann Peter Süßmilch and the Divine Order 183
Gerhard Scheuerer

Eugen Dühring and Post-Utopian Socialism 191
E. James Gay

Index 205

Contributors

Jürgen G. Backhaus
University of Erfurt, Krupp Chair in Public Finance and Fiscal Sociology, Nordhäuser Str. 63, 99089, Erfurt, Germany
juergen.backhaus@uni-erfurt.de

Christos P. Baloglou
Hellenis Telecommunications Organizations Athens, Messenias 14 & Gr. Lamprakis 143 42 Nea Philadelphia, Attikis
Greececbaloglou@ote

Hartmuth Becker
Free University of Berlin, Kaiserswerther Str. 16-18, 14195, Berlin, Germany
Hartmuth.Becker@t-online.de

Günther Chaloupek
Chamber of Labour, Prinz-Eugen-Straße 20-221041, Vienna, Austria
Guenther.CHALOUPEK@akwien.at

Arno Mong Daastoel
Utsiktveien 341410, Kolbotn, Norway
amd@daastol.com

Hans Frambach
Department of Economics, M. 13.16, University of Wuppertal, Gaußstraße 20, 42097, Wuppertal, Germany
Frambach@wiwi.uni-wuppertal.de

James Gay
University of Erfurt, Krupp Chair in Public Finance and Fiscal Sociology, Nordhäuser Str. 6399089, Erfurt, Germany
edwardjamesgay@googlemail.com

Johannes Hanel
Goethestraße 23, 99817, Eisenach, Germany
hanelq@googlemail.com

Marcel vanMeerhaeghe
Kriekenbergdreef 21, 9831, Deurle, Belgium
hvm@klaproos.be

Gerrit Meijer
Larixlaan 31231 BL, Nieuw-Loosdrecht, The Netherlands
g.meijer@hetnet.nl

Michael Montgomery
School of Economics, The University of Maine, 230 Stevens Hall,
Orono, ME, USA
michael.montgomery@umit.maine.edu

Gerhard Scheuerer
Leitender Ministerialdirektor, University of Erfurt, Krupp Chair in Public Finance and Fiscal Sociology, Nordhäuser Str. 63, 99089, Erfurt, Germany
gerhard.scheuerer@t-online.de

Karl-Heinz Schmidt
Department of Economics, University of Paderborn, Warburger Str. 10033098, Paderborn, Germany
Karl-Heinz_Schmidt@wiwi.uni-paderborn.de

Nicolaus Tideman
Department of Economics, Virginia Polytechnic Institute and State University, 3021 Pamplin Hall (0316)Blacksburg, VA, 24061, USA
ntideman@vt.edu

Introduction

Jürgen Georg Backhaus

When we started this project, the question was: is there a difference in the way seafaring and landlocked states visualise the commonwealth? The hypothesis was that Continental cultures develop utopias that are different from maritime cultures. This is clearly not true. In this sense, this volume follows the refutation of the Schumpeter Hypothesis. The question is discussed, if the hypothesis is refuted, why is it still relevant and useful? The answer provided in the book is that the Schumpeter Hypothesis remains important as it charts out an entire research program. The Hypothesis serves as a benchmarking instrument in defining the boundaries between public and private sectors in OECD countries and beyond. The Hypothesis may turn out to define the grammar of discourse for constitutional economic policy in the European and the OECD community.

The utopias presented in this book focus on the tension between the State and utopia. The contributors include background information, i.e. major economic, social, and cultural aspects that are important in the relationship between utopia and the State. For instance, Nicolaus Tideman focuses on the aspect of property in a utopian State. The question is, how can people gain claims to individual property? The answer is informed by the ideas of Pufendorf and Locke. In a second contribution, Nicolaus Tideman discusses a utopia based on the demand-revealing process[1] by Martin Bailey, who wrote "Constitution for a Future Country" as advice for a good dictator, if there were not any constraints for political legitimacy. For instance, he pursues the question how a constitution would look like, if legislators could not be influenced by a lobby. Karl-Heinz Schmidt explores the utopian elements in the formation of doctrines on the State in German State sciences; some of these utopian elements described by Schmidt we find back in Michael Montgomery's description of Mill's Stationary State. This shows the continental influence on Mill, which allows for a reinterpretation of the common view of this particular founder of

[1] The demand-revealing process is a voting procedure by Nicolaus Tideman and Gordon Tullock in the *Journal of Political Economy* in 1976.

J.G. Backhaus (✉)
University of Erfurt, Nordhäuser Str. 63, 99089, Erfurt Thüringen, Germany
e-mail: juergen.backhaus@uni-erfurt.de

J.G. Backhaus (ed.), *The State as Utopia: Continental Approaches*, The European Heritage in Economics and the Social Sciences 9, DOI 10.1007/978-1-4419-7500-3_1,

modern economics. Utopian Socialism is the topic of three chapters. The aspect of "labour and leisure" in utopian socialism is discussed by Hans Frambach, who focuses on labour.

In analysing the tension between the State and utopia, some other authors find that ideas typically considered as utopian are rather realistic instead. Examples include the contributions by Marcel van Meerhaeghe, who poses the question, "Is Montaigne a Utopian?" and Gerrit Meijer, who explores the relationship between utopia and theocracy by focussing on church and the state in Calvinist Geneva.

Some of the utopias described are hardly known yet and/or almost not reviewed in English. Examples include "The Kingdom of Ophir" by Günther Chaloupek, "Justis Concrete Utopia" by Hartmut Becker, Johann Peter Süßmilch's "Divine Rule" by Gerhard Scheuerer, "Eugen Dühring and Post-Utopian Socialism" by James Gay, Rudolph Steiner's Utopia by Arno Daastol and Johannes Hanel, and Lambulus' "Sun State," and T. Campanella's "Civitas Solis" by Christos Baloglou.

The German counter utopia of the Schlaraffenland is in this sense a continental contribution indeed. The place names indicate unvirtuous traits such as indolence, laziness, and vulgar consumption in contrast to diligence, hard work, and parsimony. The tale was made popular after the technology of printing exact maps had been developed. The tale is an old one, but it was made popular only by printing the fictitious maps – and selling the prints in the markets of major upper German cities such as Nuremberg and Augsburg, where the Fugger family showed by example the virtues of parsimony and exacting dutiful trade (Backhaus 1989).

The chapters of this book were originally presented at the 22nd annual Heilbronn Symposium in Economics and the Social Sciences, June 18–21, 2009. We are grateful to the Lord Mayor of the City of Heilbronn and the City Council for their generous hospitality and support.

Reference

Backhaus, J., December 1989. "A Transactional Approach to Explaining Historical Contract Structures", *International Review of Law and Economics*, 9, 223–226.

A Demand-Revealing Utopia

Nicolaus Tideman

A compendium of utopias would be incomplete without a description of the utopia described by Martin Bailey in his book, *Constitution for a Future Country*.[1] Bailey notes the deplorable inefficiency with which governments operate and devises a constitution that he would recommend to a benevolent dictator, who wished to provide the people of a nation with the most efficient government that can be designed with the assistance of public-choice economics.

The fundamental principle that Bailey advances in this proposed constitution is that the search for worthwhile social changes should be a search for improvements in economic efficiency, which are to be implemented in ways that are as close to Pareto improvements as is humanly possible.

Bailey begins by separating the issue of redistribution for the needy. He argues that, in view of the rent-seeking losses from public activities that are deliberately redistributive, it is best for the issue of assistance for the needy to be settled when a country's constitution is written, and then not re-opened. It would be consistent with the Bailey's perspective if the issue of provision for the needy could be re-opened, under a rule that changes could be implemented only if they were favored by majorities in all income classes. In other words, provision for the needy could be revised if shared compassion made it possible to have a revision that was an approximate Pareto improvement.

All public activities other than provision for the needy are to be financed by taxes on those who benefit, in proportion to those benefits. An intricate process of legislative proposals and citizen approval by referendum is used to develop and certify worthwhile public programs.

To deal with the perverse incentives that arise when legislators strive for election and re-election, Bailey proposes that legislators be selected by a random process and

[1]Palgrave, London, 2001.

N. Tideman (✉)
Department of Economics Organization, Virginia Tech, 3021 Pamplin Hall (0316), VA 24061, Blacksburg
e-mail: ntideman@vt.edu

J.G. Backhaus (ed.), *The State as Utopia: Continental Approaches*, The European Heritage in Economics and the Social Sciences 9, DOI 10.1007/978-1-4419-7500-3_2,

serve for fixed terms, like a grand jury.[2] Every person chosen to be a legislator would be paid 110% of whatever his or her salary had been prior to being selected.

To keep legislators from being influenced inappropriately by lobbyists, Bailey proposes that legislators and their families be housed in a community with restricted access. This can be understood as an enlargement of the idea of sequestering a jury.

This sequestration does not mean that legislators would have no access to information. Whatever expert information they needed to develop and evaluate legislative proposals would be available to them.

To guard against the possibility of a slothful legislature, Bailey proposes the combination of productivity bonuses for legislators, along with two competing legislative bodies. A legislature's productivity bonus would be based on an assessment by economic experts of the value of the laws that the legislature devised. Each legislative body would be motivated to develop its proposals as well as possible and as rapidly as possible, to secure the bonus for a good proposal before the rival legislative body removed the opportunity.

Every law proposed by either legislative body would go into effect only if it was approved by a referendum of a special type. The referendum would combine features of the demand-revealing process devised by Edward Clarke and the insurance mechanism devised by Earl Thompson.

In the demand-revealing process, each participant reports the amount of money that he or she is willing to pay to secure the adoption or the rejection of a proposal. People are motivated to report their valuations honestly, by an application of marginal cost pricing: A person is required to pay something for reporting a valuation if and only if that person's report changes the outcome. In that event, the person is required to pay the difference between the losses to those who lose from the change in the outcome and the gains to those who gain from the change, other than the person himself. All of the gains and losses are calculated from the voters' own reports.[3]

In the Thompson insurance mechanism, the government announces its estimate of the probability that a proposal will be approved. Based on this probability, voters buy insurance against the success of the outcome that they do not favor.[4]

Bailey combines the two mechanisms because the Thompson insurance mechanism is suitable for instances in which a disfavored outcome produces a loss that increases the marginal utility of money, while the Clarke procedure is suitable for instances in which a person is willing to pay for an outcome even though the disfavored outcome would not increase the marginal utility of money. Thus, Bailey's proposal is as follows:

[2]Juries are not the only example one can find of random selection of public officials. Public officials in ancient Athens were selected by a random process, and the Bible describes the choice of Samuel as the first king of the Jews by a random process.

[3]For Clarke's explanation of his idea, see Edward H. Clarke (Clarke 1971). For an explanation that is easier to understand, see Tideman and Tullock (1976).

[4]Earl A Thompson, "A Poreto Optimal Group Decision Process," in Gordon Tullock (ed.), *Papers on Nonmarket Decision Making* (charlottesville: University of Virginia,1966) pp. 133–40

When a legislative body has developed proposed legislation, it is sent to assessors who estimate the gains and losses that it would generate. Based on these estimates, compensation for those who are believed to lose is devised, to be financed by taxes on those who are believed to gain. If the proposal entails resource costs, the financing of these is spelled out as well. The combination of the proposal, the compensation and the taxes is presented to voters. Each household reports the amount of insurance it wishes to buy against the possibility of not getting the outcome it favors, along with the amount that it is willing to pay to achieve the outcome it desires, taking account of the insurance that it has bought. The decision on the proposal is based on whether the sum of the valuations of all households, from the combination of the Clarke mechanism and the Thompson insurance mechanism, is positive or negative. Bailey includes the possibility of weighting losses more heavily than gains in deciding the outcome.

Any systematic predictability in the direction in which individuals voted, as a function of characteristics that could have been used to assign taxes, is taken as an indication that the assessors did not do as good a job as they might have done in assigning compensation and taxes, and they are fined accordingly. (They are paid enough to afford some level of fines).

If the proposal is passed, the legislative body that made the proposal receives a bonus of a percentage of the net gains from the proposal.

Bailey argues that this proposal offers the best possible prospect for having a society in which new legislation is confined to changes that improve the level of well-being in the society, and these changes are *effected* as quickly as possible.

References

Edward H. Clarke, "Multipart Pricing of Public Goods," *Public Choice*, 11 (1971): 17–33.

Earl A. Thompson, "A Pareto Optimal Group Decision Process," in Gordon Tullock (ed.), *Papers on Non-Market Decision Making* (Charlottesville: University of Virginia, 1966), pp. 133–140.

T. Nicolaus Tideman and Gordon Tullock, "A New and Superior Process for Making Social Choices." *Journal of Political Economy*, 84 (1976): 1145–59.

Economic, City Planning, and Environmental Proposals by Plato in the City of Atlantis and of the Laws

Christos P. Baloglou

In Plato's unfinished dialogue *Critias*, we are told of the fertile coastal plain, 2.000 stadia by 3.000 stadia (approximately 250 by 375 miles), surrounded by a large irrigation canal. The city-polis of Atlantis is circular in shape, delineated by a round capital, or aoter, wall which sets it apart from both the fertile irrigated plain and the rest of the country. The concentric design is focused upon three artificially created islands in the center of the polis. The center-most island, shaped like a sphere, is surrounded by a canal, which in turn is encircled by another island, also encircled by a canal. A third island ring completes the interior of the polis and is set off from the main body of the capital by a final water ring. Thus, we have a series of seven concentric bodies, one within another. The circular pattern is further strengthened by a series of four internal walls, one around each of the three islands and the fourth surrounding the inner sanctum on the middle island, the Akropolis, where one finds the Temple of Poseidon, its great altar, and a stele. The islands are linked by a bridge, and have been furnished with gardens, trees, sanctuaries, and a hippodrome. An elaborate system of aqueducts irrigates the groves and provides both warm and cold water for bathhouses. Bodyguards are housed on all the islands.

As far as the technological achievements of Atlantis, Plato describes the ports and forts, which recall Piraeus and Munichia (*Crit.* 117 d-f), the mining of orichalcum (*Crit.* 114e), which seems to allude to the silver of Laurium. Orichalcum may also be (*Crit.* 114e) a composite symbol here for both the silver of Laurium and the marble of Parnassus and Hymettus. The appearance of Poseidon's temple (*Crit.* 116 d-f) resembles the Parthenon. The last item implicitly refers to the strife of Athena and Poseidon over Attica, and to the great problem of Athen's dichotomy in its agrarian and maritime components, which in turn coincides with the imperialism, wealth, and insularity of the Atlantids confronted by the virtuous farmers.

Other technological achievements of Atlantis constitute its economic force and the walls with variegated surfaces, the temple covered with metals and the Atlantid inclination for canals (*Crit.* 115d; 118d), both recalling Babylon and Ecbatana. The

C.P. Baloglou (✉)
Hellenic Telecommunications Organization, S.A. Athens
e-mail: c.baloglou@ote.gr

J.G. Backhaus (ed.), *The State as Utopia: Continental Approaches*, The European Heritage in Economics and the Social Sciences 9, DOI 10.1007/978-1-4419-7500-3_3,

case of Carthage may seem somewhat stronger: Atlantis lies in the West, and Mount Atlas and the "voracious" elephants (*Crit.* 114 e-f) point to North Africa.

Plato describes in the Atlantis the economic and social structure of the island. Poseidon with Cleito "begot five twin births of male offspring and divided the whole isle of Atlantis into ten parts" (*Crit.* 114 a); the five pairs consequently form two series, of senior and junior brothers. The decimal constitution of Poseidon's Atlantid offspring evidently reflects the cleisthenic constitution of democratic Athens with its negative by-products such as the body of the strategoi. There is also a tripartite division of the citizens, which provides the social division of labor. This division of labor has been seen as an application of justice.

The most obvious message of Atlantis is ethical: a small but just city triumphs over a mighty aggressor. It was understood by some ancient readers of the *Timaeus* and the *Critias* – notably, Theopompus of Chios (380–300 B.C.) repeats it through the picture of the *Meropian Island* with its continuities of the Machimoi and Eusebeis (FGrH 115 F 75C)-, and stressed by many modern commentators of the two dialogues.[1] Other details of the conflict between wealth and modesty, a maritime and an agrarian society, an engineering science and a spiritual force, are fully in accordance, it has been realized, with a parable of a kind to be expected from the writer of the *Laws*.

The *Laws* appears to give us a somewhat different picture of the origin of the polis (735B1–736C4) from the Republic and the Statesman. In the first place, rule is exercised by a self-controlled statesman, or someone less than that, rather than by the scientific ruler of the Statesman. Second, purity of stock is taken for granted. Third, applications for admission to the totally new colony can be rejected. The main question of the establishment of the new colony, called Magnesia, in Crete is discussed in the *Laws* (707E1–708D7). Who will be the new colonists of Magnesia? A homogeneous group has a commonality of institutions and a feeling of community but is resistant to change. The new polis requires men who will be willing to accept radically new institutions and laws, including those that prescribe a moderate and fixed level of wealth and supervision of family size (746A2–4). On the other hand, "a miscellaneous combination of all kinds of people will perhaps be more ready to submit to a new code of laws," because they lack the solidarity supplied by common institutions, "but to get them to 'pull and puff as one' (as they say of a team of horses) is very difficult and takes a long time" (708 D1–5). The solution to this problem offered by the *Laws* is that the colonists should come from Greek poleis only, but from different ones.

The commonwealth of the Laws clearly envisages the possibility of a larger polis and one of a different sort. Although the constitution of the *Republic* is acknowledged to be the best (739 D4–5), because it makes for the greatest unity, its commonality of property and family are abandoned. The code of Magnesia is framed with an eye on freedom, wisdom, and unity (701D7–9).

---

[1] For an exhaustive list of these commentators, see Dusanic (1982), at p. 25, not.2.

The variables that do enter into the determination of optimum population are items such as the purity of water supply, the fertility of the land, and the condition of the neighboring states. Of these, the Athenian Stranger selects two for special mention-that the citizenry should be large enough to defend its land area, and that the land should be able to support its given number of citizens in a life of temperance.

In the *Laws,* land is distributed to families rather than to individuals. The number of households or hearths, therefore, must be kept constant (740 B3–5). The optimum population of the polis, however, is not set at any particular number. For purposes of discussion, and especially for arithmetical convenience, the Athenian Stranger sets the number of households at 5.040.[2]

As for the proposals for city planning in the Laws, Plato proposes land for other municipal buildings, such as the law courts, the gymnasia, schools, and theaters, which will all be properly placed (779D). The spatial attributes of Magnesia have fallen into place.

Plato is a consummate planner. He adheres to the planning principle that adequate maintenance of a municipal facility or service must be an integral part of its design. To achieve this purpose, commissioners are to be charged with looking after everything. There will be urban commissioners, responsible for the upkeep of city streets and buildings, country boulevards leading to the capital, the water supply and, most crucial, the sanitation facilities. There will also be rural commissioners, who will provide for the proper run-off of rainwater and see to the beautification of springs. Their many tasks run the full gamut from securing the outlying fortifications of Magnesia against external attack, to the provision and operation of restful and recreational health spas (Laws 758, 760–761, 763, 779).

Plato shows himself to be well versed in both the theoretical and technical applications of town-planning procedures of his day. His treatment of the architectural and engineering details in the *Critias*, considerations of siting in the *Timaeus,* and discussion of the various components of the city in the *Republic* indicate his familiarity with contemporary practices. He has formulated hypothetically for us what must have been considered the proper practices.

References

S. Dusanic, "Plato's Atlantis," *L' Antiquité Classique*, LI (1982) 25–52.
G. Morrow, *Plato's Cretan City.* Princeton: Princeton University Press, 1960 [repr. 1997].

[2] See the discussion in Morrow (1960, 112–115).

Property in a Utopian State, Informed by Ideas of Pufendorf and Locke

Nicolaus Tideman

In considering the nature of a utopian state, one might begin by asking whether such a thing is a contradiction in terms. A state is a repository of power that can overcome disobedience or objection. A utopian place is conceived as a place that manifests ideal conditions. One might plausibly suppose that one component of the ideal conditions of a utopian place would be harmony that made the power of the state unnecessary. How, then, could there be a utopian state?

There are several ways of resolving this apparent contradiction. First, one might suppose that the reasoning abilities of persons are so imperfect that their expressed preferences are of no consequence in a utopian state. What is important in an ideal state, by this view, is not what people say they want but rather what those with true knowledge (Plato's Guardians) understand to be ideal. The state's power is needed to impose this.

Second, and less drastically for human freedom, one might suppose, in a way analogous to some "trembling hand" economic theories (Selten 1975), that people are generally in agreement with social policies that they would be obliged to follow in a utopian state, but they slip up occasionally, and the power of the state reduces the cost of these occasional departures from their true preferences.

I propose a different approach. I define a utopian state as one that gives expression to a conception of an ideal society that is shared by the citizens of the utopian state. The power of the state is employed to ensure that those who have a different conception of an ideal state do not interfere.

A utopian state occupies territory and does not generally include all persons. Thus one of the first questions to arise with respect to a utopian state is, how does a utopian state justify, to persons who are not its citizens, its exclusive access to the territory it occupies?

N. Tideman (✉)
Department of Economics Organization, Virginia Tech, 3021 Pamplin Hall (0316), VA 24061, Blacksburg
e-mail: ntideman@vt.edu

J.G. Backhaus (ed.), *The State as Utopia: Continental Approaches*, The European Heritage in Economics and the Social Sciences 9, DOI 10.1007/978-1-4419-7500-3_4,

Pufendorf's Contribution

Samuel Pufendorf (1632–1692) was a German natural law theorist. In his 1672 work, *On the Law of Nature and of Nations,* he propounded a theory of the origin of property. He wrote:

> It is true that God allowed men to turn the earth, its products, and its creatures, to his own use and convenience, that is, He gave men an indefinite right to them, yet the manner, intensity, and extent of this power were left to the judgement and disposition of men; whether, in other words, they would confine it within certain limits, or within none at all, and whether they wanted every man to have a right to everything, or only to a certain and fixed part of things, or to be assigned his definite portion with which he should rest content and claim no right to anything else....
>
> And yet there is no precept of natural law whereby all things are commanded to be proper to men in such a way, that every man should be allotted his own separate and distinct portion. Although natural law clearly advised that men should by convention introduce the assignment of such things to individuals, according as it might be of advantage to human society, yet on the condition that it would rest with the judgement of men, whether they wanted all things to be proper or only some, or would hold some things indivisible and leave the rest open to all, yet in such a way that no one might claim them for himself alone. From this it is further understood, that the law of nature approves all conventions which have been introduced about things by men, provided they involve no contradiction or do not overturn society. Therefore, the proprietorship of things has resulted immediately from the convention of men, either tacit or express. For although after God has made the gift, nothing remained to prevent man from appropriating things to himself, yet there was need of some sort of convention if it was to be understood that by such appropriation or seizure the right of others to that thing was excluded. But the fact that right reason suggested the introduction of separate dominions does not prevent them from going back to a human pact.[1]

In other words, property arises from human agreement. While individual property is efficient, for at least some things, it is not required. The default in the absence of agreement is that all persons are allowed to use all things: "there was need of some sort of convention if it was to be understood that by such appropriation or seizure the right of others to that thing was excluded."

There are two striking features of Pufendorf's view. First, his view entails equal initial rights of all men, and second, the separate rights of persons to individual domains of property arise only from human conventions.

The idea of equal rights to the earth for all is not as surprising as it may seem at first, if one considers the environment in which Pufendorf was writing. Learned persons of his time would be familiar with the words of Psalm 115, verse 16, "The heavens are the Lord's heavens, but the earth he has given to human beings" (New Revised Standard Version). While there is no explicit statement of equal rights here, it is a natural way to interpret the words. And learned writers understood an obligation to keep their work in harmony with biblical teaching. Furthermore, in Pufendorf's time, the question of the origin of property was a subject on which

[1]Samuel Pufendorf, *On the Law of Nature and of Nations*, Book IV, Ch. 4, Sect. 4.

many were writing, and equal initial rights to the earth was a common theme in these writings.[2]

The idea that private property arises from a convention among men requires interpretation. An alternative translation uses the word "agreement" rather than "convention" (Vallentyne and Steiner 2000). But "convention" is almost certainly the better word. "Agreement" suggests a unanimous agreement, with everyone having veto power. But Pufendorf would have understood that unanimous agreement was not reasonable to posit.

If property develops by convention rather than unanimous agreement, then the question arises as to whether the process by which such conventions emerge is adequately respectful of the rights of individuals, or whether some persons are treated unjustly in the development of the conventions of property. One can imagine property conventions arising as a consequence of conquest in which a dictator assigns nearly everything to himself. Is Pufendorf saying that all property conventions are just irrespective of their origins? I think, not.

A more plausible interpretation, it seems to me, is that Pufendorf is addressing a positive question rather than a normative one. He is not asking what makes property rules just, but rather, where do property rules come from? Pufendorf is right that there was a time before property, when no one had exclusive rights to anything, and property rules developed because people found them useful. If he had been aware of modern research on territoriality in animals,[3] he might have suggested that ideas of property in humans were built on a foundation provided by animal territoriality. But none of this addresses the question of whether the conventions regarding property that developed historically were just.

Locke's Contribution

John Locke wrote *Two Treatises of Government* in 1696, 24 years after Pufendorf's *On the Law of Nature and of Nations* had been published. I do not know whether Locke was aware of Pufendorf's work, but he was definitely aware of other writings on the subject of the origin of property.[4] In Chap. 5, *Of Property*, of Locke's *Second Treatise* (paragraph 24) he says,

> Whether we consider natural reason, which tells us that men, being once born, have a right to their preservation, and consequently to meat and drink and such other things as Nature affords for their subsistence, or "revelation," which gives us an account of those grants God made of the world to Adam, and to Noah and his sons, it is very clear that God, as King David says (Psalm 115. 16), "has given the earth to the children of men," given it to mankind in common. But, this being supposed, it seems to some a very great difficulty how any

[2] See Pufendorf, *Op. cit.*, Chap. IV, Sects. 8–13.

[3] See Konrad Lorenz, *On Aggression*.

[4] See Locke's *First Treatise*.

> one should ever come to have a property in anything, I will not content myself to answer, that, if it be difficult to make out "property" upon a supposition that God gave the world to Adam and his posterity in common, it is impossible that any man but one universal monarch should have any "property" upon a supposition that God gave the world to Adam and his heirs in succession, exclusive of all the rest of his posterity; but I shall endeavor to show how men might come to have a property in several parts of that which God gave to mankind in common, and that without any express compact of all the commoners.

In other words, Locke says that he will explain how, even though God gave the world to all mankind, it is possible for people to have individual property, and without any express compacts among people. Locke begins with the idea that people have rights to themselves:

> Though the earth and all inferior creatures be common to all men, yet every man has a "property" in his own "person." This nobody has any right to but himself. The "labor" of his body and the "work" of his hands, we may say, are properly his. Whatsoever, then, he removes out of the state that Nature has provided and left it in, he has mixed his labor with it, and joined to it something that is his own, and thereby makes it his property. It being by him removed from the common state Nature placed it in, it has by this labor something annexed to it that excludes the common right of other men. For this "labor" being the unquestionable property of the laborer, no man but he can have a right to what that is once joined to, at least where there is enough, and as good left in common for others.[5]

The last 14 words of this passage, "at least where there is enough, and as good left in common for others," are known as "Locke's proviso." The interpretation of these words has been the subject of much debate. I used to think that Locke meant that if you want to claim something in nature for yourself, you must leave as much for everyone else as you take for yourself. But, more recently, I have concluded that the proper interpretation of Locke's proviso requires that one takes into account the remainder of Locke's argument. From this perspective I now understand that Locke was dividing his argument into the easy case and the hard case. The easy case, which is covered by the proviso, is the case when natural opportunities are not scarce, "where there is enough, and as good left in common for others." If natural opportunities are not scarce, then, as a modern economist would say, the value of anything that is produced from natural opportunities is accounted for entirely by the value of other inputs. If no one is deprived of any opportunity by someone's appropriation of something from nature, then there is nothing to complain about. The person who supplied the labor is the owner of the thing.

Next, Locke argues that the easy case can apply to land:

> But the chief matter of property being now not the fruits of the earth and the beasts that subsist on it, but the earth itself, as that which takes in and carries with it all the rest, I think it is plain that property in that too is acquired as the former. As much land as a man tills, plants, improves, cultivates, and can use the product of, so much is his property. He by his labor does, as it were, enclose it from the common. Nor will it invalidate his right to say

[5] Locke, *Second Treatise*, paragraph 26.

everybody else has an equal title to it, and therefore, he cannot appropriate, he cannot enclose, without the consent of all his fellow-commoners, all mankind. God, when He gave the world in common to all mankind, commanded man also to labor, and the penury of his condition required it of him. God and his reason commanded him to subdue the earth—i.e., improve it for the benefit of life and therein lay out something upon it that was his own, his labor. He that, in obedience to this command of God, subdued, tilled, and sowed any part of it, thereby annexed to it something that was his property, which another had no title to, nor could without injury take from him.

Nor was this appropriation of any parcel of land, by improving it, any prejudice to any other man, since there was still enough and as good left, and more than the yet unprovided could use. So that, in effect, there was never the less left for others because of his enclosure for himself. For he that leaves as much as another can make use of does as good as take nothing at all. Nobody could think himself injured by the drinking of another man, though he took a good draught, who had a whole river of the same water left him to quench his thirst. And the case of land and water, where there is enough of both, is perfectly the same....

It is true, in land that is common in England or any other country, where there are plenty of people under government who have money and commerce, no one can enclose or appropriate any part without the consent of all his fellow-commoners; because this is left common by compact—i.e., by the law of the land, which is not to be violated. And, though it be common in respect of some men, it is not so to all mankind, but is the joint propriety of this country, or this parish. Besides, the remainder, after such enclosure, would not be as good to the rest of the commoners as the whole was, when they could all make use of the whole; whereas in the beginning and first peopling of the great common of the world it was quite otherwise. The law, man was under, was rather for appropriating. God commanded, and his wants forced him to labor. That was his property, which could not be taken from him wherever he had fixed it. And hence subduing or cultivating the earth and having dominion, we see, are joined together. The one gave title to the other. So that God, by commanding to subdue, gave authority so far to appropriate. And the condition of human life, which requires labor and materials to work on, necessarily introduce private possessions.

The measure of property Nature well set, by the extent of men's labor and the convenience of life. No man's labor could subdue or appropriate all, nor could his enjoyment consume more than a small part; so that it was impossible for any man, this way, to entrench upon the right of another or acquire to himself a property to the prejudice of his neighbor, who would still have room for as good and as large a possession (after the other had taken out his) as before it was appropriated. Which measure did confine every man's possession to a very moderate proportion, and such as he might appropriate to himself without injury to anybody in the first ages of the world, when men were more in danger to be lost, by wandering from their company, in the then vast wilderness of the earth than to be straitened for want of room to plant in.

The same measure may be allowed still, without prejudice to anybody, full as the world seems. For, supposing a man or family, in the state they were at first, peopling of the world by the children of Adam or Noah, let him plant in some inland vacant places of America. We shall find that the possessions he could make himself, upon the measures we have given, would not be very large, nor, even to this day, prejudice the rest of mankind or give them reason to complain or think themselves injured by this man's encroachment, though the race of men have now spread themselves to all the corners of the world, and do infinitely exceed the small number [that] was at the beginning.[6]

[6]Locke, *Op. cit.*, paragraphs 31–36.

Summarizing the argument so far without the biblical literalism, it is: People have a right to their labor. The human condition requires them to improve land to survive, so their work gives them the right to the land they improve. And no one can properly complain because there is still plenty of good, unclaimed land in America.

Locke's argument is both positive and normative. He proposes an account of how private property developed, and he argues that the process was just.

Locke claims that while some land has value apart from human labor, that contribution to value is quite small:

> Nor is it so strange as, perhaps, before consideration, it may appear, that the property of labor should be able to overbalance the community of land, for it is labor indeed that puts the difference of value on everything; and let anyone consider what the difference is between an acre of land planted with tobacco or sugar, sown with wheat or barley, and an acre of the same land lying in common without any husbandry upon it, and he will find that the improvement of labor makes the far greater part of the value. I think it will be but a very modest computation to say, that of the products of the earth useful to the life of man, nine-tenths are the effects of labor. Nay, if we will rightly estimate things as they come to our use, and cast up the several expenses about them—what in them is purely owing to Nature and what to labor—we shall find that in most of them ninety-nine hundredths are wholly to be put on the account of labor.[7]

So, Locke argues, even if there is some scarcity value to land, it is so inconsequential that it can be ignored without noticeable injustice.

> From all which it is evident, that though the things of Nature are given in common, man (by being master of himself, and proprietor of his own person, and the actions or labor of it) had still in himself the great foundation of property; and that which made up the great part of what he applied to the support or comfort of his being, when invention and arts had improved the conveniences of life, was perfectly his own, and did not belong in common to others.
>
> Thus labor, in the beginning, gave a right of property, wherever any one was pleased to employ it, upon what was common, which remained a long while, the far greater part, and is yet more than mankind makes use of. Men at first, for the most part, contented themselves with what unassisted Nature offered to their necessities; and though afterwards, in some parts of the world, where the increase of people and stock, with the use of money, had made land scarce, and so of some value, the several communities settled the bounds of their distinct territories, and, by laws, within themselves, regulated the properties of the private men of their society, and so, by compact and agreement, settled the property which labor and industry began.[8]

Thus Locke ends with compacts and agreements among men settling the rules of property.

Because Locke goes back and forth between positive arguments and normative ones, it is sometimes difficult to keep track of the thread of his normative argument. In fact, Locke leaves his normative argument incomplete by switching to positive statements. Thus to the extent that he has succeeded in his "endeavor to show how men might come to have a property in several parts of that which God gave to mankind in common, and that without any express compact of all the commoners" he has shown how it *can* happen but not how it can be *just*.

---

[7] Locke, *Op. cit.*, paragraph 40.

[8] Locke, *Op cit.*, paragraphs 44–45.

A Solution to the Puzzle

So if one starts with the premise of Pufendorf and Locke that initially all people have equal rights to the earth, how can people come to have *justly founded* rights to separate parts of the earth? Locke is right that it is important to have a solution that does not involve agreements among all persons, because there is no reasonable possibility of all persons agreeing on anything. And yet, when land is scarce, justice requires that the claims of all humanity be honored in some way.

The beginning of a solution comes from the idea of equal division. If you have left as much for everyone else as you have taken for yourself, then you are at least treating others as equals. And when there are disparate things to be allocated, values derived from market prices offer the possibility of an envy-free allocation.[9] If the market value of each person's allotment is equal to that of every other person, then no one will find another person's allocation superior to his own.

Nor need the allocations of physical resources all be equal; money can be used to compensate for unequal allocations. If each of *N* persons has a stipend that is sufficient to purchase the use of one *Nth* of the natural opportunities that are available to all, then no one can reasonably complain of receiving an inadequate share. Natural opportunities are justly allocated if they are rented at market prices and the proceeds are divided equally.

Yet, an equal division at market prices is not the complete solution to the puzzle, because there may be some natural opportunities that most of humanity does not wish to allocate to one person alone. If most of humanity views a particular rainforest as essential for biodiversity or adequate climate management, one dissenter cannot justly claim it on the ground that he is willing to pay more for it than anyone else is willing to pay. If most of humanity sees whales as companionable cousins rather than a source of tasty food, then humanity, operating on the principle of majority rule, is allowed to say that whales are not for sale at any price. It is not necessary for a person to get the agreement of humanity in order to use a resource to which all have equal right. It is sufficient to leave as much for others as one takes for oneself. But if humanity stirs itself to say, "No, most of us want this resource left undivided," then, generally, no one person can justly take it for himself.

And still there is an exception to the exception. Humanity, operating on the principle of majority rule, would be behaving unjustly if it applied majority control to so many resources that it was no longer possible for people to meaningfully express their rights to themselves.

To summarize: A utopian community would reasonably posit that people have rights to themselves, and that all persons have equal right to natural opportunities. Such a utopian community would then be faced with the question of how it explained to those who were not members of the community why it might justly exclude nonmembers from the territory that it occupied.

[9]Footnote to Foley.

Pufendorf offered a reasonable account of how it happened historically that individual property arose, but he did not address the question of how it can be just. Locke intertwined the positive question of how property arose with the normative question of how it can be just, and he left the normative question, crucially, incompletely answered at the end.

An adequate account of how individuals can justly have individual rights in the common heritage of all requires three parts. First, any division must be such that the combination of the cash and the market value of the user rights that each person receives is the same as what others receive. Second, humanity can justly, by majority rule, leave some resources out of the pool that is to be allocated to individual. Third, humanity would be acting unjustly if it managed so many resources by majority rule that people no longer had adequate opportunities to give expression to their rights to themselves.

References

Reinhard Selten (1975) A re-examination of the perfectness concept for equilibrium points in extensive games. *International Journal of Game Theory* 4:25–55.

Peter Vallentyne and Hillel Steiner (eds.) (2000) *The Origins of Left-Libertarianism*, Palgrave: Hampshire/New York, p. 30.

Duncan K Foley (1967) Resource Allocation and the Public Sector. *Yale Econ Essays* 7(1):45–98.

John Stuart Mill and the Utopian Tradition

Michael R. Montgomery

John Stuart Mill is principally remembered as one of the pre-eminent political economists and social scientists of the nineteenth century. Less remembered is that much of his thought, at its core, was heavily utopian. While Mill penned many passages thoroughly in harmony with the orthodox classical tradition, a substantial part of his work in his *Principles of Political Economy*[1] and elsewhere was lovingly dedicated to dreams and passions for the perfection of society through a total makeover of its institutions and values.

Utopian thought is a curious mixture of laudable optimism about the prospects for human improvement, coupled with an extraordinary fatuousness concerning the ease with which humanity can achieve "perfection" (or even know what such perfection actually entails). Eight propositions that characterize most utopian thought are:

- that a perfect human society is indeed possible and that the human mind can know what such a society would look like, and that humankind is also capable of creating such a society.
- that the "problem of evil" is in essence a problem of knowledge rather than a problem of human foibles. Evil is caused by ignorance of the right, not by the willful disregard of it.
- that, accordingly, the proper education and conditioning of the masses will solve all social problems through a revamping of the limitlessly malleable "character" of mankind.
- that such properly-educated masses would, under unfettered democracy, routinely place wise, just, well-meaning, and incorruptible people into positions of political power in the government.

[1] *Principles of Political Economy* (Mill 1929 [1871], Mill 1965 [1871]). The former is the famous Ashley edition, the latter the *Collected Works* edition. Each citation is followed by two page numbers, the first referring to the page of the Ashley edition, the second to the page in the *Collected Works* edition.

M.R. Montgomery (✉)
University of Maine, 5774 Stevens Hall, Orono, ME 04469, USA
e-mail: michael.montgomery@umit.maine.edu

J.G. Backhaus (ed.), *The State as Utopia: Continental Approaches*, The European Heritage in Economics and the Social Sciences 9, DOI 10.1007/978-1-4419-7500-3_5,

- that, accordingly, the problem of government is the problem of how to get the "right people" into power, *not* a problem of how to constrain those people once in power.
- that "character" is a satisfactory substitute for constraints on government power.
- that, in the private sphere, the core problem facing society is that of eradicating the "natural" human instinct of self-interest. The moral member of society thinks of the group first, him- or herself, last.
- that a perfect society will be reached when self-interest is overcome and when the replacement altruistic ideology has successfully worked its way through society, re-inventing all its institutions accordingly.

All eight of these utopian propositions are prominently featured in Mill's major works.

1. that a perfect human society is indeed possible and that the human mind can know what such a society would look like, and that humankind is also capable of creating such a society.

In the celebrated education of John Stuart Mill by his father, it was Plato – arguably the greatest utopian thinker in history – who was given some of the heaviest emphasis. Mill was thus encouraged to embrace utopian thought from an early age. In particular, the lessons of Plato's *Republic* (e.g., Kaplan 1951) were thoroughly absorbed by the young Mill. Platonic themes abound in Mill's utopian writings. *The Republic*, in many respects, can be argued to be Mill's own model of a good society. The emphasis on "character" and nobility of action, the capacity for self-sacrifice in the name of the greater good, the notion that the merchant class should not accumulate "too much" wealth, the idea that there is an upper intellectual class that should exert a disproportionate influence on society – all these are themes that Mill shares with Plato's Socrates in *The Republic*.

Mill, it appears, never doubted the major Platonic virtues or the view that such virtues practiced broadly would lead to a society far closer to the ideal than the one in which he lived. Indeed, Mill embraced the evolutionist "stage theories" of Comte and St. Simon, under which society was naturally and inevitably evolving into a higher state of being. The only question in his mind was what might be done in the present to speed up the evolutionary process.

Mill always judged the current state of mankind by its distance from the Platonic ideal (broadly defined), rather than judging Plato's utopian thought from the perspective of what a more hard-headed thinker would likely see as a constant in human behavior – rational self-interest. Mill correctly saw rational self-interest as a fatal impediment to achieving a utopia in the vein offered by Plato. However, to Mill, it was rational self-interest, not utopian visions, that needed to give way. Accordingly, Mill – despite his reputation as an economist favorably disposed to free market forces – passionately advanced argument after argument in support of the proposition that humankind would (and should) naturally "evolve" into a society of "higher" beings who spurned narrow self-interest in favor of other-centered behavioral models.[2]

2. that the "problem of evil" (at bottom, selfishness) is in essence a problem of knowledge rather than a problem of human foibles. Evil is caused by ignorance of the right, not by the willful disregard of it.

One of the constantly-recurring themes of the utopian tradition is the unlimited potential for the perfection of the human mind and spirit. Invariably, the failure of human nature to be perfected to date is, in the utopian interpretation, attributed to the corrupt state of society to date – corruption which prevents Everyman from understanding that higher state of being in which true fulfillment of his great, tragically-unrealized, potential lies. If only Everyman could be given the proper environment in which to be raised and then to live, all his false actions would naturally disappear from him, and he would emerge as a new kind of human: "higher man."

Mill's version of these utopian yearnings took two forms. First came his pronouncement, in a spirit anticipating Karl Marx, that society's self-centered institutions are *all* that stands in the way of humanity's perfection. For example, in his *Autobiography*[3] Mill writes

> Interest in the common good is at present so weak a motive in the generality not because it can never be otherwise, but because the mind is not accustomed to dwell on it as it dwells from morning till night on things, which tend only to personal advantage… (*Autobiography*, 241).

And, again,

> The deep-rooted selfishness which forms the general character of the existing state of society, is so deeply rooted, only because the whole course of existing institutions tends to foster it… (*Autobiography*, 241)

Once selfish (i.e., capitalist) institutions could be replaced by their proper other-centered substitutes, a new man would naturally arise filled with truly noble (i.e., altruistic) sentiments, and the world would change. The breach between what works (capitalism) and what is moral (altruism) would at long last be closed. The New Man would be so made as to produce prosperity in socialistic, not capitalistic, institutions.[4]

---

[2]Three thinkers who greatly influenced Mill's intellectual development – Thomas Carlyle, Claude Henri de Rouvroycomte de Saint-Simon, and Augustus Comte – all advanced various forms of "stage theories" under which human society would naturally and inevitably "evolve" into a "higher" stage featuring some version of collectivist thought. For a discussion, see Britton (1953, Ch. 1).

[3]*Autobiography of John Stuart Mill* (Mill 1981 [1873]), henceforth to be referred to as "*Autobiography.*"

[4]The *Principles* and the *Autobiography* are peppered with examples of Mill's faith in the development of a higher man who will replace mere economic man with a new one of altruistic sentiment; for example:

> The social problem of the future we considered to be, how to unite the greatest individual liberty of action, with a common ownership in the raw material of the globe, and an equal participation of all in the benefits of combined labour. … We saw clearly that to render any such social transformation either possible or desirable, an equivalent change of character must take place both in the uncultivated herd who now compose the labouring masses, and in the immense majority of their employers. Both these classes must learn by practice to labour and combine for generous, or at all events for public and social purposes, and not, as hitherto, solely for narrowly interested ones. (*Autobiography*, 239)

How might the all-encompassing self-centeredness of society be evolved into an other-centered nirvana? Here, Mill emphasized the power of "education" to effectively impart "character" into all classes of society. To Mill, "character" meant (much as it means today) the sum of one's beliefs, values, judgments, and actions. One's character determined, not only one's capacity to be honest, virtuous, altruistic etc.; not just one's capacity to find emotional pleasure and enjoyment in such noble acts; but the actual ability to see the truth broadly in life.

The thorough impartation of character into the citizenry was, in Mill's view, fully as important an educational goal as the impartation of knowledge. All society's groups could be reformed through "character." Character-laden voters would no longer be dissuaded by vague promises and appeals to self-interest into voting for the wrong leaders of society. Character-laden employers would always place the well-being of their workers ahead of their own interests. Character-laden workers would understand the value of a fair day's work in exchange for a fair day's wage.

In fact, the doctrine of "character" for Mill functions as a kind of "wild card," allowing him to escape cleanly from all sorts of intellectual predicaments. For example, Mill strongly believed in the population theories of Thomas Malthus. But Mill rejected Malthusian theory as that theory was used by classical economics to predict that human population would grow relentlessly until checked by starvation, disease, etc. Malthusian theory held that the laboring classes – predominately (in Mill's opinion) men of poorly-formed characters – could not control their basic sexual urges. Malthus and the orthodox Benthamites took men as they were and, therefore, predicted continuous problems with overpopulation in industrial societies. However, Mill's doctrine of character gave society, he thought, an escape from the Malthusian trap. Through enlightened education of the laboring classes, these men could be fundamentally changed. Character could be imparted unto these classes through education, giving them the enlightenment (and self-discipline) to resist the sexual drive and so escape the Malthusian trap. Thus, thought Mill, we need no longer fear the specter of overpopulation as laid out by Malthusian theory.

Or, what about the "deep-rooted selfishness" of mankind? Surely, any successful society must come to terms with the bottom-line need of individuals to consider one's own self-interest first? *Au contraire.* The principle of rational self-interest was just a conditional truth, a "merely provisional" (*Autobiography*, 241) feature of the state of mankind as-it-then-was at Mill's particular point in time. It was based (thought Mill) on the historically accurate, but ultimately arbitrary, assumption that the characters of men as they then were under capitalism – primitive, money-grubbing, base creatures unable to see beyond the crudest of pleasures (as Mill saw them; see, for example, the several particularly caustic quotes to be found in *Principles*, Bk. IV, Ch. 6) – would remain forever the same. Again, proper education stressing the development of noble, other-centered, altruistic characters would alter the very human clay out of which future society would be built. A new man would then emerge who was unwilling (nay, utterly unable) to act in any way that would enhance his individual well-being at the expense of broader society (*cf. Autobiography*, 237–41; Mill 1969 [1861], 227, 230–33).

3. that, accordingly, the proper education and conditioning of the masses will solve all social problems through a revamping of the limitlessly malleable character of mankind.

Mill's "doctrine of character" essentially assumes another favorite proposition of utopianism: the unlimited malleability of humankind. There is nothing wrong with the notion that there are eternal virtues and that society is healthier in proportion to the extent to which its members and leaders embody such virtues in the form of "character." Most of us would prefer to live in a value-laden society and would expect, for example, that in such a society there would be a less corrupt behavior than in more nihilistic societies. However, Mill's reliance on his doctrine of "character" runs much deeper than this. As we will see below, Mill's doctrine of character is offered up as almost a ruling principle that supersedes all other potential inputs into the "Good Society." For example, in his advocacy of voluntarist evolutionary socialism, Mill often fails to consider the relevance of the incentives-based paradigm that is at the heart of political economy (incentives he emphasized elsewhere). This is on the grounds that, in the utopian society to come, such incentives will be rendered irrelevant by the making-over of humankind into instinctively altruistic beings. Humankind, that is, is treated as a kind of utterly malleable clay, which the "educator" may shape as he/she desires.

Mill and his wife (who was, he says, co-developer of virtually all his utopian thoughts)

> saw clearly that to render any such social transformation either possible or desirable, an equivalent change of character must take place both in the uncultivated herd who now compose the labouring masses, and in the immense majority of their employers. Both these classes must learn by practice to labour and combine for generous, or at all events for public and social purposes, and not, as hitherto, solely for narrowly interested ones. But the capacity to do this has always existed in mankind, and is not, nor is ever likely to be, extinct. Education, habit, and the cultivation of the sentiments, will make a common man dig or weave for his country, as readily as fight for his country. True enough, it is only by slow degrees, and a system of culture prolonged through successive generations, that men in general can be brought up to this point. But the hindrance is not in the essential constitution of human nature… When called into activity, as only self-interest now is, by the daily course of life, and spurred from behind by the love of distinction and the fear of shame, it is capable of producing, even in common men, the most strenuous exertions as well as the most heroic sacrifices… (*Autobiography*, 239)

So, to Mill, it is simply a matter of educating, or perhaps *conditioning*, Everyman to respond to self-sacrifice with the same enthusiasm that he now reserves only for self-interested action. How Mill believes that this can be achieved is not laid out, except to point out that it would involve "successive generations" of time before it came to pass.

Though Mill does not explicitly say so, part of the explanation for his optimism likely is, that Mill's conception of "education" involved more than simply the imparting of character and knowledge to the citizen. Mill was a lifelong believer in the "associationist" doctrine of David Hartley – a prominent precursor of Skinnerian conditioning. Hartley held that ideas and particular sensations can be "associated" in a way that gives one a strong predisposition to act and believe in a particular fashion. Assume that such techniques are effective: In principle, the educator, armed with such techniques, could dramatically increase the probability that an individual will act or believe in a particular way under given circumstances requiring a reaction. James Mill, John Mill's father and teacher, was a firm believer in associationism, and the young Mill was raised accordingly. Part of Mill's famous "mental crisis," as described in his *Autobiography*, was his horror at the discovery that the "proper" associations in his mind (which he had previously taken for granted) were dissolving, leading him to question his entire education. Mill eventually decided that such methods do not work on intellectuals, since "analytical methods" tended to fray and eventually sever the carefully-laid Hartleyian bonds of ideas/actions to particular sensations. The intellectuals would, therefore, need to be taught the "why" of things if they were to assume their appropriate role in society.

Crucially, however, there was, on Mill's terms, no reason to doubt the effectiveness of Hartleyian methods on the less-introspective Everyman. The average citizen could to an extent (given the effectiveness of these methods) be *trained* to act and think "appropriately" by the Hartleyian methods. Though he never endorses them explicitly, it would not be too surprising to find Mill at least sympathetic to the use of such methods. The construction of the perfect society through the conditioning of humankind is, of course, an enduring utopian theme (see, for example, Skinner 1948).[5]

4. that such properly-educated masses would, under unfettered democracy, routinely place wise, just, well-meaning, and incorruptible people into positions of political power in the government.

Mill was a life-long enthusiastic advocate of democracy. Having postulated a more-or-less perfect educational system and as a consequence a populace correspondingly educated, it is easy for Mill to argue that, in that Higher stage of society that is to come, the problems of democracy will be easily handled. The well-educated populace is presumed to have high powers of discrimination and be fully capable of identifying the best candidates. The spectacularly-well-educated candidate-Solons are all, to a person, utterly honorable individuals, unable to even contemplate putting their personal interests ahead of those of the electors. Utopia is, therefore, "safe for democracy."

Mill's primary concern, as he considers this state of affairs, is the implicit unfairness of the "one-person-one-vote" version of democracy. In *Thoughts on Parliamentary Reform* (Mill 1977a [1859]), Mill proposed a voting scheme in which the more "cultivated" would receive multiple votes while the less "cultivated"

[5]Mill wrote that "History bears witness to the success with which large bodies of human beings may be trained to feel the public interest their own" (*Principles*, 206, 205), arguably a back-handed endorsement of the potential for the useful conditioning of the masses.

would receive only a single vote. To Mill, those with the most "proved" education invariably were also those with the most "character" (thus, Mill's scheme featured "a plurality of votes, to be given, not to property, but to proved superiority of education" [*Autobiography*, 261]).[6] We see, arguably, in such cultural elitism the lasting projection of Plato and his "philosopher-kings." Here, surely, we also spy some weaknesses not uncommon to the utopian perspective. Mill, the lifelong intellectual, naturally sees those with "proved superiority of education" as deserving of a plurality of votes. By contrast to its privileged treatment of the "better-educated," Mill's voting system grants no special status to the self-educated, self-made businessman, reflecting (and perpetuating) the longstanding contempt in the West for the "character-challenged" capitalists of the merchant "class." The school of hard knocks, apparently, was not one to which Mill subscribed.

Mill's "objective" system of determining pluralities of votes is, in fact, heavily laden with Mill's own prejudices and biases as a leading member of the "theory class" (in rebuttal to Mill, that old saw about preferring to be ruled by the first 100 persons in the Boston phonebook than by the Harvard faculty inevitably comes to mind). Whatever else formal education teaches us, practical skills that are directly applicable to the "real world" are unlikely to be dominant among them. Such skills, it might be argued, are not without value when sizing up a slate of candidates. But Mill proposed to turn elections over to an intellectual elite who, even in Utopia, would inevitably have limited experience outside the world of theory. Those with first-hand, rough-and-tumble experience of the "real world" would be correspondingly downgraded. Apparently, society can simply *think* its way to Utopia, under the wise guidance of the most "character"-laden amongst us.

5. that, accordingly, the problem of government is the problem of how to get the "right people" into power, not a problem of how to constrain those people once they are in power.

A natural accompaniment of a doctrine holds that, in essence, that "philosopher-kings" will routinely be democratically elected as heads of the State, is that in such a society little attention need be given to constraining the powers of such individuals. "Philosopher-kings" require little restraining; by definition, they are enlightened and other-centered, and also most likely to know best. Accordingly, the notion of "checks and balances" and similar constraints on government power has no place in Utopia.

While it would be an exaggeration to argue that Mill's preferred form of government is one of unrestricted power, it is interesting to see him recognize – but

[6] Mill continues: "This recommended itself to me as a means of reconciling the irresistible claim of every man or woman to be consulted, and to be allowed a voice, in the regulation of affairs which vitally concern them, with the superiority of weight justly due to opinions grounded on superiority of knowledge." "Superiority of knowledge" would be assessed via "a systematic National Education by which the various grades of politically valuable acquirement may be accurately defined and authenticated." (*Autobiography*, 261–62)

downplay – the sentiment (later to be expressed by Lord Acton) that power corrupts and absolute power corrupts absolutely. Reading three of Mill's primary political works (Book V of the *Principles*, *On Liberty* (Mill 1977b [1859]), and *Considerations on Representative Government* (Mill 1973 [1861])), it is easy to conclude that, when push comes to shove, Mill sees virtually no effective (or even desirable) limit to "the interference of government by any universal rule, save the simple and vague one, that it should never be admitted but when the case of expediency is strong" (*Principles*, 800; 804). This is as it should be in Utopia – where Mill and his wife's fondest wishes and dreams lay.

Consistent with his optimistic view of government power, Mill shows little interest in the notion that a *written* constitution (or an American-style "Bill of Rights") could offer a stronger bulwark against improper use of government power. While he speaks highly of federalism and the independent U.S. Supreme Court as valuable innovations (cf. Mill 1973 [1861], Ch. 17), Mill instead looked more (and with much greater enthusiasm) to the tweaking of voting systems as the key to democracy than he did to hard constitutional constraints.[7] But an emphasis on proper voting rules is, in its own way, a utopian conception. Mill's solution, significantly, is not the American idea of binding tightly elected rulers so that if the *wrong* people get into power they will not be able to do too much damage. Rather, Mill's is the more utopian view that the key problem of democracy is setting up the system so that the *right* people are placed in power. This accounts for Mill's fixation on optimal voting systems and the pressing need to get the voting rules "right." A properly-educated voting population, voting under well-chosen voting rules, will cause the right people to be voted into power (see, for example, his discussion in Mill 1973 [1861], 390 , where "the virtue and intelligence of the human beings composing the community" is lightly taken as an accomplished fact for the bulk of the discussion). Unfettered democratic rule will be enough to restrain self-interest in the long run. Democracy is its own defense.

By this route, the "classical liberal" Mill who is nominally concerned with checks and balances seems replaced – when it matters most – with a Mill who is optimistic about the pure motives and benevolent intentions of those making up the government (as were his own motives while serving his short stint in Parliament near the end of his life). The problem of Buchanan and Tullock (1962), concisely expressed by the philosopher Karl Britton as: "Does not any government in fact consist of a group of men, and have not these men private interests of their own?" (Britton 1953, 89), often seems far from Mill's mind in his core political passages. Such absentmindedness is even more strongly in evidence in those suggestions for government interventions that close his *Principles*. Of course, Mill believes that private interests matter in a representative government. But in his core political writings, Mill steps over the problem – one which an Adam Smith might well have placed at the very center of his approach to government. Accordingly, in his

[7] Mill is a mild *constitutionalist* in the sense that he endorses only those government actions that are allowed by a nation's laws.

assessment of, and prescriptions for, government, Mill often seems to be writing for a society of angels rather than for one of men. In this attitude, he calls to mind the modern [American] "liberal," who is generally trusting of ["other-centered"] government and suspicious of ["self-centered"] business.

Mill is, naturally, not unaware of the difficulties posed to good government by corrupt politicians and their accompanying hosts of unelected (but far from disinterested) officials. Still, he often gives the impression that a proper education for the laboring classes, combined with wisely-chosen voting rules, will fix all that and put the right kind of people into power – modern Platonic "philosopher-kings," enlightened rulers all, who will understand the felicific calculus in the manner of, well, Mill himself, and act accordingly. If such sentiments seem naive today, we must remember that Mill is writing at a time when democratic institutions are still relatively young and not yet fully formed. On the other hand, it would also be a mistake to give Mill a complete "pass" for his democratic utopianism. Either Adam Smith or David Hume (or, for that matter, his own father) could have pointed Mill towards a less utopian, more hard-headed prognostication of the likely relationship between humankind and democratic institutions.

6. that "character" is a satisfactory substitute for constraints on government power.

We have just seen that Mill worried relatively little about built-in constraints on government power. Mill's view is that democracy, tempered by properly-constructed voting rules, is its own defense against public abuse of power. Why should this be? Again, Mill's utopian views about education are his "wild card" allowing him these conclusions. Mill imagines a world of the future where all the best of society have been spectacularly well-educated. In particular, Mill assumes a future world where society's best have been through an educational process that completely eliminates the desire to do anything that is not clearly in the best interests of the public. That is, all of Mill's future leaders are brimming with "character;" all are noble representatives of the virtues emphasized by Plato. They also are ethically Christian in their altruistic attitudes towards their fellow men and women (Mill was not religious, but he admired the Christian morality).

Meanwhile, Mill's "working classes" have also had "character" imparted unto them through their education process. Perhaps they have "benefited from" a hefty dosage of Hartleyian associationist conditioning as well. Such voters – assuming appropriately weighted voting rules – are, by assumption – completely capable of identifying those who make the best candidates from the perspective of their being able to selflessly serve the best interests of society. The working classes, again by assumption, would never vote for a candidate who merely represented their own narrow interests. Such interests, due to the presumed miracle of a "character"-laden education, are no longer foremost on the working-class mind.

Why would such a utopian creation require any formal constraints on government power? As is often the case with utopian systems, there is no good reason for such constraints, *by assumption*.

7. that, in the private sphere, the core problem facing society is that of eradicating the "natural" human instinct of self-interest. The moral member of society thinks of the group first, him- or herself, last.

We have seen above Mill's sharp condemnation of self-interested behavior as the bane of a good government. In *Considerations of Representative Government*, Mill states flatly that

> [w]henever the general disposition of the people is such that each individual regards those only of his interests which are selfish, and does not dwell on, or concern himself for, his share of the general interest, in such a state of things good government is impossible (Mill 1973 [1861], 390.

Does Mill have similar sentiments towards self-interested behavior in the private sector? Surely not, one might think, since self-interested behavior is the core moving principle of the classical political economy founded by Adam Smith. Yet, matters are not so simple. Mill's attitude towards self-interested behavior and its accompanying social system – capitalism – has often been pegged as contradictory. Such a view of Mill's thought has helped to trigger a "two Mills" hypothesis [e.g., Berns 1975], which holds that Mill's thought is inconsistent. On the one hand, often in the *Principles* and elsewhere, Mill is a fine advocate of [self-centered] capitalist forces and their favorable consequences to society. On the other hand, Mill penned some of the shrillest screeds ever written attacking capitalism's self-centered incentives. The resolution of the apparent contradiction lies in the insight that Mill uses two different contexts – present-day and utopian – when discussing capitalism and capitalist incentives.

In society as it was in Mill's day (and by implication as it is also in our present society), capitalism offered the best way possible of organizing economic society.[8] Mill accordingly followed the lead of Adam Smith in endorsing such a system in his (or our) society (allowing for certain limited corrective interventions by government [see *Principles*, Bk. V, Ch. 11]). But Mill saw great flaws in capitalism, chief among them its emphasis on self-interested behavior, which Mill saw as understandable and necessary "in the existing stage of society" (*Autobiography*, 161) but still fundamentally depraved. His more utopian musings were offered as the solution to capitalism's perceived ethical failings.

In Mill's perfect utopian society, by contrast, capitalism is vanquished in favor of enlightened, voluntary socialism (see *Principles*, Bk. IV, Chs. 6, 7). This exchange of social systems would not, however, occasion any decline in economic productivity and thus human happiness, as it would in the narrowly-selfish society. On the contrary, due to the great [assumed] power of utopian educational systems, under enlightened socialism, humankind would be capable of even more productiveness than before. Individuals, liberated at last from their unclean focus on their own well-being, would joyfully produce, not primarily for themselves, but for the

[8]Ashley writes: "Until the present social system should be fundamentally changed, Mill clearly regarded the Ricardian economics as so far applicable to existing conditions as to call for no substantial revision in method or conclusions" (Ashley 1929, xxiii).

benefit of their less-fortunate brothers and sisters. Even better, these "character"-laden individuals of the New Age would find "true happiness" in extra-materialistic themes, so that the reconstituted everyman would eagerly embrace a decline in personal wealth in exchange for a "fairer" society in which wealth is distributed more "justly." Most importantly, society would at last be ethically pure: the hated contradiction between altruistic morality and selfish capitalism would be forever vanquished, allowing humankind to at last reach its full potential.

We see in this vision important utopian assumptions about the core characteristics of human nature. Mill was not religious, but his utopian vision of the nature of man is little more than the standard Christian view.[9] Christian utopianism regards man as "fallen" and insists that only through the aid of God and Christ can man regain his "true," selflessly other-loving, nature. The divine mercy of God transforms everyman into "New Christian Man." Mill took over this basic ethical perspective wholesale, but stripped it of its religious element. The *Internet Encyclopedia of Philosophy* describes Mill's attitude aptly:

> Inspired by Comte, Mill finds an alternative to traditional religion in the Religion of Humanity, in which an idealized humanity becomes an object of reverence and the morally useful features of traditional religion are supposedly purified and accentuated. Humanity becomes an inspiration… (*Internet Encyclopedia of Philosophy*, 2010)

God is thus replaced by humanity, and sacrifice for God's vision is replaced by sacrifice in the name of humanity. A society organized around such principles is "pure," "holy," and perfect. The spurning of self-interest in favor of what might now be dubbed as "enlightened altruism" creates a society in which humans can finally find and reach their "true nature" and become completely "happy."

Nestled in all this – as in Christian doctrine – is the core assumption that humanity's "true nature" has been corrupted and twisted by self-centeredness. Only when liberated from the corruption of selfishness can Everyman truly breathe free. Thus, given the replacement of selfishness by enlightened altruism as the ruling principle of Society, all things are possible in the Great Society That Is To Come – leading to the founding of a New Age of unparalleled prosperity and enlightenment. Humankind would eventually perfect itself, and utopia would come, bringing an end to all society's problems. As Mill put it, the "existing arrangements of society" were "provisional, and as liable to be much altered by the progress of social improvement" (*Autobiography*, 257). By "progress of social improvement," of course, Mill meant, enlightened evolutionary socialism of a voluntary nature.

8. that a perfect society will be reached when self-interest is overcome and when the replacement altruistic ideology has successfully worked its way through society, re-inventing all its institutions accordingly.

[9]See, for example, Britton (1953, 54), who writes that Mill, in his *Utilitarianism* (Mill 1969 [1861]), "has expressed his adherence to the most general principles of Christian morality, with modifications deriving in part from Benthamism and in part from his own moral insight."

Mill's embracement of utopian voluntarist socialism is one of the constant themes echoing through his entire adult life. His first edition of his *Principles* was quite tough on socialism – a position he later regretted and reversed. As he put it himself:

> In the first edition the difficulties of socialism were stated so strongly, that the tone was on the whole that of opposition to it. In the year or two that followed, much time was given to the study of the best Socialist writers on the Continent, and to meditation and discussion on the whole range of topics involved in the controversy; and the result was that most of what had been written on the subject in the first edition was cancelled, and replaced by arguments and reflexions, which represent a more advanced opinion. (*Autobiography*, 241)

Replacing the hard-headed analysis of the first edition were sentiments such as the following, meant to answer the notion that under socialism "each person would be excessively occupied in evading his fair share of the work…" (*Principles*, 204, 204):

> Mankind is capable of a far greater amount of public spirit than the present age is accustomed to suppose possible. History bears witness to the success with which large bodies of human beings may be trained to feel the public interest their own. And no soil could be more favourable to the growth of such a feeling, than a Communist association, since all the ambition, and the bodily and mental activity, which are now exerted in the pursuit of separate and self-regarding interests, would require another sphere of employment, and would naturally find it in the pursuit of the benefit of the community. (*Principles*, 206, 205)

Accordingly, Mill thought that "whatever may be the merits or defects of these various [socialist] schemes, they cannot be truly said to be impracticable" (*Principles*, 204, 203). Later in this chapter (the famous "Of Property" leading off Book II), Mill – a serial hedger of arguments – stated also that "we are too ignorant either of what individual agency in its best form, or socialism in its best form, can accomplish, to be qualified to decide which of the two will be the ultimate form of human society" (*Principles*, 209, 208).

But by the time we reach Book IV's last two chapters, Mill is again waxing eloquent over the doleful problems suffered by "individual agency" and the corrective future wonders to be achieved by socialism. While Mill offers praise for the newly-evolving private-sector relationship between employer and employee, his main enthusiasm is reserved for those institutions then-developing that featured laborers forming cooperative enterprises and competing directly with orthodox capitalism. In his famous and heavily influential Book IV, Ch. 7 ("On the Probable Futurity of the Labouring Classes"), Mill aggressively argues that, if labor will just stick together, then socialist co-operatives will so far outdistant their capitalist competition that

> the existing accumulations of capital might honestly, and by a kind of spontaneous process, become in the end the joint property of all who participate in their productive employment… a transformation which, thus effected… would be the nearest approach to social justice… (*Principles*, 791–2; 793–4)

As is his wont, Mill waxes rhapsodic over the favorable consequences of the [socialist] cooperative model to the working man. Such a model's superiority works

> by placing the laborers, as a mass, in a relation to their work which would make it their principle and their interest – at present it is neither – to do the utmost, instead of the least possible, in exchange for their remuneration. It is scarcely possible to rate too highly this material benefit, which as yet is nothing compared with the moral revolution in society that

> would accompany it: the healing of the standing feud between capital and labour; the transformation of human life, from a conflict of classes struggling for opposite interests, to a friendly rivalry in the pursuit of a good common to all; the elevation of the dignity of labour... (*op. cit.*, 789–90; 792)

Such fantastic utopian fantasies illustrate how, even though Mill flirts in this chapter with the notion that an evolution of capitalist institutions might improve the lot of the laboring classes, it is in reveries of nonprofit models that he finds his true hope and faith.[10]

Just how determined Mill was on a socialist future for mankind, however, can best be seen through examining one of his most famous chapters in the *Principles* – Book IV, Ch. 6, on the "stationary state." Like all the classical economists, Mill believed in a living, breathing stationary state that was utterly inevitable given the premises of classical theory – premises that classical economists regarded as accurate descriptions of the actual society in which they lived. All classical economists prior to Mill thought that, since the stationary state's arrival would end economic growth and the rise in the material standard of living, it was a state to be deplored and staved off for as long as possible.

Mill, however, relying on his utopian vision for mankind, proclaimed a highly favorable assessment of the stationary state. The great advantage Mill sees in the stationary state is that it would reign in capitalism. In one astonishing tirade[11] after another, Mill savages the self-centered materialism that is the driving force of capitalism, and aggressively advocates the well-managed stationary state as being that condition where mankind could, at long last, be freed from its vicious, soul-numbing selfishness:

> I cannot, therefore, regard the stationary state of capital and wealth with the unaffected aversion so generally manifested towards it by the political economists of the old school. I am inclined to believe that it would be, on the whole, a very considerable improvement on our present condition. I confess I am not charmed with the ideal of life held out by those who think that the normal state of human beings is that of struggling to get on; that the trampling, crushing, elbowing, and treading on each other's heels, which form the existing type of social life, are the most desirable lot of human kind, or anything but the disagreeable symptoms of one of the phases of industrial progress. It may be a necessary stage in the progress of civilization... [and] it is not necessarily destructive of the higher aspirations and the heroic virtues; as America, in her great civil war, has proved to the world... But it is not a kind of social perfection which philanthropists to come will feel any very eager desire to assist in realizing. (*Principles, ibid*; 753–4)

---

[10]He even ventures the conclusion that once such societies have "sufficiently multiplied," their appeal to the working man will be so marked as to bring forth a situation where "both private capitalists and associations will gradually find it necessary to make the entire body of laborers participants in profits" (*op. cit.*, 791; 793) (an ironic prediction to say the least, given that such an approach often characterizes modern capitalist firms' relation with their laborers, while public-sector production invariably is exclusively salary-based).

[11]The language used and heavy sarcasm applied in these passages is so unlike Mill's standard style that it is reasonable to speculate that the primary author of these passages was not Mill, but Harriet Taylor-Mill. Compare, for example, the style of these passages with the style of Taylor in her correspondence with Mill (Hayek 1951). Still, Mill clearly endorsed the sentiments, or they would not have ended up in his *Principles*.

Here is Mill waiting patiently for the Altruistic Utopia That Is Surely To Come. Mill's ideal society, realizable (he thinks) in the stationary state, is one within which, "while no one is poor, no one desires to be richer, nor has any reason to fear being thrust back by the efforts of others to push themselves forward" (*Principles*, 749; 754). If such crude leveling sentiments strike us today as "so very twentieth [and now, it would seem, twenty-first] century," we must remember how influential Mill's tome was through the early years of the 1900s. These types of "fine sentiments," however, often travel hand-in-hand with an eye-popping elitism, as Mill is quick to show us:

> That the energies of mankind should be kept in employment by the struggle for riches, as they were formerly by the struggle of war, until the better minds succeed in educating the others into better things, is undoubtedly more desirable than that they should rust and stagnate. While minds are coarse they require coarse stimuli, and let them have them. In the mean time, those who do not accept the present very early stage of human improvement as its ultimate type, may be excused for being comparatively indifferent to the kind of economical progress which excites the congratulations of ordinary politicians; the mere increase of production and accumulation.... I know not why it should be matter of congratulation that persons who are already richer than any one needs to be, should have doubled their means of consuming things which give little or no pleasure except as representative of wealth; or that numbers of individuals should pass over, every year, from the middle classes into a richer class, or from the class of the occupied rich to that of the unoccupied (*Principles, ibid*; 754–5)

It is remarkable how many hoary assumptions and illicit conclusions Mill is able to stuff into this single paragraph. There is first the assumption that the minds of those who yearn for war are motivated by the same things as those who yearn for profit (as if Watt and Napoleon had the same aspirations). Then there is the notion that the "better minds" whom Mill lauds are themselves above an interest in profit – a notion confounded by the behavior of virtually all of history's elites.[12] Next is the assumption that these elites are able and willing to educate the masses through selfless service, despite (typically) their knowing almost nothing about them, their daily lives or their values. Then we are to assume that such self-sacrifice is self-evidently the acme of morality (never mind that the sacrificer in history usually wins his laurels by sacrificing *others*, not himself, on the alter of altruistic sentiment, and never mind either that the many industrial inventions then-sparking an unprecedented revolution in living standards in England were not achieved in the name of self-sacrifice.) Then there is the downgrading of "the mere increase of production," which is, in fact, the cause of the aforementioned revolution in living standards (in a later paragraph, Mill asserts, without evidence, his view that the many capitalist innovations have failed to help the poor). Next, there is Mill's notion that someone – perhaps, one of his "better minds" – is able to determine how rich "any one needs to be." This same person also is, marvelously, able to pierce the poisonous veil of

[12] That Mill himself is quite aware of this historical tendency is made clear by him in the very next chapter, where he writes, in answer to those, like Carlyle, who would see the higher classes "protect and guide" (that is, control) the lower classes. Mill writes: "All privileged and powerful classes, as such, have used their power in the interest of their own selfishness, and have indulged their self-importance in despising, and not in lovingly caring for, those who were, in their estimation, degraded, by being under the necessity of working for their benefit" (*Principles*, 754; 759).

materialism and see how pathetically tiny is the personal pleasure Burgher X can gain from a doubling of his means of consumption. Finally, there is the supposition that those who seek to bring new inventions to market seeking profit are truly only interested in doing so, so that they may raise their "class" status (a caddish slander of inventors and a profound twisting of their history). All this from a scholar who is usually perceived as highly logical and friendly to capitalism. In fact, it is never more clear than in his chapter on the stationary state that Mill despised capitalism (or at least the incentives underlying it). In his eyes, it was a moral outrage: the worst existing system except for all of the others that were then possible, to be replaced with an "enlightened socialism" at the earliest appropriate moment.

Mill closes his stationary-state chapter with several of his favorite themes: that in the developed economies a "better distribution" is a far more pressing issue than additional production or innovation; that sharp limits on bequests and inheritances are needed to assure the less-fortunate that there are "no enormous fortunes;" and, perhaps most shockingly, that enough of the necessary technological innovations for comfortable life already have been invented (meaning that if Mill had had his way, airplanes, automobiles, air conditioning, the microchip, the modern medicines that would almost certainly have saved his beloved wife's life, and countless other things invented since the 1870s would never have existed). Thoroughly unbowed by such considerations, Mill waxes eloquent on the perils of the progrowth mind-set, maintaining that

> if the earth must lose that great portion of its pleasantness which it owes to things that the unlimited increase of wealth and population would extirpate from it, for the mere purpose of enabling it to support a larger, but not a better or a happier population, I sincerely hope, for the sake of posterity, that they will be content to be stationary, long before necessity compels them to it. (*op. cit.*, 750–751; 756)

Thus one last great advantage of the stationary state appeals to Mill – that it will help us to "Save the Earth!"

Mill was not naive about the incentive structure implicit in socialism – he saw the difficulties clearly. But, as a utopian, he was remarkably naive about the ease with which such incentive problems could be overcome through "better" education, Hartleyian conditioning, and an almost-mystical socialist transformation of the human spirit. His utopian streak encouraged him to believe that, mysteriously, humans of the future would be purged of their acquisitive imperatives and, apparently, would gladly spurn material values and warmly embrace "sustainable development" policies. *Homo Futurus* would be a "noble," happy altruist to the very core of his being.[13]

In his socialist utopian reveries of his *Principles,* his *Autobiography*, and elsewhere, Mill commits one additional sin that is worth noting – he displays a shocking

[13]With all the wreckage of the twentieth century to learn from (and, it would appear, many more learning opportunities to be forthcoming in the twenty-first), it is easy now for the reader educated in market processes to be contemptuous of such socialist dreams. But in Mill's days, those dreams were yet to be tried-and-found-wanting, while capitalism's promise seemed destroyed by Malthusian population theory. Mill's utopian voluntary socialism, naive as it seems today, can be forgiven in a way that modern coercive socialists, with all the wreckage of failed socialist experiment after failed socialist experiment to contemplate, cannot and should not be forgiven.

failure of creativity. All – or nearly all – utopian visions have proceeded along similar lines. Most notable is the naive belief, held with unshakeable determination, that selfishness is the acme of evil and that in some better time, or in some better place, humankind will be purged of this vast sin and become "saved" and finally, Whole. So, should it be; ergo, so shall it be – in that great happy "someday" of the future. More to the point (speaks the utopian): so *must* it be, in order to harmonize with my utopian dreams for the future of mankind. The great defining characteristic of utopian thought is, always and everywhere, the worship of *wish* over *fact*. Among the clearest perpetrators of this most personally selfish of indulgences is John Stuart Mill.

References

Ashley, W. J. (1929). *Introduction* to *Principles of Political Economy with Some of Their Applications to Social Philosophy*, by John Stuart Mill. London: Longmans, Green and Co.

Berns, W. (1975). "Two Mills and Liberty: [Review of] On Liberty and Liberalism: The Case of John Stuart Mill," by Gertrude Himmelfarb. *Virginia Quarterly Review* (Winter): 127–31.

Britton, K. (1953). *John Stuart Mill*. Penguin Books, Melbourne/London/Baltimore.

Buchanan, J. and Gordon, T. (1962). *The Calculus of Consent: Logical Foundations of Constitutional Democracy*. Ann Arbor: University of Michigan Press.

Hayek, F. A. (1951). *John Stuart Mill and Harriet Taylor: Their Friendship and Subsequent Marriage*. Chicago: University of Chicago Press.

Internet Encyclopedia of Philosophy (2010). "John Stuart Mill." www.iep.utm.edu.

Kaplan, J. D. (1951). *Dialogues of Plato*. New York: Washington Square Press.

Mill, J. S. (1977a [1859]). *Thoughts on Parliamentary Reform*. In *Collected Works of John Stuart Mill, Volume XIX*. Toronto: University of Toronto Press, pp. 311–340.

Mill, J. S. (1977b [1859]). *On Liberty*. In *Collected Works of John Stuart Mill, Volume XVIII*. Toronto: University of Toronto Press, pp. 213–310.

Mill, J. S. (1973 [1861]). *Considerations on Representative Government*. In *Collected Works of John Stuart Mill, Volume XIX*. Toronto: University of Toronto Press, pp. 371–562.

Mill, J. S. (1969 [1861]). *Utilitarianism*. In *Collected Works of John Stuart Mill, Volume X*. Toronto: University of Toronto Press, pp. 203–260.

Mill, J. S. (1929 [1871]). *Principles of Political Economy, with Some of Their Applications to Social Philosophy*. London: Longmans, Green and Co.

Mill, J. S. (1965 [1871]). *Principles of Political Economy, with Some of Their Applications to Social Philosophy*. In *Collected Works of John Stuart Mill, Vols. II, III*. Toronto: University of Toronto Press.

Mill, J. S. (1981 [1873]). *Autobiography of John Stuart Mill*. In *Collected Works of John Stuart Mill, Volume I*. Toronto: University of Toronto Press, 1–290.

Skinner, B. F. (1948) *Walden Two*. The MacMillan Company.

The State as Utopia: Some Thoughts on Theocracy

Gerrit Meijer

Introduction

Theocracy is the conviction that God as the Creator is the Sovereign of heaven and earth. In this sense, it is not a state form. It can be combined with several state forms. In this chapter, the concept of theocracy in Christianity is discussed. First, the relation between church and state in early Christianity is discussed. Next, the thoughts of Augustine and Aquinas on the relation between church and state are exposed. Then we turn to the discussion of anabaptism and theocracy. Special attention is given to the attempt to realize a "theocracy" in Münster as the New Jerusalem. The conceptions of the Reformation of Luther and Calvin, on the relation between church and state, will be described in the light of Geneva. The chapter will end with a conclusion.

Early Christianity on the Relation Between Church and State

In the fullness of time, God the Father sends His son Jesus Christ. The Christians formed the Christian church. The gospel was the message of salvation and eternal life, through His suffering and resurrection. With regard to the state Jesus was tempted by the Pharisees by a catch question: Is it allowed to pay taxes to the emperor? His answer was: Give the emperor what is his, and to God what is of God. This was one of a series of three catch questions posed by different groups (Matthew 22). Jesus accepted the scriptures of the Old Testament and also the Mosaic law. This clearly is evident from His so-called Sermon of the Mount (Matthew 5–7). His answer, to the question of Pilatus: Are you the king of the Jews? was that he was not the king of the Jewish people, and that His Commonwealth is not of this world. Before His ascension he told he would go to heaven and sit at the right hand of His Father and have all the

G. Meijer(✉)
University of Maastricht, Larixlaan 3 1231 BL Loosdrecht, The Netherlands
e-mail: g.meijer@hetnet.nl

J.G. Backhaus (ed.), *The State as Utopia: Continental Approaches*, The European Heritage in Economics and the Social Sciences 9, DOI 10.1007/978-1-4419-7500-3_6,

power in heaven and on earth, and that he would come back on the Day of Judgment to found His Kingdom on the New Earth: the New Jerusalem (Matthew 24).

Paul (in particular, in Romans 13) and other writers of epistles in the New Testament stress that the government as an institution is a minister of God. The authority of the rulers is from God and therefore they have to be obeyed by Christians. They are responsible to God.

In early Christianity, the state as an institution is subsidiary to the church; the church as an institution is subsidiary to the state. They are constituted by the citizens and the church members, respectively. The sovereign over both institutions is God. In this sense, the state is a theocracy. However, the same is the case with the church. However, as we will see, this does not mean that there is a hierarchy between the church and the state.

Roman philosophers (e.g., Cicero (106–143), but especially Seneca (ca 4 B.C. - 65) had influence on the Christians. Seneca is in the beginning of Christianity the most important. His writings were highly appreciated by Tertullian (ca 160–220). Sabine (1951, p.159) writes: "Seneca's interpretation of the two commonwealths was only one of the surprising parallels between his thought and that of the Christians, parallels which produced in antiquity a body of forged letters supposed to have passed between him and St Paul." Sabine also mentions that Seneca was on the one hand intensely conscious of the inherent sinfulness of human nature and that on the other hand, his ethics showed the tendency towards humanitarianism, which became continually more marked in later stoicism.

Augustine and Aquinas on the Relation of Church and State

Augustine (354–430) writes in his famous book, *The City of God* (*De Civitate Dei*), that man is a citizen of two cities, the city of his birth and the City of God. Man is body and soul. In his thinking are Manichaean influences, which have their origin and influence in Persia. He, like Mani (216–277), sees history as the struggle of good and evil. The former is the world of nature, the latter the world of grace: peace and salvation. The former is the Kingdom of Satan and the latter, the Kingdom of Christ (Cochrane, 2003).

Augustine defends the position that: under the new dispensation, the state must be a Christian state, which serves a community which is one by virtue of a common Christian faith, which ministers to a life in which spiritual interests admittedly stand above all other interests and which contributes to human salvation by preserving the purity of the faith (Sabine, 1951, p. 171). The church is autonomous, the highest authority in spiritual matters. There are two orders: one regal and one clerical, with different (earthly) jurisdictions. This dualism leads to the doctrine of the two swords (Sabine, 1951, p. 174). Spiritual matters belong to the jurisdiction of the church, which is an independent and self-governing institution.

In the Middle Ages, under the influence of Aristotle (384–322 B.C.), the ideas changed (Nemo, 1998). In the doctrines of Thomas Aquinas (1224–1277), the organic view on the state of Aristotle is combined with the doctrines of Augustine. Moreover, in fact, there was not only co-operation between the church and the state but also struggle for supremacy. On the one hand there was the secular power of the Emperor, which was contested by the church. It was also the time of the Crusades. The rise of the Islam, the false religion, to world power, was a serious threat to the Christian state (s), the Holy Roman Empire during the Middle Ages, which in the West lasted to the end of the fifteenth century and in the East to 1683 (far beyond what we call the Middle Ages). Also, there were tendencies within the church in the form of monasteries and orders of monks influenced by the doctrine of nature and grace. They were forms of asceticism (Bredero, 2000). According to Aquinas, the church, which belongs to the world of grace, became the highest authority, above the state. The state became subject to the church. The church, in its hierarchical organization with the Pope as the highest authority, had the last say in every part of life, as the only institution that is authorized – after this standpoint – for that.

Münster as the New Jerusalem-Anabaptism and "Theocracy"

In Germany, in 1525, the Peasants' War broke out. It was a revolt against feudal oppression, but its character changed into a war against all authorities, the state as well as the church. It became a movement to establish by forceful revolution "the Kingdom of God" – an ideal Christian commonwealth – with absolute equality and the community of goods. The leader is Thomas Münzer. Luther (1525) denounced this movement as anarchist, and the peasants as murderous and rapacious.

In Münster, it was tried by radical Anabaptists to establish a "theocracy" (1534/35). The leaders were Bernard Rothmann, Bernard Knipperdolling, Jan Matthys, and Jan of Leyden. The background was Anabaptism. I will spare you the bloody and cruel details John of Leyden claimed to be the successor of King David. He claimed royal honors and absolute power in the new Sion, the New Jerusalem. Community of goods was established, he legalized polygamy. He took himself 16 wives, one of whom he beheaded himself in the market place. The town was conquered back by the expelled bishop, Franz von Waldeck, on June 24, 1535. In January 1536, King John and his main followers after being tortured were executed in the marketplace. Their dead bodies were exhibited in cages, along the tower of the St. Lambert's Church. These cages are still there.

There were also Anabaptists, the most well-known is Menno Simons (1496–1561) from Witmarsum in Frisia, who opposed the use of force. He and his followers, the Mennonites never aimed at social or political revolution, they preached love of enemy and compassion. They were pacifists either by principle, or by necessity. They did not swear the oath.

When we have a closer look at Anabaptism we see that there are some doctrines that characterize this spiritual movement. They rejected child baptism, and were adherents to adult baptism. They considered themselves to be the true believers. For our subject very important is their doctrine of premillennialism or chiliasm: they believed in an earthly temporary messianic age. It is based on a (literal?) interpretation of Revelation 20: 1–6. This interpretation is seen by them in connection with some Jewish writings of the first two centuries (1 Enoch and 4 Ezra), which however are not accepted by the church as part of the Holy Scripture. In the time of the church fathers, there were different points of view on several doctrines of the church, including these two doctrines (Löwith, 1960). They were condemned by the church on the basis of the Holy Scripture.

Geneva-The Reformation and Theocracy: Luther (1483–1546) and Calvin (1509–1564)

The same doctrines (those of the church) are found in the Reformation. Art. XVII of the Augsburg Confession (1530) condemns the Anabaptists and others "who now scatter Jewish opinions that, before the resurrection of the dead, God shall occupy the kingdom of the world, the wicked being everywhere suppressed."

The form of the Anabaptism in the sixteenth century sees no principal difference between Israel and the church. This is what we find back in Zwickau (the Zwickauer Prophets, Münzer) and Münster. Luther and Calvin were afraid that their activities for Reformation of the church were seen as revolution (Sohm, 1889). This is clear from Luther's (1525) denouncement of this movement as anarchistic, and the peasants as murderous and rapacious. Also, this is evident from Calvin's letter to the king of France in 1541 in the preface to the third edition of the Institution and his letter of 1543 to the Emperor Charles V (1500–1555–9). Nevertheless, on February 14, 1544, the institution was burned in front of the Notre Dame by order of the Parliament of Paris.

The "theocracy" in Geneva has an entirely different background and character from the "theocracy" in Münster. Calvin was a humanist (Van Itterzon, 1957). He studied law and literature and wrote in 1532 on e.g., Seneca (De Clementia (Huizinga, 1936)). In 1535, he published his Institution in which he set forth the principles of Christian faith (Calvijn, 1535, 1999). For an exposition of Calvin's thinking on political and economic problems and its influence on economic and political life in Geneva see Elster (1878) and Meijer (2010).

In Geneva, since 1555, the city (state) and church more or less coincided. However, the worldly power was in the hands of the magistrates, not of the church. Not Mosaic Law but the Decalogue served as guidance. This was a difference between the Anabaptists and Calvin. The Anabaptists took as guidance the whole Law of Moses, including the ceremonial laws. Calvin saw these ceremonial laws (with the rules for priests for example) as abolished, because of the sacrifice of Jesus Christ (Praamsma, 1979). Later on, his political philosophy was elaborated (1603, 1995) and practiced by Althusius (1557–1638), as the syndic of Emden.

Calvin fought in Geneva (where he first lived from 1536 to 1538, and later from 1541 to 1564) for the independence of the reformed church in relation to the magistrates of the city. In 1555, he finally succeeded. He was not the dictator of Geneva. He was even banned from Geneva during the years 1538–1541. It was not before 1559 that he got citizenship. In 1559, he founded the Academy of Geneva.

He organized the church in a democratic way: elders (Presbyters) had to be chosen by the church members, and deacons had to take care of the sick and poor people. Law and order by the magistrates under the influence of the preaching of the reformed church were improved in the spirit of the Decalogue and the principles of economics and politics of Calvin, which were in favor of trade (and industry) and freedom of contract, private property, and Christian moral values. He stimulated also by practical proposals on economic and social problems, especially the improvement of employment to fight poverty.

The political philosophy of Calvin and later on Althusius influenced especially the development of events in the Netherlands (Kossmann, 1987). In the century between about 1560 and 1660 in the Republic of the Seven Netherlands (a federation of seven independent republics), the discussion on tolerance was an important subject (Janssen 2004; Meijer unpublished manuscript; Meijer 2000). William of Orange in this respect held ideas about this that were not accepted by all Calvinists. The ideas were strongly influenced by the fact that the Republic was at war with Spain. Mennonites in service of the Republic were dispensed from swearing the oath. The religious conflict in 1618/9 between remonstrants and contra-remonstrants had, as a background, the difference of opinion on foreign policy during the ceasefire from 1609 to 1621. The Peace of Münster (1648) not only ended the war with Spain. The Netherlands became independent, and the Tract was also an agreement on the position of the different religions. The freedom of conscience and, therefore, tolerance became, in the train of thinking of Calvin, the overruling principle.

Conclusion

Theocracy in the meaning of the Reformation is not a state form. It concerns the question of sovereignty. It means that God as the Creator is the Sovereign. This conception can be combined with monarchy, democracy, aristocracy, etc. In Calvin's Geneva, it was combined with democracy as a form of government in church and state. When we compare Münster and Geneva, one of the most important differences is the world avoidance of the Anabaptists. They try to realize a New Jerusalem. It is a destructive utopia, because it undermines the foundations of Christian society. In Geneva, it was the objective to realize a commonwealth adapted to the will of God, as revealed in the Bible. It gave rise to a society that was conducive to a well-organized and prosperous city life. It is not a New Jerusalem that is strived after.

References

Althusius, J., 1995, Politica. An abridged translation of Politics Methodology Set Forth and Illustrated with Sacred and Profane Examples. Edited and translated, with an introduction by Frederick S. Carney. Foreword by Daniel J. Elazar, Indianapolis; Liberty Fund. Originally Politica Methodice Digesta et exemplis sacris et profanes illustrate, 1603, Herborn: Christophorus Corvinus

Bredero. A.H., 2000, 3e druk, De ontkerstening der Middeleeuwen. Een terugblik op de geschiedenis van twaalf eeuwen christendom. Kampen: Agora

Calvijn, J., 1535, 1999, 13e druk, Institutie of onderwijzing in de christelijke godsdienst. Vertaling van A. Sizoo. Zoetermeer: Meinema

Cochrane, C.N., 2003, Christianity and Classical Culture. A Study of Thought and Action from Augustus to Augustine, Indianapolis: Liberty Fund. Originally 1940, Oxford: Oxford University Press

Elster, L., 1878, Johann Calvin als Staatsmann, Gesetzgeber and Nationalökonom. Jahrbuch für Nationalökonomie und Statistik, Bd. 30 (Jena)

Huizinga, J., 1936, 3e druk, Erasmus. Haarlem: H.D. Tjeenk Willink

Janssen, G., 2004, Om de theocratie. Honderd jaar van strijd om de verwerkelijking en vormgeving van de theocratische gedachte, Middelburg: Stichting de Gihonbron

Kossmann, E.H., 1987, Politieke theorie en geschiedenis. Verspreide opstellen en voordrachten. Amsterdam: Bakker

Löwith, K., 1960, Wereldgeschiedenis. Wijsgerig en Bijbels gezien, Utrecht/Antwerpen: Het Spectrum. Originally: Meaning of History (1949), Chicago: Chicago University Press. In het Duits: Weltgeschichte und Heilgeschehen. Stuttgart: Kohlhammer

Luther, M., (1525), Wider die räuberischen und mörderischen Rotten der Bauern, in: Werke. Kritische Gesamtausgabe in 120 Bänden, Band 18, 1888. 357–361. Weimar: Verlag Hermann Böhlaus

Meijer, G., 2000, The Idea of Subsidiarity in Dutch Economic and Political Thought, in G. Meijer, W.J.M. Heijman, J.A.C. van Ophem, B.H.J. Verstegen (eds.), ISINI Papers Maastricht, Volume II, 2000, pp. 415–420. Maastricht: Shaker

Meijer, G., 2010, Calvin über Wirtschaft und Staat: Die Reformation und ihre Wirkung, in J.G. Backhaus (ed.) 2010, Religion und Wirtschaft: Die Bedeutung der Reformation. Berlin, Münster; LITverlag

Meijer, G., 2010, Calvin on Economics and Politics: The Reformation and its Impact with Respect to Calvin, in J.G. Backhaus (ed.) 2010, The Reformation. New York: Springer

Meijer, G., The Peace of Münster at the background of the History of Thought (unpublished manuscript)

Nemo, Ph., 1998, Histoire des idées politiques dans l'Antiquité et au Moyen Age, Paris: Presses Universitaires de France

Praamsma, L., 1979, De kerk van alle tijden. Verkenningen in het landschap van de kerkgeschiedenis. Vier delen, Franeker: Wever

Sabine, G.H., 1951, 3e druk, A History of Political Theory. London: Harrap

Sohm, R., 1889, De geschiedenis der kerk in hare grondtrekken geschetst. Nijkerk: Callenbach. Vertaling door L.H.F.A. Faure; met voorwoord van H.G. Kleyn van Sohm's Kirchengeschichte im Grundrisz, 1887. Leipzig: Böhme

Van Itterzon, G.P., 1957, 2de druk, Calvijn, in Christelijke enyclopedie, Deel II, Kampen: Kok, 76–82

Justi's Concrete Utopia

Hartmuth Becker

Introduction

To begin with, the paradoxical title of this chapter has to be explained: As is well known, utopias are considered incomprehensible or abstract (what is more, utopia comes from the Greek for "no place," which speaks for itself). This is down to the fact that – according to today's understanding – utopian ideas are extrapolated into the future, which implies uncertainty. If the talk here is nevertheless of a "concrete utopia," it should be mentioned that Justi has reflected his ideas precisely. He designed a normative model of state to which the government and administration should orientate themselves. In Justi's writings, the ideal-typical structural elements of a utopia are found: reason, necessity, and utility. All three are important to realize the *common good* (lat. "bonum commune").[1] Even though the title illustrates his volition precisely, Justi has not, as far as I know, used the word utopia in his writings explicitly. This term was regarded as problematic in the early eighteenth century. Even if a utopia was considered to serve as a model, it was quite clear, that it could be just an idealistic long-term objective. Critique of the term outweighs by far its acceptance, in the eighteenth century anyway. Christian Wolff regards the description of a perfect state as a touchstone or rather as a mirror, whereby we can see the incompleteness of our states, but otherwise as superfluous.[2] Nevertheless, we can make the observation: Orientation toward the future and not looking back in the past was Justi's point in building a new state.[3] Thus follows his construction of a utopia implicitly as a continuity of how it had been existing since the middle of the eighteenth century. Unlike Thomas More's novel *Utopia*, which was then seen as a contempoaneous fiction, the utopias of the eighteenth century were located in the

[1] See Nitschke (1996), 36.

[2] See Dierse (2001), 512.

[3] See Marchet (1885), 294.

H. Becker (✉)
University of Erfurt, Nordhäuser Str. 63, 99089, Erfurt Thuringen, Germany
e-mail: becker.hartmuth@t-online.de

J.G. Backhaus (ed.), *The State as Utopia: Continental Approaches*, The European Heritage in Economics and the Social Sciences 9, DOI 10.1007/978-1-4419-7500-3_7,

future. In other words, we find here a switch of high quality in the meaning of the term. In the future, according to the teleological idea of progress, it may work out, and the utopia will become a reality. This change in the social consciousness of time emerged, because a number of important technical innovations happened, that seemed to allow an unconditional control of nature[4] – like Watt's "steam engine," Hargreaves' "Spinning Jenny," Herschel's "reflecting telescope," Montgolfier's "hot-air balloon," and Volta's "battery." Later in the twentieth century, wicked utopias like Aldous Huxley's *Brave new world* or George Orwell's novel *1984*, arose.

The chapter is subdivided into two sections in which, along the usual lines, at first some brief notes about the person are mentioned, although the analysis of the work shall be presented in the foreground. After this, Justi's work will be discussed in the context of his contemporaries, such as Christian Thomasius, Christian Wolff, and Charles de Secondat Baron de Montesquieu, whereupon the key concept of his work, which is the felicity, will be discussed. A selected part of his oeuvre shall be considered as a manifestation of his "concrete utopia." And this is not easy, as he was regarded as a prolific writer on cameralism, having written in the period from 1741 to 1771 at least 48 books (according to Meusel's dictionary), which in some cases consist of several volumes.[5] If the translations are counted independently, there are even 67 books (according to the Ketterer catalog no. 224 from the year 1998).[6] The critics remarked early on, that many of his later works merely represented revisions or long-winded variations of former works. It was inevitable that literal repetitions appeared.[7] Most books had been written with "witty carelessness,"[8] stated Roscher. I have chosen *Der Grundriß einer guten Regierung* from the year 1759, the treatise on *Die Natur und das Wesen der Staaten* from the following year, and his relevant writings about the *science of police* and the *science of cameralism*. Moreover, the *Staatswirthschaft* from the year 1755, which can be considered as an essential outline, has to be consulted, too.

Justi, His Life and Work in the Context of His Time

Remarks about the Person

It still remains uncertain, up to now, exactly when Johann Heinrich Gottlob von Justi was born in Brücken (county of Sangerhausen) in Thuringia. In recent literature, different versions of the basic facts of his life can be found.[9] He presumably

---

[4] See Garber (1996), 99–100.

[5] See Roscher (1868), 82.

[6] See Reinert/Reinert (2009), 19.

[7] See Klein (1961), 146.

[8] Roscher (1868), 84. *Note: direct quotations have all been translated from German into English.*

[9] See Reinert (2009), 36.

was born on Christmas day in 1717, as an entry suggests in the local baptismal register. There is no doubt about the day of his death, he died in the Prussian fortress Küstrin on July 21, 1771, as a prisoner. Judgment of the person and oeuvre by his contemporaries and the posterity is controversial. In the years 1741–1742, Justi was engaged as a soldier in Saxonian services in the first Silesian War. After that he studied in Wittenberg. To this day, it is not certain, whether this important representative of the *science of cameralism* and of the *science of police* switched to the Roman Catholic faith in Austrian services (1751–1754 at the Theresianum), although evidence suggests so. It is also uncertain, whether he was ennobled at this time or had rather incorrectly used the title following his Viennese time. His further adventurous destiny is known, however. His short stay in Göttingen (1755–1757) had been appreciated in detail by Frensdorff, a time, in which the first systematic textbook for the *science of police* was written. His time period in Göttingen overlapped with the beginning of the Seven Year War (1756–1763).[10] In 1758, he was in attendance in Danish services. The Bavarian academy of sciences in Munich took him as a member in 1762.[11] In 1765, was Justi nominated by Frederick II., the Great, as head of the state mines in Prussia. Three years later he was arrested because of alleged misappropriations. Again, there are diverse opinions in the literature about the reasons for his detention and the progress of the lawsuit.[12] By the way, Justi was initially under domiciliary arrest, however, as it cost him two Talers daily for the Prussian guards to protect (and watch) him, he decided instead to go to prison in the fortress Küstrin.[13]

Wolff, Thomasius, and Montesquieu

One can often read that Justi's ideas had been influenced by the German enlightenment philosophers Wolff and Thomasius. This does not come as a surprise. These two philosophers from the University of Halle had been ever-present at Justi's time. Both were important representatives of the science of natural justice and rational law. They presupposed a natural justice, accessible to human reason, which attained validity independently of social agreement or the existing positive state laws. Starting from supreme principles, they tried to deduce a canon of valid laws by an exact deduction. Thomasius and Wolff had been uncritical of religion, unlike the French enlightenment philosophers, but their attempt at rationalistic explanation belonging to the rational law caused difficulties with church authorities. So, Wolff came under suspicion of atheism.[14]

[10] See Frensdorff (1901), passim.

[11] See Deutsch (1889), 561.

[12] See Obert (1992), 9–10, 17–18, 22–23.

[13] See Inama-Sternegg (1881), 750, see Dittrich (1974), 707–709, see Klueting (2005), 333–336.

[14] See Hirschberger (1988), 257–266.

Just like Thomasius, who was the first German enlightenment philosopher who combined English empiricism and French rationalism for his own independent philosophy, Justi was an opponent of Aristotelianism. Also diverging from Melanchton, who tried as a protestant church reformer, to re-establish the scholasticism outside of the Catholic background.[15] At all times, Thomasius stood firmly against Aristotelianism and scholasticism. It was definitely usual in the early stage of the German enlightenment to cultivate a secular awareness of the self – like Thomasius – which had to cause a clear contrast to Aristotle's metaphysics, who saw human beings in their totality.[16] There is also another practical reason to mention, which suggests a turning away from Aristotelianism by Justi. With the implementation of the cameralistic subjects, and primarily the *science of police*, it had to come to a dissociation from the older academic subject of politics based on Aristotle. Politics in that sense did not represent the given challenges of a modern statehood.[17] Presumably, this was an important reason for the implementation of the *science of cameralism* itself. Moreover, Justi borrowed the idea of the sovereignty of the people from Thomasius, which becomes obvious when one reads the *Staatswirthschaft*.[18] Highlighting and decline of the modern social contract theories took place in the eighteenth century. Just like Thomasius, Justi stands against the social contract theory, which is represented by Thomas Hobbes, John Locke or Jean-Jacques Rousseau. In *Natur und Wesen*, it is stated clearly: "We have shown in the proceeding chapter that republics arise likely nearly unnoticed. No one has thought either of a contract or of decrees."[19] If Justi uses the word "by agreement"[20] in another context, he speaks about a constitution: In other words, about the control of power and not about a social contract.[21]

In his work, Justi rests on Wolff's moralistic system of duties.[22] This is seen obviously from Chap. 7 on *Natur und Wesen* that deals with the mutual obligations of ruler and people as a central theme.[23] Justi writes there about the narrow relationship between sovereign and people and particularly about the obligations of the people. Things in common are found between Wolff and Justi on how they both view the authority of the state, the *constitution* (Grundgesetz), and the peoples' right to resist.[24] Incidentally, contrary to Thomasius, Wolff was also involved in teaching metaphysics. From Wolff, who supports an enlightened absolutism, Justi obtained the motivation to give the *science of cameralism* a socio-philosophical foundation. Justi adopted Wolff's abstract-deductive method as well, which was obviously different from the inductive method of Montesquieu. Divergences

[15] See Rüdiger (2005), 146–147.

[16] See Hirschberger (1988), 257–258.

[17] See Maier (1986), 164–177.

[18] See Justi (1758), I, 34–35.

[19] Justi (1760), 41.

[20] Justi (1759), 8.

[21] See Justi (1760), 76.

[22] See Marchet (1885), 291–292.

[23] See Justi (1760), 215–264.

[24] See Obert (1992), 165.

between Justi and Wolff are, however, found there where no one would have expected them superficially. Divergences are to be found in the perception of eudaimonia, in the interpretation of the idea of felicity, which we will speak about in the following chapter. While Wolff relates his perception of natural justice with an objective moral commandment, Justi connects it with a subjective survival instinct. The idea of felicity is for Wolff an ethical doctrine that gives the idea of the welfare state, a proof of identity.[25] For Justi, the common welfare and the term felicity are merely a secondary effect of a strong state.[26] Even despite all the specified, undeniable dependence on Wolff, Justi himself seems to lose this dependency as he approaches towards Montesquieu. However, personal reasons may also have contributed to the later estrangement from Wolff, because Wolff verbally attacked him in connection with Justi's award-winning essay about Leibniz' Theory of Monads, written for the Prussian academy of sciences in 1747.[27]

Since the year 1752, Justi dealt with Montesquieu, in the beginning because of his job as an Austrian censor. In Justi's writings, Montesquieu is mentioned from about 1757.[28] Already in the second edition of the *Staatswirthschaft* from the year 1758, various references in the footnotes to Montesquieu could be found.[29] Marchet even talks of a preference for this French author. Also, Remer calls Justi one of the best Montesquieu experts of all.[30] His literature, especially Justi's book *Natur und Wesen* from the year 1760, was often seen as dependent on Montesquieu. A proof of this is that you can find the same rejection of the so-called hypothetical contractarian theories by Montesquieu and Justi.[31] Also, both have the same assumption of the *natural state* (Naturzustand) and the same idea of the relativity of the legislation, which results "from the nature of the things."[32] The opinion, that Justi's *Natur und Wesen* is only an amendment of Montesquieus' *Esprit des lois*, and is in addition tedious and imprecise, has lasted up to today.[33] This might have been caused by the authority of Roscher, who reproached Justi, that he "would stay essentially on the shoulders of Montesquieu, although he would often argue against his master."[34] For example, it can be observed with the question whether there are special natures or driving forces behind the different forms of government, which does not appreciate Montesquieu, or when Justi applies a dichotomic model of division of powers into legislation and executive, he is going against Montesquieu's most modern division of powers into legislation, executive, and jurisdiction.[35] But this opinion does not fully appreciate that Justi wanted an

[25] See Sommer (1925), 210–212.

[26] See Maier (1986), 183.

[27] See Backhaus (2009), 8–9.

[28] See Unruh (1969), 13.

[29] See Adam (2009), 86.

[30] See Remer (1938), 20.

[31] See Marchet (1885), 292, 303.

[32] Justi (1760), 266.

[33] See Schelp (2001), 71.

[34] Roscher (1868), 84–85.

[35] See Justi (1759), 156.

independent outline, as he has formulated it emphatically in *Natur und Wesen*: "In the meantime, no one should think that I am trying to disprove or blame Montesquieu everywhere. No!… You can consider my work a *Spirit of the Laws* itself."[36]

Felicity as a Contemporary Watchword of Everyone

The "concrete utopia" of Justi can be fixed to the idea of felicity, which Immanuel Kant once called the "watchword of everyone" (Losungswort aller Welt).[37] The word, which was used in the eighteenth century in an excessive way, had a similar meaning to the models of social security and justice today. It forms the secular counterpart to the eternal blessedness at which religion is aimed.[38] The phrasing describing felicity as the final aim of all states is found in Justi's writings dozens of times.[39] Justi seems to recognize an "optimum optimorum": The universal monarchy – which causes the "greatest felicity"[40]. Analogous to his automatic opinion about nationhood, which was typical for the whole century,[41] Justi had no methodological-individualistic position, but a holistic point of view, although the idea of felicity cannot be removed from individual references. Even if it is ultimately the individual, that shall be in bliss, the entire entity is considered to be more than the sum of the individual parts. However, this profound methodological conflict is hidden, because individual interests and collective interests harmoniously complete each other. Justi and other enlightenment philosophers regard these interests as in principle in harmony. It is because of this that he can use terms like felicity of states, felicity of subjects, felicity of families or felicity of citizens synonymously without regarding this is a problem.[42] Felicity is explained by Justi in the words of labor ethics. Any hard-working subject shall come into the possession of material commodities and immaterial goods. That is what a good government has to guarantee. Now, how does Justi define the concept of felicity?

"Therefore I understand by the felicity of the subjects, such a good implementation and composition of a state, that anyone can enjoy liberty and is enabled to acquire those moral goods and material commodities by their diligence, which a subject needs for an enjoyable life here."[43] He adds the limitation immediately: "No one should understand too much by the enjoyable life of the subjects.… The human nature is satisfied with few goods."[44]

---

[36] Justi (1760), preliminary report.

[37] Kant (1798), 262.

[38] See Justi (1760/61), II, 15.

[39] See for ex. Justi (1756), 5, Justi (1761), I, preliminary report.

[40] Justi (1761), II, 235.

[41] See Stavenhagen (1969), 27.

[42] See Engelhardt (1981), 50–51.

[43] Justi (1758), I, 66.

[44] Justi (1758), I, 67.

In the literature, sometimes Justi's idea of felicity is criticized as a circular argument. This was mentioned by Franz Joseph Bob, a representative of the *science of police*.[45] As it is well known, laws and rules are adequate, if they transport the felicity. But for Justi, felicity is not only relevant for examination, but is itself a final aim. Thus, a tautology emerges.[46] We want to follow the critics and see felicity in the logic of the eighteenth century as the final aim.

Justi's Oeuvre as a Manifestation of the "Concrete Utopia"

Foreign politics and inner security are necessary, although by no means sufficient to Justi to make the described objective of felicity come true. In addition, they require the wealth, meaning: national income and states income.[47] State politics is responsible for foreign politics and inner security. Still, the economic police guarantee inner security per procurationem. Police are also responsible for the administration. Justi saw his own undeniable merit for the *science of cameralism* as a result of attempts to replace the common *particular cameralism* with a universal approach.[48] *Universal cameralism* is not limited to the financial system (chamber) alone, but rather includes the *politics*, the *science of police*, the *science of commerce*, and the *economics* as a whole.[49] It seems quite obvious then that his approach of *universal cameralism* is a comprehensive one.

Philosophy and Politics of the State

Justi gives a conception of state, related to the perception of the rational law that regards the state as having an independent nature with its own personality.[50] The state is a physical machine,[51] according to Justi, or a simple moral body.[52] According to an operating state mechanism, no individual will, which goes directly against the common will, can be tolerated. Justi justifies the prior-ranking position of the state compared to the families. The common good is ranked higher than private goods of families. In a wider sense, all private goods are at the disposal of the state, but not at the disposal of the ruler personally: "The state has the access to all goods of the private people. This is the result of the unification of wills and forces. Because the state

[45] See Marchet (1885), 414.
[46] See Justi (1758), I, 35–36.
[47] See Justi (1758), I, 69.
[48] See Justi (1758), I, XXXI.
[49] See Justi (1758), I, 52.
[50] See Marchet (1885), 291.
[51] See Justi (1759), 392.
[52] See Justi (1760), 176.

is a simple moral body, however, the goods of these families also belong to them without doubt."[53] This means there is a power of control, but not nationalization. Nowadays, Justi's view is considered modern.[54] He appreciates the value of individuals and families to the felicity of the entire state. No longer, as in the Middle Ages, is the main attention on the ruler only. The attention is now on the ruler *and* the people, which gives rise to the common good. Justi seems to venture a new approach.

The concretization of his conception of the state is described in his four-element doctrine. The state is based on two visible bases and two moral bases, under which families, the country, the unification of wills and the unification of families' strength have to be counted in detail.[55] Justi said: "Not the size of the republics alone is important, rather, the more numerous and the stronger the families are, the more the state becomes secure. The composition of the families is important here."[56] The internal structure and efficiency of the families is the analytical subject of the *science of police*. Furthermore, the national territory is the second visible basis for every republic.[57] Justi was still far away from founding a theory of region. It seems most important that the connection of the families becomes durable. According to Justi, the first moral basis of a state is the unification of wills. The unification of the families' strength is the second moral basis of a republic. Both arguments are complementary: "If the families unite their wills; they also must unite all their strengths."[58] The ultimate authority of the state then arises, which is nothing more than the complete strength of the single parts.[59] Justi is not interested in a historical genesis of the state but in the logical context of his four-element doctrine.

Justi describes the legitimacy in a whole chapter in *Natur und Wesen*,[60] since a state will not reach its final aim "if it has no good and wise laws."[61] He also tells about the laws of natural justice.[62] Justi orientates himself to the *Esprit des lois*, which he mentions several times. "The united will of the people cannot reveal itself other than by laws… If the people decide, how the ultimate authority of the state should be, then there is a constitution."[63] In other words, the form of government is established constitutionally. Justi shows three forms of government: monarchy, aristocracy, and democracy;[64] ; he conceded, that each of them has a special nature. The special driving force within a monarchy is the honor or the desire

[53] Justi (1760), 80.
[54] See Justi (1760/61), II, 101–105.
[55] See Justi (1760), 31–44.
[56] Justi (1760), 31.
[57] See Justi (1760), 37.
[58] Justi (1760), 38.
[59] See Justi (1760), 39
[60] See Justi (1760), 265–488.
[61] Justi (1760), 265.
[62] See Justi (1760), 335–354.
[63] Justi (1759), 7.
[64] See Justi (1760), 104–105.

for merit,[65] in an aristocracy the moderation,[66] and last but not the least, the driving force for democracy is the love of equality.[67] He prefers the constitutional monarchy: "The most perfect balance and relationship under the internal forces take place in the restricted monarchies or in forms of mixed government."[68] A constitutional monarchy is different from an (at that time largely established) absolute monarchy. A constitutional monarchy is not despotic but rational and able to initiate the required reforms. It is also different from a democracy. A monarchy only can guarantee the (for this purpose, necessary) central organization. Through this hint, you can see that Justi wanted to have a moral relationship as the ultimate authority of the state. He balanced out the position of sovereignty from the people on the one hand and the power of the monarch on the other hand.[69] That reason you can find in the *Grundriß*: "If the people delegate their power to the ultimate authority of the state, then this force is still based on the people, since it has arisen from the unification of wills and the strengths of the subjects."[70] From this, incidentally, a right to resist is derived, although he clearly distanced himself from the radical position of the Monarchomachs, to whose view the German lawyer Johannes Althusius subscribed. The right to resist is only relevant in the improbable case, when a monarch reveals himself openly as "enemy of the people."[71]

Justi expressed an opinion, which surprisingly, gets close to a thesis of the state as an *end in itself* (Selbstzweck), which is assigned in German literature first to Idealism or assigned to Romanticism. Obviously, this pioneering thesis is justified jusnaturalistically. The wording is found in the *Grundriß*: "The basis of all moral actions of the people is self-love; and the state as a moral body can have no other basis, than the love of itself, of its nature and form. This love is so natural, that is has to fill rulers and subjects, and through this, all parts of the state's body will revive."[72] As far as I know, the consequences of this passage for the state's philosophical judgment of the philosophy of enlightenment have not been investigated.

Science of Police, Science of Commerce, and Economics

Justi uses an economic term for police as it cannot be found either before him or after him in this intensity in literature. Moreover, he was the first writer, who precisely and analytically separated the disciplines of politics and police from each

[65] See Justi (1760), 193.

[66] See Justi (1760), 198.

[67] See Justi (1760), 199.

[68] Justi (1761), II, 24.

[69] See Marchet (1885), 302.

[70] Justi (1759), 6–7.

[71] Justi (1758), I, 346.

[72] Justi (1759), 10.

other. Justi defines the *science of police* as follows: "The science of police teaches how wealth can be gained in a durable way for the state."[73] Justi, as the first systematic thinker on the *science of police*, has contributed two important books to that topic. The *Grundsätze der Policey-Wissenschaft* from the year 1756 fitted to the requirements of a textbook, and the two-volume work from the years 1760 and 1761: *Die Grundfeste zu der Macht und Glückseeligkeit der Staaten; oder ausführliche Vorstellung von der gesamten Policey-Wissenschaft* contained even more material. That second book, however, was shown only as a "comment"[74] on the first one, which was probably wrong. Different from the *Grundsätze,* which is still held in the style of the older cameralism, the *Grundfeste* pertains to a free spirit, which primarily stresses the significance of the individuals and families for the community.[75] The felicity of states is essentially dependent on the wealth of the subjects. The word "wealth" has to be understood in the double meaning of the German word "Vermögen": as capital on the one hand, and as the abilities of a working population to be productive and creative on the other hand.[76]

The *Grundsätze* covers in four chapters[77]: the "culture of the countries," "the moral condition of the subjects and preservation of a good order," the "means to a blossoming sustenance," and also "the principles of police." On the one hand, the police contribute to a sufficing wealth of the state by promoting the sources of the wealth. Measures for the growth of population by supporting births and promoting immigration, a topic which is current today once more, are part of it; also, the support of the foreign commercial trade through obtaining an active trade balance, although not at any "mercantilistic" price; and the use of domestic raw materials. And, on the other hand, the police try to mobilize the wealth, for example, through governing trade to enable the circulation of commodities. The police support the banks as financial intermediaries, try to stop monopolization, enact laws against profiteering, and provide for the development of domestic production.[78] Justi also suggests not to tax (or to tax them only moderately) the end-products made for export, as well as the foreign raw materials at import, which are indispensable for the domestic production. Dispensable luxury goods should, however, be highly taxed at import as should the exportation of domestic raw materials. Justi gives a politico-economic reason: "People, who give raw materials to other foreign people, reduce the sources of their own wealth…"[79] Justi's great strength is due, among other things, to seeing the connection between laws and political meanings in a politico-economic context. He correctly pleads for a coordinated system of laws of police and the other laws.[80]

---

[73] Justi (1766), 4.

[74] Funk (1863), 500.

[75] See Maier (1986), 182–183.

[76] See Backhaus (2001), 8.

[77] See Justi (1756), passim.

[78] See Engelhardt (1981), 78–79.

[79] Justi (1760/61), I, 468.

[80] See Schulze (1982), 93, see Justi (1760/61), II, 516–517.

While the emancipation of the *science of police* came out (leaving the *science of cameralism*), the subject of administration raised undreamt-of possibilities. The police measures encompass many social areas now, for example, scientific research and education.[81] A consequence of that is the remodeling of the doctrine of regalian rights, which is now a part of cameralism as well as the police. Although the original purpose of the regalian rights to generate state earnings has still survived, the regalian rights are predestined for the use of the economic police. The economic police could use the regalian rights to control the economic participants in a politico-economic sense. "The regalian right to issue coins has stopped being a simple fiscal instrument and has become an institution of the police; with that the degradation of struck coins had to disappear from the agenda. The regalian rights of traffic are no longer used merely to ransack the traffic but to raise the traffic, because the importance of the effect is now recognized."[82] The same applies to the regalian right of mining, which can be similarly a cameralistic issue as well as an issue of the police.[83] Also seen at the raising of tolls, customs, and excises the state should take care not to obstruct the circulation of commodities.[84] Some objectives are in conflict between the *science of police* and the *science of cameralism*, and this Justi pointed out as a central theme.

The *science of police* is completed by the *science of commerce,* which refers to the business trade. The police finally shall contribute; "to establish commerce in a country and lead it to a blossoming condition…"[85] Justi finally mentions *economics*, which he had already mentioned in the *Staatswirthschaft*. Nevertheless, the private economy has nothing directly to do with the public sector, except that economic activities increase with the national income. After all, the income of the state can be filled up from the national income, for example by raising the tax rates. *Economics* deals namely with "how the wealth of the private people can become increased."[86] Your knowledge is of interest to the policeman as a representative of the "good order". In other words, the considerations of Justi on the impact of the families, find their expression not only in the explanation of state interaction in the four-element doctrine, but also relating in practice to their work in the private economy and in the agricultural sector. This is where we find the main sphere of influence of the families. Their domestic home production is less important. It is true that in the field of *economics* the cameralists were not epoch making. According to Schumpeter, the approach of the economic police was: "Laissez-faire plus surveillance."[87] Only when it may seem absolutely necessary, for example in the case of a market failure, the private activities of the subjects were complemented by state intervention.

[81] See Marchet (1885), 325.

[82] Marchet (1885), 398.

[83] See Justi (1758), I, 243–258, II, 245–275.

[84] See Justi (1756), 131.

[85] Justi (1758), I, 61.

[86] Justi (1758), I, 61–62.

[87] Schumpeter (1965), 230.

Science of Cameralism

The real *science of cameralism* is older than the specific disciplines, and especially older than the above-mentioned *science of police*. The first chairs for the *science of cameralism and economics* were set up by Frederick William I. in 1727, who was a sponsor of practical sciences, in the newly founded universities of Halle and Frankfurt/Oder.[88]

Justi has written down his opinion about the financial system in some works. The second volume of the *Staatswirthschaft* from the year 1755 already treats comprehensively the revenues and the expenditures as well as the financial administration of the state in a traditional way.[89] Later, he has striven for another specification in the *System des Finanzwesens*.[90] It should particularly be stressed that Justi paid attention to the aspects of the modern financial administration, which was remarked upon by no one else in his day. The older domestic character of his approach can still be recognized by the fact, that he puts the domain income above the fiscal revenue, which absolutely represented the fiscal relevance at the time.[91] Interestingly enough, Justi argued in favor of abolition of indirect taxes, because the excise would have negative effects on personal liberty, trade, and commerce. In the end, he reduced them for a reason, which seems irrelevant today and referred to the high collection costs of this tax in the past.[92]

The *science of cameralism* is a practical science, in which an immediate reference between the consultant and the ruler exists. Success or failure of consulting becomes obviously fast.[93] The difficulties surrounding cameralism are becoming clearer now, too. As Justi criticized, that the representatives of cameralism are too interested in the benefits of their princes,[94] it applies equally today, although self-referentially, that an objective consulting of politics stands behind a subjective consulting of politicians. Justi ergo is far away in the practise of consulting to be at the side of the fiscal governmental concern. Representatives of cameralism should not only pay attention to the maximization of the budget alone, but also take care that their own behavior does not counteract the necessary politico-economic activities, for example through a false thrift. He sharply criticizes the so-called *increase doers* (Plusmacher) in particular, whose orientation is only fiscal.[95] But he also writes in the visitors' book of the monarch, that he has to distinguish between his

---

[88] See Timm (1964), 84–85.

[89] See Justi (1758), II, 59–466, 467–658, 661–744.

[90] See Peukert (2005), 216–224.

[91] See Roscher (1868), 101–102.

[92] See Justi (1762), 103–112.

[93] See Backhaus (2001), 9–10.

[94] See Justi (1758), I, XXXII.

[95] See Justi (1766), 83–85, see Peukert (2009), 125.

personal belongings and the belongings of the government.[96] Justi trusts in the ability of the ruler to recognize that in the long run he leads better, if he increases the public welfare instead of merely exploiting the country for his personal advantage, which will work out only in the short-term, for example when the ruler manipulates the currency.[97] It seems that this appeal can be understood by a monarch, but not by democratic politicians, who are orientated to a short-term legislative period.

As it is well known, Justi criticized the so-called particular cameralism. Through the emancipation of the *science of police,* amongst other things, from the *science of cameralism,* which evidently was down to Justi, the problem has worsened. The conflict has continued up to the present day, which can be seen when, for example, a chancellor of the exchequer has to deal with the claims of the department ministers to finance various political measures. The result shows that the *science of cameralism* still remains of the greatest importance, after the separation of the other sciences of political economy, or as Justi puts it: "It is easy to see, that the *science of cameralism* is connected with all other economic sciences with the utmost meticulousness… It teaches not only, how to use the wealth wisely for the best of the state, which *politics*, the *science of police*, the *science of commerce*, and *economics* contribute to. The *science of cameralism* also leads the inward budgeting in the large economy of the state."[98]

Conclusions

The idea of the feasibility of plans with regard to governmental policy corresponds with the mechanical perception of Justi, which was typical for the eighteenth century. This becomes obvious in the vocabulary: scale, clock, driving force, and wheelwork. In connection with that, we can talk about a *state programming of aims* (Zweckprogrammierung). It is not surprising that the planning of the state in the sectors of economy and administration is amongst the most outstanding achievements of cameralism. The cameralistic state has become a role model for today's welfare state, which has developed in the German-speaking regions. Justi's achievement is down to the fact that he worked on this project of the modern age. In his work, despite his interest in details, he never missed the greater context. One may therefore talk about a "concrete utopia."

---

[96] See Justi (1759), 224.

[97] See Peukert (2005), 217.

[98] Justi (1758), II, 23.

Bibliography

Primary Sources

Justi, J. H. G. von (1756). *Grundsätze der Policey-Wissenschaft in einen vernünftigen, auf den Endzweck der Policey gegründeten, Zusammenhange und zum Gebrauch academischer Vorlesungen abgefasset*, Van den Hoeck: Göttingen.

Justi, J. H. G. von (1758). *Staatswirthschaft oder systematische Abhandlung aller ökonomischen und Cameralwissenschaften*, two Vol., 2nd ed. ([1]1755), Bernhard Christoph Breitkopf: Leipzig.

Justi, J. H. G. von (1759). *Der Grundriß einer Guten Regierung in Fünf Büchern*, Johann Gottlieb Garbe: Frankfurth; Leipzig.

Justi, J. H. G. von (1760). *Die Natur und das Wesen der Staaten, als die Grundwissenschaft der Staatskunst, der Policey, und aller Regierungswissenschaften, desgleichen als die Quelle aller Gesetze*, Johann Heinrich Rüdigers: Berlin; Stettin; Leipzig.

Justi, J. H. G. von (1760/61). *Die Grundfeste zu der Macht und Glückseeligkeit der Staaten; oder ausführliche Vorstellung von der gesamten Policey-Wissenschaft*, two Vol., Johann Heinrich Hartungs Erben/ Gebhard Ludewig Woltersdorfs Wittwe: Königsberg; Leipzig.

Justi, J. H. G. von (1761). *Gesammlete Politische und Finanzschriften über wichtige Gegenstände der Staatskunst, der Kriegswissenschaften und des Cameral- und Finanzwesens*, three Vol., Rothensche Buchhandlung: Koppenhagen; Leipzig.

Justi, J. H. G. von (1762). *Ausführliche Abhandlung von denen Steuern und Abgaben nach ächten, aus dem Endzweck der bürgerlichen Gesellschaft abfließenden Grundsätzen, und zur Wohlfahrt der Völker dienlichen Maaßregeln*, G. Ludwig Woltersdorffs Wittwe: Königsberg; Leipzig.

Justi, J. H. G. von (1766). *System des Finanzwesens, nach vernünftigen aus dem Endzweck der bürgerlichen Gesellschaften, und aus der Natur aller Quellen der Einkünfte des Staats hergestellten Grundsätzen und Regeln*, Rengersche Buchhandlung: Halle.

Secondary Sources

Adam, U. (2009). Justi and the Post-Montesquieu French Debate on Commercial Nobility in 1756, in: Backhaus, J. (Ed.): *The Beginnings of Political Economy. Johann Heinrich Gottlob von Justi*, Springer: New York, 75–98.

Backhaus, J. (2001). *Alte oder Neue Finanzwissenschaft? Ein Plädoyer für das Alte und Bewährte*, Antrittsvorlesung Universität Erfurt, Erfurt.

Backhaus, J. (2009). From Wolff to Justi, in: Backhaus, J. (Ed.): *The Beginnings of Political Economy. Johann Heinrich Gottlob von Justi*, Springer: New York, 1–18.

Deutsch, G. (1889). Johann Heinrich Gottlob von Justi. Ein Beitrag zur Geschichte der Kameralwissenschaften in Deutschland, in: *Zeitschrift für die gesamte Staatswissenschaft*, Vol. 45, Tübingen, 554–567.

Dierse, U. (2001). Utopie, in: Ritter, J. et al. (Ed.): *Historisches Wörterbuch der Philosophie*, Vol. 11, Darmstadt, 510–526.

Dittrich, E. (1974). Justi, Johann Heinrich Gottlob, in: *Neue Deutsche Biographie*, Vol. X, Berlin, 707–709.

Engelhardt, U. (1981). Zum Begriff der Glückseligkeit in der kameralistischen Staatslehre des 18. Jahrhunderts (J. H. G. v. Justi), in: *Zeitschrift für historische Forschung*, Vol. 8, Berlin, 37–79.

Frensdorff, F. (1901). *Die Vertretung der ökonomischen Wissenschaften in Göttingen, vornehmlich im 18. Jahrhundert, in: Festschrift zur Feier des hunderfünfzigjährigen Bestehens der Königlichen Gesellschaft der Wissenschaften zu Göttingen*, Berlin, 495–565.
Funk, F. X. (1863). Die Auffassung des Begriffes der Polizei im vorigen Jahrhundert, in: *Zeitschrift für die gesamte Staatswissenschaft*, Vol. 19, Tübingen, 489–555.
Garber, J. (1996). Utopiekritik und Utopieadaption im Einflußfeld der "anthropologischen Wende" der europäischen Spätaufklärung, in: Neugebauer-Wölk, M., Saage, R. (Ed.): *Die Politisierung des Utopischen im 18. Jahrhundert: vom utopischen Systementwurf zum Zeitalter der Revolution*, Niemeyer: Tübingen, 87–114.
Hirschberger, J. (1988). *Geschichte der Philosophie, Vol. 2: Neuzeit und Gegenwart*, 13th ed., Herder: Freiburg.
Inama-Sternegg, T. von (1881). Justi, Johann Heinrich Gottlob v., in: *Allgemeine Deutsche Biographie*, Vol. 14, Leipzig, 747–753.
Kant, I. (1798). *Reflexionen zur Anthropologie*, Vol. XV, Akademie-Ausgabe (http://virt052.zim.uni-duisburg-essen.de/Kant/aa15/262.html).
Klein, E. (1961). Johann Heinrich Gottlob Justi und die preußische Staatswirtschaft, in: *Vierteljahrschrift für Sozial- und Wirtschaftsgeschichte*, Vol. 48, Wiesbaden, 145–202.
Klueting, H. (2005). Justi, Johann Heinrich Gottlob von, in: Reinalter, H. (Ed.): *Lexikon zum Aufgeklärten Absolutismus in Europa*, Wien, 333–336.
Maier, H. (1986). *Die ältere deutsche Staats- und Verwaltungslehre*, reprint of the 2nd ed., dtv: München.
Marchet, G. (1885). *Studien über die Entwickelung der Verwaltungslehre in Deutschland von der zweiten Hälfte des 17. bis zum Ende des 18. Jahrhunderts*, Oldenbourg: München.
Nitschke, P. (1996). Der doppelte Sieg der Nützlichkeit: Zur Interdependenz von Staatsräson und Utopie in der politischen Theorie der Aufklärung, in: Neugebauer-Wölk, M.,Saage, R. (Eds.): *Die Politisierung des Utopischen im 18. Jahrhundert: vom utopischen Systementwurf zum Zeitalter der Revolution*, Niemeyer: Tübingen, 27–39.
Obert, M. (1992). *Die naturrechtliche "politische Metaphysik" des Johann Heinrich Gottlob von Justi (1717–1771)*, Peter Lang: Frankfurt a. M.
Peukert, H. (2005). Justi's Moral Economics and his System of Taxation (1766), in: Backhaus, J. G. (Ed.): *Essays on Fiscal Sociology*, Peter Lang: Frankfurt a. M., 211–237.
Peukert, H. (2009). Justi's Concept of Moral Economics and the Good Society, in: Backhaus, J. (Ed.): *The Beginnings of Political Economy. Johann Heinrich Gottlob von Justi*, Springer: New York, 117–132.
Reinert, E. S. (2009). Johann Heinrich Gottlob von Justi – The Life and Times of an Economic Adventurer, in: Backhaus, J. (Ed.): *The Beginnings of Political Economy. Johann Heinrich Gottlob von Justi*, Springer: New York, 33–74.
Reinert, E. S.; Reinert, H. (2009). A Bibliography of J.H.G. von Justi, in: Backhaus, J. (Ed.): *The Beginnings of Political Economy. Johann Heinrich Gottlob von Justi*, Springer: New York, 19–31.
Remer, J. (1938). *Johann Heinrich Gottlob Justi. Ein deutscher Volkswirt des 18. Jahrhunderts*, Kohlhammer: Stuttgart; Berlin.
Roscher, W. (1868). Der sächsische Nationalökonom Johann Heinrich Gottlob von Justi, Ein Beitrag zur innern Geschichte von Deutschland um die Mitte des vorigen Jahrhunderts, in: *Archiv für die Sächsische Geschichte*, Vol. 6, Leipzig, 76–106.
Rüdiger, A. (2005). *Staatslehre und Staatsbildung. Die Staatswissenschaft an der Universität Halle im 18. Jahrhundert*, Niemeyer: Tübingen.
Schelp, R. (2001). *Das allgemeine Staatsrecht – Staatsrecht der Aufklärung: eine Untersuchung zu Inhalt, Anspruch und Geltung des naturrechtlichen Staatsrechts im 17. und 18. Jahrhundert*, Duncker & Humblot: Berlin.
Schulze, R. (1982). *Policey und Gesetzgebungslehre im 18. Jahrhundert*, Duncker & Humblot: Berlin.
Schumpeter, J. A. (1965). *Geschichte der ökonomischen Analyse*, 1st part, Vandenhoeck & Ruprecht: Göttingen.

Sommer, L. (1925). *Die österreichischen Kameralisten in dogmengeschichtlicher Darstellung*, 2nd part, Konegen: Wien.

Stavenhagen, G. (1969). *Geschichte der Wirtschaftstheorie*, 4th ed., Vandenhoeck & Ruprecht: Göttingen.

Timm, A. (1964). Preußische Wirtschaftspolitik des 18. Jahrhunderts, in: Koenigswald, H. von; Merkatz, H.-J. von (Ed.): *Besinnung auf Preußen*, Gerhard Stalling: Oldenburg; Hamburg, 83–91.

Unruh, G.-Ch. Von (1969). *Subjektiver Rechtsschutz und politische Freiheit in der vorkonstitutionellen Staatslehre Deutschlands*, Hansischer Gildenverlag: Hamburg.

The Kingdom of Ophir – A "Realistic Utopia"

Economic Concepts of the Utopian Tract of 1699 and Mercantilist Economic Doctrines

Günther Chaloupek

The Tract "Ophir" in the Context of Contemporary Writings on Social Philosophy, Politics, and Economics

"*Der wohleingerichtete Staat Des bishero von vielen gesuchten/aber nicht gefundenen Königreichs Ophir/...*" ("Ophir") is the first utopian tract of a German author written in German (Wagener, p. 11). First published in 1699, it was re-issued under a different title in 1704 (Swoboda 1972b, p. 167), and fell into oblivion thereafter, to be reprinted only in 1987. It was published anonymously in Leipzig, from which the distance to Halle is short, so that the author has been supposed to come from the University of Halle. In 1692, Veit Ludwig von Seckendorff had been appointed chancellor of the newly established university, but he died in that same year, so that it appears impossible that he might have been the author of Ophir. Other suggestions for authorship are Heinrich and Samuel Cocceiji, Christian Thomasius, Christian Wolff[1] (Swoboda 1972b, p. 168). As yet, no detailed investigation about probable authorship by comparison of the style of writing has been made. The fact that the major part of the content is devoted to description and discussion of legal matters of various kinds permits the conclusion that the author has been a legal scholar, rather than a cameralist economist (Wagener, p. 15).

As a fictional model, Ophir's position is between the pious, god-agreeable ideal state represented by Johann Valentin Andreä's "*Christianopolis*" (1619), and the utopian tracts – primarily of French origin – inspired by the philosophy of enlightenment. Ophir's approach to religion has been characterized as "Lutheranism modified by rationalist critique" (Wagener, p. 26). In Ophir, tendencies towards sectarianism which would put social peace and unity of the state at risk are preempted by procedural rules by which all issues of interpretation of the Bible are to be decided by a supreme council of the church, and by imposing strict limits on

[1] Wolff's authorship is implausible for the simple reason that he was only 20 years old when the tract appeared.

G. Chaloupek (✉)
Chamber of Labour, A-1040 Wien, Print Eugen-Stresse 20, Austria
e-mail: guenther@chaloupek.eu

J.G. Backhaus (ed.), *The State as Utopia: Continental Approaches*, The European Heritage in Economics and the Social Sciences 9, DOI 10.1007/978-1-4419-7500-3_8,

theological sophistry. The tract does not discuss matters of substance of religion. The aim of these provisions is to ensure that religion and religion-based education of the whole population can be used as a solid base for a system of social morals.

	Utopian tracts	Philosophy and law	Economists
1600	Thomas Morus, *Utopia* (1516)		
	Johann Valentin Andreă,		
	Christianopolis (Tübingen 1619, German translation 1741)		
1650	Denis de Vairasse, *Histories Severambes* (1675)	Samuel Pufendorff 1632–1694	Veit Ludwig von Seckendorff 1626–1692
		De officio hominis et civis juxta legem naturalem (1673)	*Teutscher Fürstenstaat* (1656, 1664[2])
			Johann Joachim Becher 1635–1682
		Gottfried Wilhelm Leibniz 1646–1716	*Politischer Discurs* (1668)
		Christian Thomasius 1655–1728	Philipp Wilhelm von Hörnigk 1640–1714
			Österreich über alles… (1684)
1700	*Ophir* (Leipzig 1699)	Johann Christian Wolff 1679–1754	Johann Georg Leib 1670–1727
	Johann Gottfried Schnabel	Vernünftige Gedanken von dem gesellschaftlichen Leben des Menschen Halle 1721	*Vier Proben, wie ein Regent Land und Leute verbessern… könne* Leipzig 1708
	Insel Felsenburg (1741/43)		
	Morelly, *Code de la nature…* (1755)		

Kirchenheim (1892/1985), Swoboda (1972a,1972b), Dittrich (1974)

The underlying social philosophy of Ophir shows a strong influence of the ideas of early enlightenment as represented in the writings of Johann Christian Wolff. According to the preface to his "*Vernünftige Gedanken von dem gesellschaftlichen Leben der Menschen.*" Wolff's intention is to show that men can promote their happiness by uniting their powers, and if they were conducted by reason and virtue, then everybody would honestly and voluntarily contribute to the common good. But in reality, ignorance and malice do not permit the realization of the common good. But even if it is impossible to establish a perfect state in reality, efforts to describe such a perfect state are not futile.[2] They could serve as a mirror, in which the

[2]"Wäre bei allen Menschen Verstand und Tugend, so würde ein jeder aufrichtig und freiwillig zur gemeinen Wohlfahrt beitragen… es ist freilich wahr, dass es in keinem gemeinen Wesen besser gehen

imperfections as well as the good elements of existing states could be discovered. Although written 22 years after publication of Ophir, the essence of Ophir's particular type of utopianism appears well expressed in Wolff's words.

Basic structures and institutions in Ophir's model of an ideal state are, to a large extent, taken over from existing reality. A higher degree of perfection is achieved by specific improvements in institutions, in the laws governing men's actions, and in moral standards conducive to socially responsible behavior of men. The tract ends with a sceptical note that the changes necessary to achieve the intended higher degree of perfection were unlikely to occur. Hence, compared to most other utopian tracts, Ophir is characterized by a distinctly realistic-pragmatic approach, with only a few genuinely utopian elements. There is no fundamental critique of the existing social order in Ophir, as is implicit or explicit in Thomas Morus' Utopia or in French utopian tracts of the eighteenth century. No fundamental changes of the socio-economic order are envisaged.

In particular, Ophir's economy is based on private ownership and private economic activity, with money as means of exchange as well as store of value. The social order is hierarchical, with the king at the top and the other ranks according to the traditional structure of European society. Ophir's constitution is conceived of as an electoral monarchy, in which princes are preferred successors if they are likely to conform to the standards of benevolent autocratic government. The essential function of the governmental bodies is to advise the king who makes the final decision. The state is not omnipotent. Moral education of the population of all classes based on "the true Christian religion" is the key instrument to achieve a high degree of social consciousness and of socially conforming behavior of individuals. Otherwise, the state does not interfere with the private conduct of life. The family, in its traditional form, is the basic unit of society. No presumptions are made that punishment and prisons would be unnecessary in the ideal state – detailed descriptions of punishable behavior of citizens and of state officers are numerous. Ophir is not hermetically secluded from the rest of the world, as most other utopian states are.

Because structures of state and society in Ophir in most respects are very similar to those found in existing states of the German Reich, it is not surprising that the characterization of Ophir as a utopian tract has been questioned.[3] Yet, there are two

---

würde, als wo alles mit Vernunft geschähe, das ist, wo jedermann in allen vorkommenden Fällen zureichenden Verstand und genug Tugend hätte: allein da wir solche Menschen auf unserem Erdboden nicht antreffen, lässet sich auch hier kein so vollkommener Staat einrichte. Nun wäre wohl nicht alle Mühe vergebens, wenn man dergleichen vollkommenen Staat beschreiben wollte: denn er wäre ein Spiegel, darinnen wir die Unvollkommenheit unsrer Staate erblicken können, und ein Probier-Stein, daran sich das Gute in unseren Staaten zu erkennen gäbe". (Wolff 1721/1991, p. 9f).

[3] Saage (1991) does not include Ophir in his comparative analysis of political utopias. Kirchenheim (1892–1985) admits that with its obtrusively instructive paragraphs Ophir resembles a textbook, but emphasizes that it is a true picture of the ideal model of the welfare state of the early German enlightenment (p. 172f). Swoboda characterizes Ophir as "Utopie vom Policey-Staat, vom perfekten Wohlfahrts – und Verwaltungsstaat landesväterlicher Prägung, wie er für das Staatsideal des 17. und 18. Jahrhunderts vielfach charakteristisch war"(1972b, p. 167).

elements by which Ophir as a state and as society appears in stark contrast to existing societies: peaceful conflict resolution, or rather pre-emption of conflict about religious matters, and a high degree of economic and social equality which goes hand in hand with the practical elimination of poverty.

Social peace, above all, requires peaceful co-existence of different religious confessions. There is a dominant religion in Ophir in which unity is maintained. There are no quarrels and divisions within the church because in matters of religion it is not permitted to use other terms than those of the Bible. The unity of faith is preserved by the church council,[4] which decides about questions of faith and exercises censorship over books with religious content. It appears that certain differences in the practice of religion are allowed, but any debates about issues of faith between members of different confessions are forbidden.

That social equality is a utopian element in Ophir has remained largely unnoticed in the secondary literature. Ophir's legal system does not aim at complete elimination of social distinctions. e.g., there are dress codes for the different social ranks. But sumptuary laws impose strict limits on conspicuous consumption. Regulations restrict the wealthy classes from making full use of their purchasing power, especially with respect to the use of land. The social order and economic regulations provide that the lower classes enjoy a decent standard of living which includes, e.g., the consumption of meat and beer. Domestic servants are entitled to the fivefold amount of the wage if it has been unjustly withheld by their lord. At the same time, there are many provisions in Ophir, which ensure that sufficient public revenues are available at any time to prevent the lower classes from falling into poverty. Begging is not permitted, beggars are either provided with sufficient livelihood, or encouraged to seek work. The elimination of poverty ensures a high degree of security in all public places in Ophir.[5]

Agricultural and Industrial Policies in Ophir

Agriculture and Provision of Foodstuffs (Chap. 14)

The goals of equality and elimination of poverty are the dominant aspects of policy prescriptions for the agricultural sector. Wealthy classes are prohibited from withdrawing fertile soil from productive use. In order to ensure maximization of grain

[4]"Und weil niemanden/auch den Lehrern selbst nicht zugelassen ist/andere Redens-Arten und Terminos, als in der heiligen Schrift befindlich sind/unter sich oder ihren Glaubens-Genossen zu gebrauchen/so sind Wort-Gezäncke und Spaltungen daselbst etwas unerhörtes. Wie dem auch zu Erhaltung der Einigkeit im Glauben/nicht wenig beyträget/ein daselbst… auffgerichteter allgemeiner und stets-währender Kirchen-Rath" (p. 11f).

[5]"Dannenhero wird man in dem gantzen Königreiche nicht leicht einen Bettler zu Gesicht bekommen/kann auch die Besuchenden bis unter die Thüre begleiten/auff der Gassen ungehindert stehen und gehen/und zu den Fenstern frey heraus sehen/ohne von Bettlern mit großem Ungestüm/wie in vielen Oten Europae zu geschehen pfleget/angeschryen und überlauffen zu werden" (p. 318f).

production, gardens and parks merely for pleasure and entertainment may be laid out only with approval from the authorities. Cultivation and the choice of crops are supervised by the authorities who take care to ensure that soil is not wasted for growing daintiness ("*Leckerey*") and other unnecessities. In the same vein, in the construction of roads due consideration must be paid to the priority of agricultural use of land. Woods may be cleared in the interest of opening up more land for production of grain, which has priority over the predilection of noblemen for hunting.

Each year, the price of grain is fixed by authorities, with due consideration to conditions of supply. Export of grain is prohibited, with the sole exception that good crops provide for a surplus that is available for exports. Adequate stocks of grain must be kept in public magazines ("*Kornhäuser*") situated throughout the country, which are to be made available for food supply to the lower classes in periods of shortage, and, if necessary, also as seed-corn. Forestalling of grain of which the Jews are suspected is strictly forbidden and put under severe punishment.

Flour mills are under strict control. Complete documentation of sales and purchases from the farmer down to the producer of the final good (the baker) is ensured by excise bills ("*Accis-Zettul*"), in order to guarantee the correct application of differentiated percentages of excise taxes (see below section "Taxation (Chap. 18)"), and also to prevent the diversion of food supplies from public markets. Grain or flower must not be used for production of brandy, of starch for linen or bookbinding, etc.

The price of bread is also regulated. Bakers are required to post these prices, and also to maintain a stock of flour sufficient a least for 1 month's production of bread. Authorities have the right of access to inspect the stocks any time.

Regulations are also concerned with ample supply and price of beer and meat, in order to ensure that the poor can afford it. Therefore, pastures have to be primarily reserved for cattle. Horses may be kept as draft animals on the countryside and in smaller numbers also in cities and towns, where their use for taking a drive for ostentation is prohibited. State regulations for forestry ensure a sustainable supply of wood for heating and cooking at permanently fixed prices.

The Crafts, Trade, and Commerce (Chap. 16)

Prosperity of manufacturing and commerce in Ophir is based on mercantilist policies. Exports of raw materials are prohibited. The government welcomes and promotes the immigration of artisans and craftsmen from abroad, who may be granted tax exemptions for limited time periods. It offers financial support for inventions of new goods and "artificial works" (p. 395).

Only a few paragraphs are devoted to crafts and their organization. If privileges ("*Freyheiten*") of craft guilds are granted by the king, the wording of the tract is ambiguous as to what extent the content of guild regulations is left to the corporations themselves, or prescribed by the state (p. 398). Masters are obliged to teach their apprentices properly, and to ensure that feasts do not become drinking bouts. Journeymen are allowed to travel to foreign countries only with the state's permission, and if their savings provide sufficient funds to support their living. They must never disclose the secrets of their handicraft.

A flourishing commerce is the best way to promote prosperity of the manufacturing crafts. In Ophir, this is ensured by a comprehensive system of companies ("*Compagnien*") through which manufactures are distributed and traded throughout the whole kingdom. Nine such companies are entrusted with the monopoly of inter-regional trade within their sector (e.g., for gold, silver, luxuries; for iron and nonferrous metals and respective manufactures; for silk and linen manufactures; for woollen manufactures; for wood manufactures; etc.). The directors of the companies have to report to the commercial council ("*Commercien-Rath*"), which acts as the supreme authority to advise the king on matters of policies with respect to commerce and manufactures. The commercial council (pp. 241ff) supervises the companies, establishes new branches of manufactures, and issues directives and recommendations for measures to promote economic activities.

Only experienced and honest tradesmen can become members of the companies. The companies' profits (and losses) are distributed among them according to the capital contributed; 10% of profits must be withheld to build up reserves. The monopoly of companies pertains only to interregional and external trade. For local distribution of goods, independent tradesmen are also admitted; yet, they are not allowed to transport goods to other regions of the kingdom. Bankruptcy is punished with prison where the debt has to be paid back by work. Foreign tradesmen are admitted only for imports of such goods which are deemed necessary, but which cannot be produced in Ophir.

Each company may also enter banking business and establish a "*Banco di Cambi*" (p. 408), which can take deposits and make loans. Interest on deposits must not exceed 6%, whereas the upper limit of interest charged for loans is only 4%. The same rate applies to all loans in the kingdom. No commissions may be charged for deposits. The banks' statutes include the provision that the king will not borrow from the companies' banks, but will obtain credit for his own needs and for the state from other sources at six, seven or even more percent interest.

Constant standards of currency are strictly enforced in Ophir through a system of supervision and threats of severe punishment. In order to pre-empt corrupted foreign currency to enter circulation in the kingdom, proceeds from exports must be spent for merchandise abroad.

Taxation (Chap. 18)

The tract suggests a division of state finances in Ophir between the exchequer of the king ("*Hoff-Kammer*") and the general exchequer for other state expenditure. The king's expenses are covered by the revenues from the royal domains. Other current state expenditure is financed by excise taxes, which is considered the fairest ("*billigste*") form of taxation which taxes everybody according to his consumption. Excise taxes can be collected conveniently "with small percentage," "quasi unnoticed and without execution" (p. 475).

To keep the burden of taxation of the less well-to-do classes within tolerable limits, rates of taxation are differentiated by urgency of needs. Excises on wry bread are lower than those on white bread, on white bread lower than on pastry, wine is more heavily taxed than beer, cloth less than silk, etc. Taxes on imports are higher than on goods from domestic production. There are no exemptions from excise taxes, which must be paid even by the king.

Clerks of the exchequer's office receive fixed salaries. All state offices are strictly obliged to pay their bills when they are due. All units of state administration (cities, counties) have to present annual accounts to the administrative council ("*Policey-Rath*") and to the financial council ("*Cammer-Rath*").

Taxation of property is used only as "extra-ordinary contribution," which is made necessary by war expenses. In that case, a modest tax ("*nicht zu hoch*") can be levied proportionally on the property of all subjects, without exemptions (p. 459).

Mercantilist Economic Thought in Ophir

Only a minor part of the tract is devoted to economic aspects of an "ideal state." The three chapters of predominantly economic content comprise 21% of the text (not counting the 104-page index). If other parts relevant with respect to economic issues are included, economic content amounts to one quarter of the total volume. Major parts are devoted to religion (18%, including schools and education), to the king, the education of the princes and to the court (19%), the rest to matters of constitutional and private law and administration. Compared to Seckendorff's "*Teutscher Fürstenstaat*," of which only a very small part (including the *Additiones*) deals with agriculture, the crafts and trade, economic matters figure rather prominently in the tract Ophir.

Distinctly mercantilist in its orientation, the economics of Ophir appears to a considerable extent as a combination of Becher and certain parts of Seckendorff.[6] By assumption, the kingdom is conceived of as a state of considerable extension and transcends the narrow perspectives of the typical small state within the German Reich. Therefore, much less attention is paid to matters of administration of royal domains and income thereof, than in Seckendorff's tract. In this sense, Ophir as a tract is primarily mercantilist and less cameralist in its basic approach.

As a title, Ophir is meant as a paradox. If the legendary biblical kingdom is associated with gold as expression of its wealth, the preface ridicules the belief that Ophir's gold

[6] For a comparison of Becher and Seckendorff see Chaloupek (2005).

mines are the source of the kingdom's wealth. To the contrary, it is the organization of church and state, the system of good governance, which lays the foundations for its superior standards of living, and which is, therefore, made the subject of this book of travels.

In matters of industrial and commercial policy, Ophir is highly indebted to Johann Joachim Becher's ideas. Without referring to Becher's theory of *Monopolium/Propolium/Polypolium*, Ophir adopts his main thesis that trade and commerce is the principal driving force of a prosperous economy. Becher points to the example of the Dutch economy with trading companies at the heart of its economic success. As an ideal form of organization of commerce, he proposes a certain type of trading company in which several private tradesmen and capitalists co-operate. The companies that exist in Ophir are clearly modeled according to Becher's proposal. The sectoral organization of the nine companies in Ophir follows more or less Becher's description of the structural division of trade and industry[7], although Becher in his Political Discourse (1673–1688) does not propose a comprehensive sectoral organization of trading companies.[8] Another important idea which Ophir borrows from Becher is the establishment of publicly administered magazines to guarantee continuity of an adequate supply of foodstuffs for the population.

In his memorandum of 1666 to emperor Leopold I., Becher had proposed to establish a commercial council ("*Kommerzkolleg*") in the Austrian crownlands to which several tasks were assigned: co-ordination and supervision of the trading companies' activities, communication between the emperor and the other state authorities and the trading companies, and promotion of new industrial activities (Hassinger 1951, p. 146ff). In Ophir, the commercial council is established as a superior authority entrusted with the co-ordination of the activities of the nine trading companies. The idea appears to be borrowed from Becher, but Ophir establishes an encompassing system of companies subordinated to a commercial council. This somehow, albeit vaguely, foreshadows J.H.G. Justi's concept of "*Universalkommerz*,"[9] although it remains unclear as to how many functions are to be taken over by the councils, and to what extent co-ordination is left to the market mechanism.

With respect to banks, Ophir's system in which banks are an extension of other activities of trading companies is distinctly different from Becher's proposals. In Becher's proposals, banks played an important role in his concept of commercial and industrial policy, according to which banks were established as separate enterprises.

[7]Instead of Ophir's nine, Becher divides trade and industry into 14 branches (Hassinger 1951, p. 105f).

[8]In his memorandum of 1666 to emperor Leopold, Becher had proposed to establish five companies in Austria (silk, linen, cloth, leather, fancy goods) (ibidem, p. 147).

[9]On Justi's concept of "*Universalkommerz*" see Chaloupek (2009).

If most German cameralists advocate legislation against the consumption of luxuries, the reason is that many luxuries are imported (from France), and are therefore, a drain on the balance of payments. In Ophir, restrictions on conspicuous consumption are imposed for quite different reasons, namely to reduce economic and social inequalities.

In the excise tax controversy ("*Akzisenstreit*"), which was sparked off by Tenzel's tract "*Christianus Teutophilus Entdeckte Goldgrube…*" of 1685,[10] Ophir is entirely on the side of the advocates of excise taxes, which are the only form of taxation in normal times. Taxes on property and income are excluded. Only the need for extraordinary contributions to cover the expenses for war is seen as sufficient justification for taxing people's property.

Like Seckendorff's *Teutscher Fürstenstaat*, the tract Ophir is intensely concerned with many specific details of administration, education, and moral qualification. Many pages are devoted to describe in great detail the administration of the king's court and of the ideal education of the prince by which he is taught the morals which qualify him to become the ruler of the country. Much emphasis is placed on comprehensive education of the whole population. The school system is part of the organization of the church – church and schools mutually serve each other's general purpose.[11] Piety and a high average level of education are both essential elements of the welfare state concept of early enlightenment. Fear of God is considered essential for socially responsible conduct of life, while literacy, vocational skills, and science are considered – in modern language – as preconditions of high productivity which is the basis of a decent standard of living for the whole population of Ophir.

Special care is taken in Ophir to ensure that only persons with appropriate moral qualification are selected for functions in the administration of state and church. Yet, moral education is no guarantee for socially responsible behavior of Ophir's officials, civil servants, and citizens. To keep deviating forms of conduct in check, there is a comprehensive system of supervision and control in Ophir. All units of administration are requested to report regularly on their activities to their superior bodies.

Concluding Remarks

The kingdom of Ophir is an ideal model of the welfare state which the German philosophers, jurists, and economists of the earlier periods had in mind. Intended as a utopian tract, it lacks elements of fantastic speculation, which characterize most other contemporary utopian tracts, especially those of French rationalism. Due to the tract's realistic approach, Ophir's basic institutions and structures are very similar to

[10] On this controversy, see Roscher (1874, p. 319ff).

[11] "Die Kirchen sind nichts anders als gemeine und große Schuhlen/die Schuhlen aber besondere und kleine Kirchen"(p. 52).

those in existing states of the German Reich, but a superior degree of perfection has been achieved in Ophir by deliberate changes in the design of institutions and policies which are orientated towards the goals of social equality and peaceful society. Mercantilist policies play an important role in achieving a high standard of living of the whole population through a prosperous economy and a well-functioning administration ("*gute Policey*"). In the spirit of German protestantism, high standards of social morals guide the actions of members of all social ranks in the public as well as in the private sphere.

But where is Ophir?

> Wo die wahre Christliche Religion in reiner Lehre und heiligem Lebens-Wandel sowohl der Lehrer als Zuhörer fleißig im Schwange gehet/da ist das rein-gediegenste Gold; wo Recht und Gerechtigkeit ohne Unterscheid gehandhabet wird/da ist feinstes Silber; Wo Handel und WAndel in gutem Flor seyn/da ist das vielen Nutzenbringende Helffenbein; Wo die Unterthanen nichts als Christ-löbliche Thaten ihres Regenten vor sich sehen/da sind die besten Assen; Wo alle Königlichen Bedienten für das Heil ihres Herren und Auffnehmen des gemeinen Besten unermüdet sorgen/da sind die Wachsamsten Pfauen; Wo aber dies alles/da ist das Königreich Ophir (p. 608).

References

(Anonymus) (1699), Der wohleingerichtete Staat des bishero von vielen gesuchten/aber nicht gefundenen Königreichs Ophir…, facsimile reprint, herausgegeben und eingeleitet von Hans Wagener, Mitarbeit: Laurence G. Lyon, Verla Peter Lang, bern 1987

Backhaus, J. (ed.) (2009), The Beginnings of Political Economy. Johann Heinrich Gottlob von Justi, Springer, New York, Berlin

Chaloupek, G. (2005), Seckendorff as an Economist in Comparison with Contemporary Writers, European Journal of Law and Economics, 19, 235–247

Chaloupek, G. (2009), J.H.G. Justi in Austria: his writings in the context of economic and industrial policies of the Habsburg empire in the 18th century, in: pp. 147–156

Dittrich, E. (1974), Die deutschen und österreichischen Kameralisten, Wissenschaftliche Buchgesellschaft, Darmstadt

Hassinger, H (1951), Johann Joachim Becher, Verlag Adolf Holzhausens Nachfolger, Vienna

Kirchenheim, A (1892), Schlaraffia politica. Geschichte der Dichtungen vom besten Staate, Leipzig, reprint Antiquariat Frank Pflaum, Sandhausen 1985

Pankoke, E (ed.) (1991), Gesellschaftslehre. Bibliothek der Geschichte und Politik Vol. 18, Deutscher Klassiker Verlag, Frankfurt

Roscher, W. (1874), Geschichte der National-Ökonomik in Deutschland, Verlag R. Oldenbourg, München und Berlin (reprint 1924)

Saage, R. (1991), Politische Utopien der Neuzeit, Wissenschaftliche Buchgesellschaft, Darmstadt

Seckendorff von, V.L. (1664/1976) Teutscher Fürstenstaat, with the Additiones. 2 vol., Frankfurt a.M. Reprint of the 3rd edition 1976, with a preface by Ludwig Fertig, Verlag Detlev Aufermann, Glashütten im Taunus

Swoboda, H. (1972a), Utopia, Europaverlag, Wien

Swoboda, H. (ed.) (1972b), Der Traum vom besten Staat, Deutsctier Tascher buchver lag, Munich

Wolff, J.C. (1721), Vernünftige Gedanken von dem gesellschaftlichen Leben der Menschen, excerpts reprinted in Pankoke 1991, pp. 9–18

Is Montaigne a Utopian?

Marcel van Meerhaeghe

Pourquoi fatiguer ton esprit d'éternels projets qui le dépassent.

Michel de Montaigne

Le poète en des jours impies
Vient préparer des jours meilleurs
Il est l'homme des utopies
Les pieds ici, les yeux ailleurs.

Victor Hugo

While discussing the subject of this conference with Professor Backhaus, he kindly drew my attention to White's *Famous Utopias* (1946). After ordering the book I discovered that White considers Montaigne and Shakespeare as utopian authors. This is unusual. I did not find these authors in previous books on, or surveys of, utopian writers. They are also absent in similar, recent works.[1] I even consulted the *Dictionary of Literary Utopias* (Fortunati and Trousson 2004),[2] but no mention of Montaigne. In this note, I challenge White's opinion and I try to substantiate my own point of view.

Perhaps it is because I became (accidentally) an economist, but I have never understood the permanent interest in, even enthusiasm for, utopias, in novels too. In recent French literature, for example, two authors (one of them a Nobel laureate) lay the scene in utopias.[3] Of course there are many pretexts of writing utopian fantasies. As French poet Alphonse de Lamartine (1790–1869) puts it: "Utopias are often only premature truths."[4] And Mikhaïl Saltykov (1826–1889), Russian author of social-utopian publications, concurs: "Without utopias no really fruitful activity is possible."[5]

[1] See, for example, Rouvillois (1998). Allemand (2005) quotes Montaigne, but in connection with the history of thought, not as the author of utopian publications.

[2] Fortunati V. and Trousson R. (ed.).

[3] See Rufin (2004) and Le Clézio (2006).

[4] Les utopies ne sont souvent que des vérités prématurées.

[5] Sans utopies, une activité véritablement féconde n'est pas possible.

M. van Meerhaeghe (✉)
K riekenbergdreef 21, 9831,Deurle, Belgium
e-mail: hvm@klaproos.be

J.G. Backhaus (ed.), *The State as Utopia: Continental Approaches*, The European Heritage in Economics and the Social Sciences 9, DOI 10.1007/978-1-4419-7500-3_9,

I share Cioran's pessimism: "society being as it is, they (*viz* the utopian authors) do their utmost to conceive an entirely different society." But he adds: "How is so much naïveté, so much folly possible?"[6] (Cioran 1995, p. 1035). In fact, most utopians wrote no master-pieces. Cioran censures Campanella's "ludicrous accuracy" ("minutie risible" – Cioran, p. 1037), "Fourier's, Cabet's and Morris' nonsense" ("les … fadaises dans les ouvrages … d'un Cabet, d'un Fourier ou d'un Morris"), and the numerous Russian blueprints (Cioran Ibid.).

Nevertheless, White believes there are not enough utopians and "creates" new ones. I shall examine his arguments, refer then to Montaigne (1962) text, deal with his pessimism, and formulate a conclusion.

White

White's thesis is mainly based on Chapter XXXI (Des Cannibales), Book I of Montaigne (1962) *Essais* – which, according to White – "skeptically examines the pretensions of his own (*viz* Montaigne (1962)) civilization by comparing it to that of the South American native" (White (1946), p. 139). Parts of Des Cannibales are reproduced in *Famous Utopias* (a translation of John Florio of 1603, "with some changes" by White: White (1946), p. 140). But the following quotations are based on Donald Frame (1958) better translation.

Moreover, White observes:

> Montaigne weaves together, from fact and fantasy, a portrait of the noble savage, which serves at once as an attack against things as they are and a justification for a more natural way of life
>
> (White (1946), p. xviii).

and further

> The primitive society of the Brazilians he finds so 'natural' that it surpasses his own in many points
>
> (White (1946), p. 140).

Shakespeare

Since White contends that Shakespeare "read … Montaigne's portrait and defense of a primitive or natural utopia"' (Ibid.), and expressed the same idea in "The Tempest," Shakespeare is also "promoted" a utopian writer.

That Montaigne influenced Shakespeare is not disputed, but discussions originated over the degree of this impact and they continued for centuries (see, for example, Robertson 1909). Later, G. Taylor concludes diplomatically:

---

[6]… la société étant ce qu'elle est, certains se soient évertués à en concevoir une autre, toute différente. D'où peut provenir tant de naïveté, ou tant de folie?

> … one may say with a fair degree of assurance, whether one believes … that Shakespere's library was relatively large, or … that it was relatively small, that there was in it from 1603 to his death one volume, Florio's Montaigne, which he prized above a dukedom.'
>
> (Taylor 1925, p. 46).

And Lanson ascertains:

> One observes some traces of Montaigne in several pieces of Shakespeare; in the *Tempest*, for example, and probably already in *Hamlet*. If they are not more numerous and more certain, this can perhaps be explained by the strong personality of the English poet that digests and transforms what it absorbs[7]
>
> (Lanson 1958, p. 346).

Why this special interest for Shakespeare? After all, many other writers and scientists read Montaigne and commented on his ideas or leant on his opinions. During secondary education my daughter had to use *An English Anthology* that still called Shakespeare "the greatest of all poets" (Tavernier and Lommée 1946, p. 31). Nowadays, there is a more balanced view. In his "A reader against Shakespeare" George Steiner, a *connoisseur*, draws attention on Wittgenstein's essential reservations about the place Shakespeare occupies in Western culture (Steiner 1986, p. 115) and writes not without reason.

> The contrast with Dante, with Goethe, with Tolstoï, *die Dichter par excellence,* is glaring. Where is there a Shakespearean philosophy or intelligible ethic?
>
> (*Ibid.*, p. 124).

As Shakespeare is only adventitiously involved in this discussion, I shall henceforth concentrate on Montaigne (1962).

Montaigne

Des Cannibales represents only 14 pages of Montaigne (1962) complete works or about 1% of the total. It is based on the evidence given by a man who lived "10 or (sic) 12 years" (Montaigne (1962), p. 200) in South America. Montaigne believes he is reliable (Montaigne (1962), p. 202) and does not mention additional sources of information. Moreover, White seems to ignore other parts of the *Essais* which deal with related subjects, for example, Chapter VI of Book III entitled Des Coches (Montaigne (1962), pp. 876–894) in which Montaigne, *inter alia*, opposes the Conquistadors' duplicity and the natives' loyalty:

> … the beauty of their workmanship in jewels, feathers, cotton, and painting, show that they were not behind us in industry either. But as for devoutness, observance of the laws, goodness,

[7]On aperçoit quelques traces de Montaigne dans plusieurs pièces de Shakespeare; dans la *Tempête*, par exemple, et probablement déjà dans *Hamlet.* Si elles ne sont pas plus nombreuses et plus certaines, cela tient peut-être à la forte personnalité du poète anglais qui digère et transforme ce qu'elle absorbe.

liberality, loyalty, and frankness, it served us well not to have as much as they: by their advantage in this they lost, sold, and betrayed themselves.

As for boldness and courage, constancy, resoluteness against pains and hunger and death, I would not fear to oppose the examples I could find among them to the most famous ancient examples that that we have in the memories of our world on this side of the ocean[8]

(Frame (1958), p. 693–94).

Montaigne seems sometimes too credulous, for example, when he repeats that the inhabitants who have problems with illness or old age are rare, and that they dance the whole day (Montaigne (1962), p. 205). He has few criticisms as regards their way of life. In fact, he makes no real "analysis" (see above), nor "comparison" (see above). He delivers only loose, unsystematic thoughts such as, for example, the following:

... I think there is nothing barbarous and savage in that nation, from what I have been told, except that each man calls barbarism whatever is not his own practice, for indeed it seems we have no other test and reason than the example and pattern of the opinions and customs of the country we live in. *There* is always the perfect religion, the perfect government, the perfect and accomplished manners in all things. Those people are wild, just as we call wild the fruits that Nature has produced by herself and in her ordinary progress[9]

(Frame (1958), p. 152).

Those nations, then, seem to me barbarous in this sense, that they have been fashioned very little by the human mind, and are still very close to their original naturalness. The laws of Nature still rule them, very little corrupted by ours

(Frame (1958), p 153).[10]

and

So we may well call these people barbarians, in respect to the rules of reason, but not in respect to ourselves, who surpass them in every kind of barbarity[11]

(Frame (1958), p. 156).

[8]... la beauté de leurs ouvrages en pierrerie, en plume, en cotton, en la peinture, montrent qu'ils ne nous cedoient non plus en industrie. Mais, quant à la devotion, observance des loix, bonté, liberalité, loyauté, franchise, il nous a bien servy de n'en avoir pas tant qu'eux; ils se sont perdus par cet avantage, et vendus, et trahis eux mesme. Quant à la hardiesse et courage, quant à la fermeté, constance, resolution contre les douleurs et la faim et la mort, je ne craidrois pas d'opposer les exemples que je trouverois parmy eux aux plus fameux exemples anciens que nous ayons aus memoires de nostre monde par deça (Montaigne (1962), p. 887).

[9]Or, je trouve ... qu'il n'y a rien de barbare et de sauvage en cette nation, à ce qu'on m'en a rapporté, sinon que chacun appelle barbarie ce qui n'est pas de son usage; comme de vray, il semble que nous n'avons pas d'autre mire de la verité et de la raison que l'exemple et l'idée des opinions et usances du païs où nous sommes. Là est toujours la parfaicte religion, la parfaicte police, perfect et accomply usage de toutes choses. Ils sont sauvages, de mesme que nous appelons sauvages les fruicts que nature, de soy et de son progrez ordinaire, a produicts... (Montaigne (1962), p. 203).

[10]Ces nations me semblent donq ainsi barbares, pour avoir receu fort peu de l'esprit humain, et estre encore fort voisines de leur naifvté naturelle. Les loix naturelles leur commandent encores, fort peu abastardies par les nostres (Montaigne (1962), p. 204).

[11]Nous les pouvons donc bien appeler barbares, eu esgard aux regles de la raison, mais non pas eu esgard à nous, qui les surpassons en toute sorte de barbarie (Montaigne (1962), p. 208).

But, notwithstanding Montaigne's bias in favor of the natives, nowhere do we find suggestions to imitate their life style or parts of it. It is not because he finds the native society less barbarous than the French society that it is an utopian society.

Montaigne is an enthusiast in respect of some aspects of native life. An example is the polygamy, which is encouraged by native spouses, because it enhances the prestige of their husbands. And he notes:

> It is a remarkably beautiful thing about their marriages that the same jealousy our wives have to keep us from the affection and kindness of other women, theirs have to win this for them[12]
>
> (Frame (1958), p. 158).

He even refers to the Bible and the wives of August and Dejotarus:

> In the Bible, Leah, Rachel, Sarah, and Jacob's wives gave their beautiful handmaids to their husbands and Livia seconded the appetites of Augustus, to her own disadvantage: and Stratonice, the wife of king Dejotarus, not only lent her husband for its use a very beautiful young chambermaid in her service, but carefully brought up her children, and backed them up to succeed to their father's estates[13]
>
> (Frame (1958), p. 158).

But, once again, Montaigne does not make any proposal to introduce polygamy in his country.

It does not mean that he does not draw attention to points he approves. The cannibals do not have many rules, but at least they have some rules for everybody. "Resoluteness in war and affection for their wives" (Frame (1958), p. 154) (vaillance contre les ennemis et l'amitié à leurs femmes: Montaigne (1962), p. 2006). Montaigne was not a model in respect of the last "quality": he was more interested in passion than in love (cf. Gide 1929, p. 24).

Planning and Scepticism

In other words, Montaigne does not much criticize most manifestations of the natives' lives, but he does not consider them as examples to follow; they are not living in an utopian society. He does not even refer to a utopian nation. Neither does he deal with the typical features of a utopian society, such as perfection, harmony and the social conditions leading to it (for example, peace, satisfaction of wants,

[12]C'est une beauté remarquable en leurs mariages, que la mesme jalousie que nos femmes ont pour nous empescher de l'amitié et bien-veillance d'autres femmes, les leurs l'ont toute pareille pour la leur acquerir (Montaigne (1962), p. 211).

[13]...Lia, Rachel, Sara, et les femmes de Jacob fournirent leurs belles servantes à leurs maris, et Livia seconda les appetits d'Auguste, à son interest; et la femme du Roy Dejotarus, Stratonique, presta non seulement à l'usage de son mary une fort belle jeune fille de chambre qui la servoit, mais en nourrit soigneusement les enfans, et leur feit espaule à succeder aux etats de leur pere (Montaigne (1962), pp. 211–212).

absence of a discretionary authority). He was too cautious a man to propose another kind of society: *pas d'histoires*! Montaigne cannot criticize the authority of a king under age, but a "cannibal" can do (Montaigne (1962), p. 159).

Moreover, a utopian society implies a minimum of order and planning. But that is something absent in the *Essais*, "a living weave of echos and citations" (Steiner 1986, p. 7). Vauvenargues (1715–1747) dealing with Montaigne's style is brief, but clear: "admirable in the details, incapable of forming a whole" ("Admirable dans les détails, incapable de former un tout," de Vauvenargues 1981, p. 292). As Jean d'Ormesson, one of the most successful French novelists, puts it in his "other history of French literature."

> There is no plan in the *Essais*. The whole work is a perpetual efflorescence, a permanent *excursus* that starts in all directions and always comes back to you
>
> (Ormesson, tome 1, p. 39).[14]

Montaigne's attitude is quite normal, because he is known as a sceptic: somebody who believes nothing can be known with certainty; a person inclined to doubt and question; distrustful, incredulous, pessimist. Nietzsche is one of the many philosophers who like his "courageous and joyful scepticism" (die tapfere und frohmutige Scepsis eines Montaigne: Nietzsche 1999, p. 552). And as a rule, sceptics do not draft or build utopian societies.

I shall examine whether Montaigne *is* indeed a sceptic. For that purpose I shall consult a few experts; a few because the literature on Montaigne is enormous.[15] His scepticism alone has given rise to numerous writings.

Montaigne is reviving ancient traditions: Pyrrho of Elis, the first sceptical philosopher, and especially Plutarch (first-second centuries), and Sextus Empiricus (third century). Two definitions of scepticism came in vogue: one suspends judgment, and does not even affirm or deny that certainty is possible (the Pyrrhonian version), the other does not go so far, but recognizes the fallibility of all judgments and rules out the possibility of certain knowledge.

> Confronted with the breakdown of the ancient Greek-scholastic world, Montaigne always attached to scepticism, tries to renew it, to adapt it to the new, emerging configurations … (Stratius 1997, p. 170) … He is the father of modern scepticism[16]
>
> (*Ibid.*, p. 171).

Albert Thibaudet the great scholar reminds us of the main sources of Montaigne's scepticism:

---

[14] Il n'y a pas de plan des *Esais*. L'œuvre entière est une efflorescence perpétuelle, un *excursus* permanent qui part dans tout les sens et qui finit toujours par retomber sur vos pieds.

[15] I am grateful to Dr. A. Roose (French department, Faculty of Letters and Philosophy, Univ. of Ghent, Belgium), author of *La curiosité de Montaigne* (Roose 2009) who put me up to the ropes of the Montanian bibliography, for his comments on a draft of this text.

[16] … confronté à l'effondrement du vieux monde gréco-scolastique, Montaigne, toujours attaché au scepticisme, s'efforce de le rénover, de l'adapter aux nouvelles configurations qui émergent … Il est le père du scepticisme moderne.

> the aversion to the ungainly dogmatism of scholars and magistrates with whom he grew up and lived *and* the aversion to the dangerous dogmatism that provoked the wars of religion
>
> (Thibaudet 1963, p. 273).[17]

Brahami points out to the main differences between Montaigne's scepticism and that of the Ancients: first, he discovers the secret dogmatic basis of pyrrhonism itself; second, the existence of God: the laws of logic do not apply to him[18] (Brahami 2004, pp. 893–94). Friedrich (1967) tries to characterize the scepticism of the French author: it is

> an opening scepticism with respect for the superiority of the pure appearance of a thing over the always imperfect explanation of that thing[19] (p. 9). His scepticism is outlook-broadening wisdom, no mind to destroy[20] (p. 123). There is a big difference between such opening scepticism and the later, elucidating scepticism such as advocated by a Fontenelle, a Bayle, a Voltaire. In fact, the last one is a dogmatism of the sound human common sense. But Montaigne considers possible what the sound common sense does not see[21] (p. 129).

A is usual in the social sciences there is no terminological unanimity and scientists lose much time with terminological disputes. This is also the case with scepticism. Lanson, for example, does not like the word:

> *Subjectivism, positivism, relativism,* are terms that define better Montaigne's position than the very diffuse word "scepticism," certainly suitable for his time[22]
>
> (Lanson 1958, p. 162).

Before – his 1963 book assembles earlier texts – Thibaudet wrote that Montaigne's scepticism is in fact, subjectivism and pragmatism (Thibaudet, p. 317). I wonder whether 'fatalism' is sometimes not a better characteristic. Many of Montaigne's aphorisms, for example the one that starts this essay, reflect this fatalism.

A few authors would "invent" anything to "prove" their originality. One tortures his imagination to explain what Montaigne *really* meant and to insinuate that he is, in fact, not a sceptic:

> His scepticism is an 'average' scepticism, a scepticism of irresolution. This scepticism is as enwrapped or bordered with another philosophy. Montaigne *is* not a sceptic, because he

[17] le dégoût du dogmatisme balourd des savants et des magistrats entre lesquels il avait grandi et vécu', and le dégoût du dogmatisme dangereux qui avait provoqué les guerres religieuses.

[18] This conclusion is less apparent in Brahami (1997).

[19] … eine erschliessende Skepsis mit der Ehrfurcht vor der Überlegenheit der reinen Erscheinung einer Sache über die immer nur unvolkommene Deutung der Sache.

[20] Seine Skepsis ist blicköffnende Weisheit, nicht Zerstörungslust.

[21] Es liegt ein grosser Unterschied zwischen solcher einschliessender Skepsis und der späteren aufklärerischer Skepsis von der Art eines Fontenelle, eines Bayle, eines Voltaire. Diese nämlich ist ein Dogmatismus des gesunden Menschenverstandes … Montaigne aber hält gerade das für möglich, was dem gesunden Verstand nicht einleuchtet (p. 129).

[22] *Subjectivisme, positivisme, relativisme*, sont des termes qui définiraient pour nous la position de Montaigne, plus exactement que le mot très lâche de *scepticisme*, bon assurément pour son temps.

See an analogous observation in Faguet (1982) who does not like "scepticisme," but prefers "éclectisme et dilettantisme" (p. 414). Gide calls Montaigne's scepticism "inconsistant" (p. 19).

> is it only when he likes it, only sometimes, and in his way. For him, scepticism works as an indispensable background for what is not sceptic in his thought[23]
>
> (Sève 2007, p. 352).

But apart from such exceptions – *qui confirment la règle* (which confirm the rule) – nobody denies that Montaigne is a sceptic. Thibaudet's summing up is to the point:

> He took an interest in three doctrines: stoïcism, epicurism, pyrrhonism. He admired the first, applied the second, adopted the third, and these three attitudes concurred to engender a unique thought[24]
>
> (Thibaudet 1963, p. 570)

As is well-known Montaigne was surrounded in his library by 57 sentences he let paint on the beams (nine of them from Sextus Empiricus). They illustrate his 'scepticisme et épicurisme chrétien' (Thibaudet and Rat in Montaigne (1962), p. 1427). Some are reproduced below:

* Because I see that we, all of us, are no more than phantoms and light shades.
* Oh, unhappy spirits of men, oh, blind hearts, the very short time at our disposal passes away amidst the obscurities of life and great perils.
* Did you ever see a man who believes to be wise? A demented will give you more hope.
* This can be or cannot be.
* Man, you do not know whether this or that is best for you, or whether both can do.
* The man who relies on his knowledge, is not yet aware of what it represents.
* Who knows whether to live is not to die, and whether to die is not to live.
* All things are too difficult for men to understand them.
* Keep within bounds, observe the limits, and respect nature.
* Enjoy the present, the rest is not in your power.
* Each reasoning can be opposed a reasoning of the same force.
* I do not decide anything.[25]

---

[23] Son scepticisme est un scepticisme "moyen," un scepticisme de l'irrésolution, Ce scepticisme est comme enveloppé ou bordé d'une autre philosophie. Montaigne n'est' pas sceptique, parce qu'il ne l'est que quand il lui plaît, parfois seulement, et à sa manière. Le scepticisme fonctionne chez Montaigne comme un fond indispensable au déploiement de ce qu'il y a de non sceptique dans sa pensée.

[24] Trois doctrines l'ont interessé: le stoïcisme, l'épicurisme, le pyrrhonisme. Il a admiré le premier, pratiqué le deuxième, adopté le troisième, et ces trois attitudes forment le jeu d'une pensée unique.

[25] Car je vois que tous, tant que nous sommes, nous ne sommes rien de plus que des fantômes ou une ombre légère.

O malheureux esprits des hommes ! O cœurs aveugles ! En quelles ténèbres de la vie, et dans quel grands périls s'écoule ce tout petit pas de temps que nous avons.

As-tu vu un homme qui se figure sage? Un dément donnera plus que lui à espérer.

Cela peut être et cela peut ne pas être.

Homme, tu ne sais si ceci ou cela te convient plus, ou l'un et l'autre également.

L'homme qui présume de son sçavoir ne sçait pas encore ce que c'est que sçavoir.

Qui sait si vivre est ce qu'on appelle mourir, et si mourir c'est vivre?

Toutes les choses sont trop difficiles pour que l'homme puisse les comprendre.

Gardes la mesure, observer la limite et suivre la nature.

Jouis agréablement du présent, le reste est en dehors de toi.

A tout raisonnement on peut opposer un raisonnement d'égale force.

Je ne décide rien.

Conclusion

By all means, Montaigne being a sceptic, is not "a famous utopian of the Renaissance." He has read the "utopians" Rabelais and Thomas More and sometimes it finds expression in some pages but as was usual at that time no quotations! Other passages may give the *impression* that he is in favor of "cannibal" practices, but he does not take risks: he wants to stay on good terms with State and Church.

He did not need this "utopian" attribution for his glory. He remains an important philosopher pleading for scepticism and tolerance. The author of the Essais is, in some way, a "universal" author because everybody will recognize in this work his or her views: the believer and the nonbeliever, the sceptic and the nonsceptic, the conservative and the revolutionary[26] (according to Voltaire, Montaigne "is a man who will always be loved": "un homme qui sera toujours aimé"). Of course, he is only a link, though an important one, in the history of scepticism. Moreover, he made available, in a pleasant way, the wisdom of the ancient world.

Apart from being the inventor of the essay and a founder of modern scepticism, with Rabelais the most important French prose-writer of the sixteenth century,[27] he is a forerunner of the French *moralistes* and other authors,[28] and still more important, a precursor of modernity. To wind up with Thibaudet:

> In respect of a great deal of philosophical questions Montaigne was the disciple of the Ancients. But on the principal social problems he was a modern. His thought was never behind the times, but always ahead of his time: a hundred years in matters of witchcraft, two hundred years in respect of laws, three hundreds on the subject of seducation[29]
>
> (Thibaudet, *Ibid.*).

References

Allemand, R. (2005), *L'utopie*, Ellipses, Paris.
Brahami, F. (1997), *Le scepticisme de Montaigne*, PUF, Paris.
Brahami, F. (2004), Scepticisme, in *Dictionnaire de Michel Montaigne*, ed. P. Desan, Honoré Champion, Paris.
Cioran, E. (1995), *Œuvres*, Gallimard, Paris.

[26]A similar, still more general observation in Gide (p. 39): Chacun peut glaner dans les *Essais* ce qui lui plaît, qui souvent est ce qu'aura dédaigné tel autre (Everyone can take in the *Essays* what he likes. often what somebody else looks down upon).

[27]See d'Ormesson 2003, p. 418: '... le merveilleux XVIe siècle, illustré dans la prose par Rabelais et Montaigne.'

[28]One of them is Jean de La Fontaine (1621–95). Montaigne is the author from whom he 'borrows' most though he quotes him little (Orieux 1976, p. 126). See also p. 409 and p. 428.

[29]S'il a dit sur un grand nombre de questions philosophiques le mot d'un disciple des Anciens, Montaigne a dit sur les principaux problèmes sociaux le mot d'un moderne. Il a pensé jamais en retard, mais toujours cent, deux cents ou trois cents ans à l'avance. Cent ans quand il s'agit de la sorcellerie, deux cents quand il s'agit des lois, trois cents quand il s'agit de l'éducation.

Faguet, E. (1928), in *The Essayes of Michael Lord of Montaigne translated into English by John Florio and with an introduction by Desmond MacCarthy*, Vol. III, J.M. Dent, Toronto and E.P. Dutton, New York, Appendix.
Fortunati, V. and Trousson, R. ed. (2004), *Dictionary of literary utopias*, H. Champion, Paris.
Frame, D. (1958), trans., *The complete essays of Montaigne*, Stanford Univ. Press, Stanford.
Friedrich, H. (1967), *Montaigne*, 2nd ed., Francke, Berne and Munich.
Gide, A. (1929), *Les pages immortelles de Montaigne choisies et expliquées par André Gide*, Corêa, Paris.
Lanson, G. (1958), *Les Essais de Montaigne*, Etude et analyse, Mellottée, Paris.
Le Clézio, J. (2006), *Ourania*, Gallimard, Paris.
Montaigne, M. (1962), *Œuvres complètes*. Textes établis par Albert Thibaudet et Maurice Rat. Introduction et notes par Maurice Rat, Bibliothèque de la Pléiade, Gallimard, Paris.
Nietzsche, F. (1999), *Sämtliche Werke*. Kritische Studienausgabe, ed. G. Colli and M. Montinari, de Gruyter, Berlin.
d'Ormesson, J. (1998), *Une autre histoire de la littérature française*, Nil, Paris, 2 tomes.
d'Ormesson, J. (2003), *Et toi mon cœur pourquoi bats-tu?* Gallimard, Paris.
Orieux, J. (1976), *La Fontaine ou la vie est un conte*, Flammarion, Paris.
Robertson, J. (1909), *Montaigne and Shakespere*, Albert and Charles Black, London.
Roose, A. (2009), *La curiosité de Montaigne*, Campion, Paris.
Rouvillois, F. (1998), *L'utopie*, GF Flammarion (Corpus), Paris.
Rufin, J. (2004), *Globalia*, Flammarion, Paris.
Sève, B. (2007), Montaigne. *Des règles pour l'esprit*, PUF, Paris.
Steiner, G. (1996), *No passion spent*, Essays (1978–1996), Faber and Faber, London and Boston.
Stratius, P. (1997), *Le réel et la joie. Essai sur l'œuvre de Montaigne*, Kimé, Paris.
Steiner, G. (1986), *A Reading Against Shakespeare*, University of Glasgow.
Tavernier, J. and Lommée, D. (1946), *An English anthology* With a short survey of the history of English literature, Verbeke-Loys, Bruges.
Taylor, G. (1925), *Shakespere's debt to Montaigne*, Harvard University Press, Cambridge.
Thibaudet, A. (1963), *Montaigne*, Texte établi par Floyd Gray d'après des notes manuscrites, Gallimard, Paris.
Vauvenargues, L. de (1981), *Œuvres*. Edition de 1747 suivie de textes posthumes et de textes retranchés. Chronologie, introduction, notes et index par Jean Dagen, Flammarion, Paris.
White, F. (1946), *Famous utopias of the Renaissance*, Hendricks House. Farrar, Straus, New York.

Labor in Utopian Socialism

Hans Frambach

Theories of the so-called prescientific socialism, meaning the socialistic theories before Karl Marx, are often described as *utopian socialism*. The utopian socialists criticized the existing social order, but expected a renewal of the order by force of ideas alone. Not the aims but the means were described as utopian. The central category of utopian socialism was labor, which was central, too, for most early nineteenth century economic theories. The utopian socialists interpreted labor in peculiar ways and took it as a starting point for different socialist attempts to put theory into practice. This paper looks at the content and range of the labor concept propounded by the utopian socialists that influenced German economic thought, and analyzes some of the directions taken by utopian socialism, namely the beginnings of socialism in Germany, interventionism, Saint-Simonism, cooperative socialism, and anarchism. To keep the essay succinct, each of these approaches will be exemplified in (for the most part) one main figure.

The Foundations of Utopian Socialism in Germany (Lorenz von Stein)

To analyze the understanding of labor proposed by the utopian socialists, the ideas of the national economist, sociologist, and theoretician of constitutional law, Lorenz von Stein (1815–1890), are particularly important. Although not a socialist himself, and even a critic of socialism – as he, toward the end of his life, experienced it – his ideas of economic history anticipated and formed central elements of the socialist era that followed. Stein is the first theoretician to provide a realistic analysis of societal movements and at the same time a theory of revolution and class struggle. He expressed his idea of labor as follows:

H. Frambach (✉)
University of Wuppertal, Dept. of Economics – Schumpeter School of Business and Economics
Gaußstraße 20, 40897 Wuppertal, Germany
e-mail: frambach@wivi.uni-wuppertal.de

J.G. Backhaus (ed.), *The State as Utopia: Continental Approaches*, The European Heritage in Economics and the Social Sciences 9, DOI 10.1007/978-1-4419-7500-3_10,

> Labor is the realization of the infinite mission in life which a person sets himself, making his own certain aspects of the outer world and thus forcing them to become part of his own inner world.
>
> (Stein 1964a, 99).

More concretely, Stein defined work as "that human activity whose purpose is to form a specific matter to fulfill a need" (Stein 1964b, 138). Human labor is, therefore, the sum of all the activities a person performs for the satisfaction of needs – e.g., production, purchase, exchange of goods (Stein 1964b, 138). Stein calls it *real labor* if it is done for a concrete purpose (Stein 1964b, 141). Real labor is subdivided into *mechanical* labor (using only physical energy, the production of material goods in particular) and *formative* or *free* labor. Formative labor refers to activities that reunite components of mechanical work into a whole, set the aims of labor in advance, or direct and control labor etc. (Stein 1964b, 142). Regarding the satisfaction of need as the innate purpose of human nature, to be protected above all else, labor – as the means of satisfying need – becomes "the activity of free self-determination of the individual within nature" and, in that sense, the realization of personal freedom: *labor is the development of personal freedom.* That is why it is absolutely necessary; and it is precisely this that Stein means when he says that *humans are made to work* (v. Stein 1964b, 138).

Stein's theory of societal development is penetrated by socialist thoughts and ideas. At a time when socialism was still unknown in Germany – it seemed to Germans to be a "fairytale from far abroad" – it was first spread by Stein's book *Socialism and Communism in Today's France* of 1842 (Roscher 1874, 1020). Throughout the periods of physiocracy, classical economy, and the historical school, labor was seen in relation to the nation, national economy, and national system of political economy, but this changed with the French Revolution. From then on, labor was discussed not in a geographically restricted context but in that of the "political-revolutionary nation." François Babeuf was the first to posit a general obligation to work in a national community, and Stein saw in Babeuf's "first school of pure communism" the seminal idea of an *organization of national labor.* Thus, Stein used the notion of national labor, which came in 1848 from France to Germany, explicitly in terms of state socialism. In France, the provisional government had issued a decree, drafted by Louis Blanc, guaranteeing the workers a *right to work* and safeguarding their livelihood (the revolutionary government obliged itself to give jobs to all workers and guaranteed them the proceeds of their work). The right to work and the right to receive the revenue of work thus became a national matter. The "organization of labor," Blanc's famous slogan even before the Revolution, was politically more clearly defined by Stein's notion of the "organization of national labor by state authority" (Conze 1972, 208).

In the first part of *Socialism and Communism,* Stein elaborates the details of the theory of class struggle. He starts with the dualistic separation of society and ends with the striving of the proletariat to seize all political power by overcoming the state. Like Karl Marx later, Stein chooses labor as *the* criterion of the dualistic class division, the confrontation between the propertied class and the dispossessed. The propertied class is not forced to work but is able to satisfy its needs without work because it forces the poor class to work for its own benefit – Stein calls it "income without labor." Hence, the propertied class is not only privileged but also workless, receiving its income from the work of others. Consequently, there is a polarization between property and non-property, and furthermore, between property and labor (Stein 1972, 91).

Capital and labor are initially explained as two sides of a coin, the result of a natural process, corresponding to the principle of reciprocal needs and following the order of a society built on labor income (Stein 1972, 105–106). But this harmony is interrupted as soon as the interests of capital – striving for higher profits via wage reduction – begin to contradict those of labor – striving for the satisfaction of needs via wage growth (Stein 1971, 35; 1972, 107–108). The natural interests of capital to keep wages low makes it impossible for labor to build capital ("those without capital cannot build capital" – Stein 1972, 109). A hardening of the societal order and class structure follows, and an increasing contradiction develops between the rigid persistence of class structures and the permanent change characteristic of labor – this contradicts the idea of freedom. Consequently, the conditions for a political revolution are given (Stein 1971, 39–40; 1972, 109).

However, in contrast to the protagonists of real and scientific socialism, Stein neither supports revolution nor any form of utopia. Nevertheless, his goal is *social reform* in which labor is ranked higher than capital. This begins with the idea that the value of things derives from labor, that wealth is the product of labor, and that capital is nothing else than accumulated labor (Stein 1972, 117). What must happen is that the contradiction between capital and labor be overcome, because this devastates freedom. In Stein's view, the possibility to work, and thus to reach a higher level of satisfaction, is threatened by the interests of capital (i.e., capital prevents the development of freedom), for freedom and labor are identical:

> If freedom and labor are identical [and in this respect Stein follows Hegel – H. F.] and if the revenues of labor (because of its privileged nature) belong to the workers, there has to be a societal order where this idea of labor and its inherent rights are realized.
>
> (Stein 1972, 117).

As to what this order might be, Stein weighs up socialism against communism. Socialism is the clear winner, but still in the sense of a second best solution, because socialism must necessarily abolish ownership, which is the goal of individuality and freedom (Stein 1972, 118). Social reform should be implemented by achieving a harmony of interests and not by abolishing the social classes. The paramount principle is the safeguarding of freedom. Freedom expresses the ability to achieve by virtue of one's own activity, continuous personal self-determination (i.e., independence from the external circumstances of life by overcoming them). In a society built on labor, power is capital. This means that personal freedom in a labor society can be ensured only by providing all the workers with the opportunity (Stein speaks of ability) to acquire capital (Stein 1972, 135–136). Whether this is at all possible in a society built on labor is a question left open.

Interventionism (J. C. L. Simonde de Sismondi)

Jean Charles Léonard Simonde de Sismondi (1773–1842) stands in the tradition of Adam Smith. Sismondi relates his own experiences with capitalist society in his *New Principles of Political Economy*, which sees free competition as increasing the existing overbalance of economic power rather than establishing a harmony of interests. Already meager livelihoods will be more and more destroyed and workers increasingly forced to accept unfavorable conditions of employment. It may be true that free competition causes a considerable increase in production, but it utterly fails to solve the issue of distribution, because the assets and incomes of the rich increase on the one hand, but on the other those who have no property are rapidly reduced to the status of an impoverished proletariat. Defining wealth, Sismondi adopts a classical national economic stance. Wealth arises from the three continuing *sources of wealth*: land, capital, and life (labor) – and neither land nor capital can produce income without the support of labor (Sismondi 1971, 96–97). While land is able to unfold productive forces at least to a certain extent, the function of capital (accumulated labor) consists only in the payment and employment of labor (incidentally, in this theory the institution of property remains inviolate). The decisive connection between the three sources of wealth is, therefore, labor. Without labor, land and capital are economically devoid of sense or value, and capital is not even thinkable.

Sismondi notices that the capital, which employs and pays labor, is generally owned by the capitalist and is not in the hands of those who work. The interest of the capitalist is to leave the worker at subsistence level and to maximize added value, which means the amount the worker produces above subsistence level (Sismondi 1971, 98). The worker fights for a greater share of the value she or he has produced, but against the capitalist the worker is always in the worse position. The capitalist (the rich individual) dictates to the worker (the poor individual) how he or she should live: 1. If the capitalist has higher expenses than income, further expenditure can only be incurred by the use of capital, which should really be productively invested in order to maintain or expand production and secure the incomes of the workers. These incomes are inevitably cut when capital expenditure is reduced. Thus, Sismondi concludes that the rich man dictates the poor man's way of life. 2. If the rich save part of their income (profits) to increase capital, production will also increase, which will in turn increase the income of the workers. The income of the workers thus increases in direct proportion to reduction in the income of the capitalist; in this respect, the rich provide for the poor. With increased wages, the population will also increase, but in the long run an adjustment of wages downward will follow (Sismondi 1971, 100–101). The poor receive income only from their labor, and are, therefore, fundamentally dependent on the owners of capital. Workers must sell their labor before they receive an income, and they can sell it only to those who are willing to exchange their residual capital for the labor the workers can provide. It follows that the willingness of the capitalist (the demand for work) substantially determines the price of work, and the amount the employee can spend varies with that price (i.e., wage) level (Sismondi 1971, 106).

The failure of the process of free competition, the totally distorted distribution of power, income and property and, last but not least, the dependence of the work force on capitalists are the reasons why Sismondi demands concrete measures in the form of state intervention (Sismondi 1975, 265–266). He trusts only in the state to restore equilibrium between the spheres of production and consumption, and to reconcile the different interests involved. Wealth should be seen in relation to general and individual welfare and not only from the viewpoint of increasing the material production of an economy. This is the only way to reach a more equitable distribution of capital and income and to protect workers from exploitation. Further tasks of the state include the ban on child labor and Sunday working, the restriction of working hours, and the imposition of an obligation on employers to pay the costs of illness, unemployment, and aging, and to grant the right of free association to their workers (Amonn 1949, 214–215).

Following a more general consideration of Sismondi, state intervention is necessary if economic theory is seen as a theory not only of maximizing wealth but also of achieving "the greatest happiness." It hardly makes sense to work as much as possible, and to sell one's labor at the lowest possible price, if one must abandon all the advantages of the wealth he has worked for: "one would increase his efforts and rob himself of enjoyment." The task of the state must be to protect everybody against the attacks of others. Therefore, economic theory (political economy) can be interpreted as an expression of social knowledge. It teaches that the social interest of all must be observed: that nobody be overtaxed on the one hand or go away empty-handed on the other. It also teaches that social interests must be coordinated with individual interests, a process which entails that everybody must receive an adequate wage for their work because they make an effort even at the lowest price. Thus, the state is the "protector" of the individual (Sismondi 1975, 262–263). The restrictions of liberty accompanying state intervention are understood as a concession of the individual to the community, which would not exist at all in unbridled competition. For Sismondi, the state and its intervention in the economic process become a feature of civilized societies; he does not assign any particularly higher degree of civilization to the mechanism of free competition. In comparison with a modern capitalist, the employer of a slave-holder society would have paid (just enough) for the needs of his slaves; the modern employer disposes of such obligations to his workers by passing them (the obligations) on to society (Sismondi 1975, 274–278).

Saint-Simonism (C.-H. Comte de Saint-Simon)

Claude-Henri de Rouvroy, Comte de Saint Simon (1760–1825), recognizes in the modern worker the continuation of the tradition of slavery and exploitation of man by man. Although the exploitation of man does not show the horrendous character it did in ancient times, it is no less actual or relevant at present. The worker is not, like the slave, the property of a master: the situation is determined by a contract concluded by both sides; nevertheless, this situation is always variable. Because of their material situation, workers are in a predicament; however, they have no other option than to enter the contract ("He must accept the contract on pain of death, since his daily food depends solely on the work of the day before" – Saint Simon 1962, 105).

Saint-Simon's theory is the first in which the separation of property from labor, and the clear divorce of the class of capitalists from that of proletarians, is openly discussed, and this explicitly in the face of the impoverishment of the workers and the concentration of capital – both factors resulting from the principle of unrestricted competition (Saint-Simon 1962, 114, 123). Saint Simon does not deny the economic success of political and economic liberalism; however, he finds fault with leaving the social question unanswered. The root cause of the differences and tensions between the different classes lies in unequal political and economic power, evident above all in a system of capital distribution that generates a one-sided disadvantage for the workers – who alone support economic and social progress – and a one-sided advantage for the ruling class, which is regarded as economically unproductive and useless (Saint-Simon 1962, 12–14, 110–111).

On the basis of his theory of historical and philosophical development, Saint Simon began to elaborate a positive conception of a future social order. His social theory is dominated by the idea of economic upswing. The insight is central that economic factors rather than a political constitution are the foundation stone of social life. Economic factors, which Saint Simon primarily sees as determined by property conditions and the economic inclination and abilities of the people, have gained increasing importance in the course of the social development process. This importance alone explains the transition from the feudal to the industrial system.

For Saint-Simon, the economy is the main conditioning factor of the political and social structure; from this principle, he derives the task of creating a new kind of social order corresponding to the new type of (industrial) economy.[1] As a means to this end, he demands harmony rather than class struggle because people should merge to improve their mutual welfare. In the industrial system, which for Saint-Simon represents the end of progressive development, the principle of industrial equality is realized. In accordance with this principle, "everybody should be paid according to his abilities, any ability according to its performance" (Saint-Simon 1962, 14, 127–128). This ideal, Saint-Simon realized, is only attainable with a new morality that puts behind it the oppression of labor. Nevertheless, he wants to maintain private property and the inheritance law (in contrast, e.g., to his pupil Saint-Amand Bazard, who wants to make the state the sole heir). Saint Simon always has the growth of economic productivity and of the national product in mind, and hopes for a wealth creation resulting exclusively from work and thrift. He holds thoroughly liberalist ideas and cannot, therefore, be unambiguously assigned to socialism.

[1] The term *industry* includes all economic activities, like agriculture and trade, and also science and art; it is the most important source of material prosperity. Industry, furthermore, includes all activities that are useful for society, e. g. intellectual work, because it is science that leads the economy in the form of technology. Industry is thus understood as an order where a new organization of society will be carried out by the application of science (Saint-Simon 1962, 28, 44–45, 119).

Cooperative Socialism

Of all the representatives of cooperative socialism, Charles Fourier (1772–1837), Robert Owen (1771–1858), and Louis Blanc (1813–1882), it is Blanc who is responsible for the most realistic and sustainable concepts. Blanc sees in the foundation of *social workshops* (*productive worker-cooperatives*) an effective measure to redress the negative results of liberalism and competition (the exploitation of labor) and to build a society on the socialist principles of equality and justice. He strives for a mutual labor organization, a community of workers where revenues are distributed in relation to the individual level of labor and capital invested (Pechan 1929, 93). To guarantee this, the individual must be protected from the negative consequences of competition. However, only the state can accomplish this task, and that only if the state is controlled by the workforce. Therefore, Blanc propagates a general right to vote, which permits employees to assume political power. Blanc's economic program thus aims at a systematically directed organization of the economy and the elimination of private ownership of capital equipment (Pechan 1929, 91).

The state, directed by workers, is required to found the social workshops. To accomplish this, the state has to buy the existing workshops, production locations, and estates, and make them available to the workers (the state holds property) – thus Saint-Simon argues in his book *Organisation du Travail*[2] of 1840 (Blanc 1848, 117–121). The state becomes the "supreme head of production" with the task of destroying competition by direct participation in the economic process. The state raises loans and establishes common workshops (productive cooperatives) for the most important branches of industry. It designs statutes, which acquire legal force, obtains the necessary tools, and regulates wages in the initial phase. The workers carry out the distribution of the work themselves. Profit is divided into three segments: (1) a share for the old people, the invalid, and the sick, as well as for the support of other branches of industry; (2) a share that is distributed evenly to all members of the productive cooperatives; (3) a share to finance capital equipment for new community members. In this way, a productive cooperative will compete with private industry in every main sector of industry (Blanc 1848, 118–119). Because productive cooperatives have a much higher degree of common life – and are, therefore, in Blanc's eyes superior – private industry will be forced to organize itself according to the example of these cooperatives, and consequently also under the direction of the state (Blanc 1848, e.g. 120). But Blanc is careful not to disturb the prevailing ownership relations such as the private ownership of consumer goods, as well as the law of inheritance.

While Blanc starts with the rebuilding of the state, Charles Fourier – and later, his pupil Victor Prosper Considérant (1808–1893) – begin their social reform with

[2] *Organisation du Travail* is a collection of articles written in 1839 which were all originally published in the journal *Revue du Progrès politique, social et littéraire*. This journal was also founded by Saint-Simon.

a new construction of the municipalities. Their aim was the organization of what was not yet organized: labor. Particularly in the area of industry, everything seemed left to the arbitrariness and the mood of single individuals, who fought each other in endless competition – a remedy could only be found in the organization of labor (Considérant 1906, 48). Fourier's *phalange* consisted of 1,500–2,000 persons. The number could not be smaller because the range of different characters, leanings, and dispositions must be varied enough to provide willing workers for all kinds of labor – this was necessary in order to produce goods for the different needs of society. The number could not be larger, because otherwise the social mechanism would become too complex and susceptible to disruption. All members would live in common quarters (*phalanstère*) in the middle of the basic area of the communal *phalange*. For whatever property the members of the phalange brought in to the community at the time of their accession, they would get an equivalent in the form of share certificates in the total value of the *phalange*. These share certificates would be fully transferable and saleable. The institution of private property was thus maintained in Fourier's theory, but with the construction of the *phalanges,* the attempt was made to reconcile the distinction between capital and work without revoking it (Adler 1906, 22, 25–28, Considérant 1835, I, 369–374; 1906, 5457; Gide and Rist 1921, 266–271). The members of the *phalange* would be allotted to specific divisions in accordance with the existing types of labor (agricultural, trade, domestic, educational, etc.), which in turn were subdivided into smaller groups. Every member was to be trained and employed according to his dispositions, abilities, and interests, but work could also be changed. Heads were to be elected by the groups and divisions, and it was their task to make suggestions, advise, and implement decisions. The heads would have no authority to command, because the principle of social harmony excluded coercive rules. Every member would receive a minimal income for his most essential needs and, furthermore, a certain remuneration for his individual working hours. Labor done for "useful needs," however, was to be paid more highly than labor for "bare conveniences." Fourier believed that he had in this way reconciled the principles of the division of labor and the harmonious association of work in a manner most favorable for production (Considérant 1835, 375–381).

Every individual would be free to choose the job they wanted, and thus the way in which they could best satisfy their needs. It was also assumed that the monotony of one-sided activities, as well as the isolation of the single worker, would no longer exist in the system of the *phalange*. These were considerable advantages over an economic system in which every individual wanted to destroy his competitors, and where the different interest groups – capital owners, dealers, workers, producers, and consumers – incessantly clashed with each other. In such a comparison, the current economic system was doomed to extinction. The "greatest happiness" of mankind would, for Fourier, be fulfilled if the system of private economy were relinquished in favor of communal economic organization. He saw scattered individual features of a cooperative economy realized in the social mechanisms of civilization, from the great East India Company down to associations of poor villagers. The problem of developing such single organizations (including their earlier forms) into one great uniform mechanism could only be solved, however, if people could be persuaded to "unite out of an inner drive to common work." The prerequisite for this was that individuals should be completely free in their choice of work, they should be allowed to follow their drives unrestrictedly, and be completely assured of a high yield from their labor (Adler 1906, 24–25).

Fourier saw a central problem for societies in the arduous nature of wealth production: "Labor is repulsive." (Considérant 1906, 58). His reasons were insufficient wages, working conditions that were damaging to people's health, loneliness (isolation during work), the constant one-sidedness of work, and lack of competition. A solution (making labor attractive) could be reached by a change of occupation (division of labor), a boost in competitiveness, the use of different individual character traits, the unfolding of ambition, the communal and free election of foremen, etc. (Considérant 1906, 61–68). Gide and Rist describe the attraction of work as the key issue of Fourierism. Fourier did not want a social situation in which individuals were forced to work by the need to earn their living, by profit seeking, or by the commandments of social or religious duty etc. People should work for pleasure; they should "be attracted by work" (Gide and Rist 1921, 273). Of course, from Fourier's point of view, the organization of the *phalange* would be the perfect way to realize such goals, and thus the central step toward solving the social problem.

Anarchism (P. J. Proudhon)

The anarchist Pierre Joseph Proudhon (1809–1865) criticized both classical national economics and the different lines of socialism. Socialism, because it stood, just like communism, in opposition to the liberty of the workers: Proudhon condemned every kind of state organization because all these presupposed conditions of power and oppression. He reproached the existing social order for allowing an income to be received without work although work alone was productive (Diehl 1968, e.g. 65, 99). Because only labor could generate value, all incomes received only on the basis of the existing ownership rights were described as "workless incomes." Proudhon consequently remarks that the employer pays every employee to the value of his individual performance, but withholds for himself the product of their communal work (which is the fruit of the increased collective strength of all involved in the production process and exceeds the sum of all individual performances) (Stavenhagen 1957, 133). Proudhon replaces the coercive legislation of the state with the organization of economic forces in the form of contracts entered into between citizens, single social groups, organizations, and corporations. Order arises from the free activity of everyone, because the field of activity of each individual is determined by the natural division of labor, free choice of occupation etc. In his system, there is no government, no authority, no political parties, but solely the absolute liberty of the people as individuals and citizens (Diehl 1968, 109).

Summary and Conclusions

Socialism criticizes the social evils of economic and social liberalism and the unequal and unjust distribution of income and wealth produced. Socialists are far more radical in their demands than other groupings, e.g. they seek the complete reorganization of society, equal income distribution and the abolition of the mechanisms of competition, and the market. Following German idealism, however, early (prescientific) socialism also conceived of labor as freedom: Lorenz v. Stein equates labor with the development of freedom as people must satisfy their needs by work (the primeval mode of free self-determination is seen in the satisfaction of need). Stein's book *Socialism and Communism in Today's France* contributed substantially to the spreading of the socialist body of thought in Germany. In contrast to the representatives of the so-called real and scientific socialism, he stood for social reform rather than revolution. And the solution proposed by social reform consists, in this view, in the guarantee of freedom for every individual. More concretely, it must be possible for each individual to have access to power, i.e. capital acquisition must be open to all, down to the last worker.

The supremacy of capital owners over workers is lamented also in the interventionism of Simonde de Sismondi. The worker is always in the worse position as his "way of life" is dictated to him by the capitalist. In the conflict of interests between capitalists and workers, the latter are the losers. Because of this unequal position of power, and the lopsided income and capital distribution resulting from the failure of free competition, Sismondi demands concrete state intervention. He believes that only the state can provide for a convergence between the interests of capitalists and employees. The restriction of freedom following state intervention must be understood as a concession of the individual to the community. This "price" is considered to be not unreasonable as in the opposite event unbridled competition and self-interest would make the very emergence of a community impossible.

In their assessment of the negative sides of capitalism, the representatives of Saint Simonism hold the opinion of the other socialist movements, but they appreciate more highly the economic successes of capitalism. Saint Simon's theory is dominated by the awareness of economic upswing: for him economic (and not political) factors form the basis of social cooperation. Therefore, a social order adapted to the "new economic system" (i.e., of industry) is required. But, as opposed to capitalism, the new social order will be dominated by harmony in the sense of the orientation of individual interests toward the public welfare. However, a prerequisite of this order is a system of morals that is also oriented toward the public good, and a reform of the property order (without abolishing private property).

Such utopian ideas take concrete shape among the representatives of cooperative socialism. For Louis Blanc, for example, social workshops are the most effective measure with which the state can proceed against competition and its negative consequences. Considérant takes up Fourier's idea of the *phalange* to prove the superiority of social harmony and communal organization over the private economic system. If low wages, unreasonable working conditions, and the enduring monotony of labor, etc. are abolished, and ways of changing work and self-realization in the workplace are provided, work will lose its arduous and offensive character and become "attractive." While most socialists, like Blanc and Fourier, trust in the state's abilities to redesign the social and economic system, the anarchist Proudhon rejects state authority altogether, because it immediately presupposes power and oppression. The organization of economic forces must – according to Proudhon – take the place of state legislation, because order arises only from the free activity of all beyond the boundaries of any superimposed power or authority.

References

Georg Adler, 1906. Fourier und der Fourierismus, in: Victor Prosper Considérant, 1906. Fouriers System der sozialen Reform, transl. of Exposition abrégée du système phalanstérien de Fourier, suivie de Études sur quelques problèmes fondamentaux de la destinée sociale, Paris 1844, orig. ed. Paris 1840, Leipzig: C.L. Hirschfeld, pp. 7–42.

Alfred Amonn, 1949. Simonde de Sismondi als Nationalökonom. Darstellung seiner Lehren mit einer Einführung und Erläuterungen, Vol. I: Die „Neuen Prinzipien". Kritik des Liberalismus, Neubegründung des Interventionismus, Sozialpolitik, Bevölkerungslehre, Krisentheorie, Bern: A. Francke.

Louis Blanc, 1848. Organisation du Travail, 5. Aufl. (Paris), 1. Aufl. 1840, Brüssel: J.P. Meline, Cans et Cie.

Werner Conze, 1972. Art. Arbeit, in: Otto Brunner, Werner Conze and Reinhart Koselleck, eds. Geschichtliche Grundbegriffe. Historisches Lexikon zur politisch-sozialen Sprache in Deutschland. Stuttgart: E. Klett, pp. 154–215.

Victor Prosper Considérant, 1835. Destinée sociale, 3 Bde. (1835–1844), Paris: Libraires du Palais-Royal.

Victor Prosper Considérant, 1906. Fouriers System der sozialen Reform, transl. of Exposition abrégée du système phalanstérien de Fourier, suivie de Études sur quelques problèmes fondamentaux de la destinée sociale, Paris 1844, orig. ed. Paris 1840, Leipzig: C. L. Hirschfeld.

Karl Diehl, 1968. Pierre Joseph Proudhon. Seine Lehre und sein Leben, repr. of vol. Jena 1888 (Die Eigentums- und Wertlehre), Aalen: Scientia.

Charles Gide und Charles Rist, 1921. Geschichte der volkswirtschaftlichen Lehrmeinungen, transl. Of the 3. french ed. Histoire des doctrines économique depuis les physiocrates jusqu'à nos jours, 1909, Jena: Gustav Fischer.

Hermann Pechan, 1929. Louis Blanc als Wegbereiter des modernen Sozialismus, Jena: Gustav Fischer.

Wilhelm Roscher, 1874. Geschichte der National-Oekonomik in Deutschland, München: R. Oldenbourg.

Claude-Henri de Rouvroy, Comte de Saint-Simon, 1962. Die Lehre Saint-Simons, transl. of the orig. ed. 1828/1829, Neuwied: Hermann Luchterhand.

Jean Charles Léonard Simonde de Sismondi, 1971. Neue Grundsätze der Politischen Ökonomie oder vom Reichtum in seinen Beziehungen zur Bevölkerung, vol. I, transl. of the 2. ed. (Paris 1827) of "Nouveaux Principes d'économie politique" (orig. ed. 1819), Berlin: Akademie-Verlag.

Jean Charles Léonard Simonde de Sismondi, 1975. Neue Grundsätze der Politischen Ökonomie oder vom Reichtum in seinen Beziehungen zur Bevölkerung, vol. II, transl. of the 2. ed. (Paris 1827) of "Nouveaux Principes d'économie politique" (orig. ed. 1819), Berlin: Akademie-Verlag.

Gerhard Stavenhagen, 1957. Geschichte der Wirtschaftstheorie, 2nd ed., orig. ed. 1951, Göttingen: Vandenhoeck & Ruprecht.

Lorenz von Stein, 1964a. Die Gesellschaftlehre, repr. of the orig. ed. Stuttgart 1856, Osnabrück: Otto Zeller.
Lorenz von Stein, 1964b. System der Staatswissenschaft, repr. of the orig. ed. Stuttgart 1852, Osnabrück: Otto Zeller.
Lorenz von Stein, 1971. Proletariat und Gesellschaft, text of the 2nd ed. of Der Sozialismus und Kommunismus des heutigen Frankreichs, 1848, orig. ed. 1842, München: Wilhelm Fink.
Lorenz von Stein, 1972. Geschichte der sozialen Bewegung in Frankreich von 1789 bis auf unsere Tage, 3 vol., repr. of the ed. 1921, orig. ed. 1850, Darmstadt: Wissenschaftliche Buchgesellschaft.

Iambulus' "Sun State" and T. Campanella's "Civitas Solis": Some Comparative Parallels and Links of Two Utopias

Christos P. Baloglou

Introduction

The fifteenth-century rediscovery of Plato and Plutarch stimulated the early modern "best state" exercise and encouraged a debate on constitutions that replicated the seed-bed out of which the classical utopia had sprung.[1] If we define utopia as the envisaging of a best commonwealth, or ideal society, of sinful human beings in a fallen world without benefit of divine agency, then more may be said to have reinaugurated the exercise. More's "Utopia" identified itself, in the text as well as in the prefatory and appended letters and verses, as a product of a humanist concern with literature, language, and moral philosophy.[2] However, the axis of the work is the suggestion that there is a conceivable social ideal in which fallible humans live in a society of moral dignity and worth without the aid of revelation and that, moreover, such an ideal cannot be arrived at by moral effort in a curial context or even by the legislative effort[3] of good men struggling in a corrupt world. However imaginative, fictional, or satiric the device, More has to suggest ways in which political and social arrangements could be made, which would conduce to that end. The first stage is the solution of the problem which was a work of supreme artifice: The creation of an artificial island by manual excavation. The second was to construct a constraining social and institutional order, which would oblige fallible human beings to behave in ways compatible with social harmony and morality.[4] Human beings always acted reasonably in pursuing their interests as defined by circumstance. The point was, therefore, to reconstruct social circumstance so as to reconcile

[1] Ferguson (1975), p. 28; Manuel and Fritzie (1997), pp. 95–100.

[2] Davis (1991), p. 335.

[3] More (1965), p. 103.

[4] Davis (1991), p. 335.

C.P. Baloglou (✉)
Messevias 14, 14342 Nea Philadelphia Attikis, Hellas Hellenic Telecommunications Organization, Athens, Greece
e-mail: cbaloglou@ote.gr

J.G. Backhaus (ed.), *The State as Utopia: Continental Approaches*, The European Heritage in Economics and the Social Sciences 9, DOI 10.1007/978-1-4419-7500-3_11,

private and communal interest. Accordingly, since private property inspired only private interest, communal property must be substituted for it.[5] The institutional, legal, and educational apparatus of "Utopia" was carefully designed, in extension of this, to guide flawed individuals into better social performance.

Almost a century later, Campanella's "City of the Sun" pursued the same themes. The name given by Campanella to his island is similar to the corresponding island given by Iambulus, the Greek "novelist" of the Hellenistic Times. This paper attempts to analyze some parallels and similarities between the socioeconomic ideas of these two distinguished authors. Such a comparison has not been made yet systematically, as far as we know.[6]

Iambulus' "Sun State"

Iambulus' Itinerary

Iambulus, after a youth devoted to study, became a merchant when his father died (Diodorus Siculus 1935, *Bibliotheca Historica*, II 55 (1)). On the way across Arabia, he and his fellow travelers were seized by brigands, who made shepherds of them. Subsequently captured by the Ethiopians, they were put into a boat with 6 months' provisions and cast out to sea as an expiratory offering that was made every 600 years; Iambulus and his comrade were threatened with death if they should turn back. By sailing directly south, after a 4-month voyage, they came upon a group of seven islands similar in size and equidistant from one another (Diodorus Siculus 1935, *Bibliotheca Historica*, II 55 (1–6)). After 7 years, Iambulus and his fellow traveler were forced to leave because of their bad habits. After a voyage of more than 4 months, Iambulus' companion lost his life in a shipwreck on the Indian coast. Iambulus was conducted to the King of Palimbothra by friendly villagers. The King was well educated and friend of the Greeks. He sent Iambulus to Persia with an escort when he was later able to return to Greece. There he wrote an account of his adventures and related many matters about India that had not been known before (Diodorus Siculus 1935, *Bibliotheca Historica*, II 60).

Iambulus' itinerary can easily be traced: Syria or the land of Nabaters, South Arabia, i.e., Yemen[7] – Ethiopia – the Archipelagus of the Seven Islands in the Indian Ocean – the Delta of Ganges – Palibothra – the State of Seleucides. The work is in accordance with the historical facts, as the caravans of the merchants

[5]More (1965), pp. 237–239.

[6]It is interesting to note that Jowett presents in his preface to Plato's "Politeia" an abstract of Campanella's "City of the Sun." Cf. Schumpeter (1994), p. 207, n.3. A brief reference to a comparison between Iambulus and Campanella is given by Winiarczyk (1997), p. 153.

[7]Some authors – Rohde (1900^2), p. 244, n. 1; Kroll (1914), col. 681; Weinreich (1962), p. 11; Baldassari (1973), p. 305, n. 6 – adopted the view Iambulus went to Somalia. It is more probable that Iambulus went to Felix Arabia because there was the main center of trade of frankincence and myrrh in the Ancient World. Altheim and Stiehl (1964), vol. I, p. 84; Schwarz (1983), p. 45.

would normally set out for Arabia Felix, because of incense and myrrh, and the King of India, who was friendly towards the Greeks, is evidently a ruler belonging to the Maurya Dynasty (ca. 31–185).

Description of the Island

The island was round in general shape, and 5,000 stades in circumference (Diodorus Siculus 1935, *Bibliotheca Historica*, II 55 (6)). The era of the utopic poleis of Phaleas and Hippodamus is over; the frontiers of the new states that are always expanding are at the same time expanding the political thought in a larger radius.

Since the island was located near the equator, night and day were of the same duration. The surrounding waters were sweet, the climate mild; hot and cold springs abounded; fruits were plentiful and ripened throughout the year as in Homer's land of the Phaecians (Homer 1919, *Odyssey*, 7, 120–121) cited by Iambulus for comparison. To his paraphrase of Iambulus on the fertility of the islands and the lushness of all growing things, Diodorus appends a tacit structure against contemporary gluttons. The islanders "do not indulge in the enjoyment of his abundance without restraint, but they practice simplicity and take for their food only what suffices for their needs. Meat and whatever else is roasted or boiled in water and prepared by them, but of all the other dishes ingeniously concocted by professional cooks, such as sauces and the various kinds of seasonings, they have no notion whatsoever" (Diodorus Siculus 1935, *Bibliotheca Historica*, II 78–79).

Description of the Society

Because of their abstemiousness or not, the inhabitants have certain physical characteristics. Four cubits in height, they have flexible bones and more muscular bodies than other men. Their skin was soft to touch, and their bodies smooth and hairless. Beautiful and graceful in appearance, they had very wide nostrils that closed and opened like an epiglottis. Their tongues were split in some fashion all the way down to the roots. This enabled them to imitate every human speech as well as the sounds of birds. They were even able to carry on two conversations at the same time (Diodorus Siculus 1935, *Bibliotheca Historica*, II 57 (1–7)).

The inhabitants are rarely afflicted with disease, but after reaching the stipulated age of 150 they take their own lives by lying down upon a special plant with the property of lulling them to sleep and imperceptibly killing them (Diodorus Siculus 1935, *Bibliotheca Historica*, II 57 (5–6)).

Their social organization is simple. They lived together in associations (κατά συγγενείας καὶ συστήματα) 400 members each. The oldest man in each group acted as ruler until he reached the age of 150; he was then succeeded by the oldest survivor (Diodorus Siculus, *Bibliotheca Historica*, II 57 (1)).

As far as the familiar relations are concerned, the natives of the "Sun State" had no marriages, held women in common and the children whose parentage was thus unknown, were equally dear to everyone (Diodorus Siculus 1935, *Bibliotheca Historica*, II 58 (1)). They were never troubled by civil strife. Each association maintained a huge bird for the purpose of testing the young children. Only those who would fly fearlessly on the bird's back were deemed worthy to be brought up (Diodorus Siculus 1935, *Bibliotheca Historica*, II 57 (3)).

The "Sun State," as described by Diodorus, is based on agriculture. Foods grew wild. From the white fruit of a certain reed they prepared a meal which they used in cooking sweet cakes. There were both hot and cold springs in abundance and the water from them was healthful (Diodorus Siculus 1935, *Bibliotheca Historica*, II 59 (1–4)). Although food was abundant, the natives were moderate in their eating. Ignorant of complicated sauces, they cooked everything by baking or boiling. They were skillful fishermen and fowlers. Nuts were plentiful, as also were plants yielding oil or wine (Diodorus Siculus 1935, *Bibliotheca Historica*, II 59 (5)).

There is an absence of slavery, and the natives of the islands live equally, without social discriminations and property. The land does not belong to anyone, and its products belong to all (Diodorus Siculus 1935, *Bibliotheca Historica*, II 59).

There is an absence of money, and there prevails the type of barter economy. So, the inhabitants cannot produce "chrematistics."

The absence of slaves creates the necessity of the obliged labor by the adults. The time of labor is not very long because most products are given by nature without cultivation. In the long time of "schole," they are occupied with music and fine arts, especially with astronomy: "They paid attention to every subject to education, but particularly to astrology" (Diodorus Siculus 1935, *Bibliotheca Historica*, II 57 (13)). The recognition of the annoyance created by the uniform daily labor conducts in the degree of the alternation in the occupation of the productive work. As Diodorus survives: "They pursue their occupations in turns: at any given time some will be in attendance on others, some will be fishing, some busied in crafts, some busy about other useful duties, and some engaged in public duties according to a regular round, with the exception of the aged" (Diodorus Siculus 1935, *Bibliotheca Historica*, II 59 (6)).

The Author

The author of the work is considered Iambulus, though this has not been proved.[8] Brown considers that Iambulus' description is familiar with Swift's "Gulliver's Travels."[9] Winston considers it more probable that Iambulus is the name given to the narrator rather than the author's won name.[10] F. Altheim[11] traced the origins of the name in a more precise manner, thus proving that his name derives from the

[8] Winiarczyk (1997), p. 132.

[9] Brown (1955), p. 61.

[10] Winston (1956), pp. 59–60.

[11] Altheim (1948), p. 155; Altheim and Stiehl (1964), vol. I, pp. 83–85.

Arabian. In his opinion, such name (ynbl or ynblw) was familiar with the Nabaters. Altheim accepted that the information set out in the beginning of the work – Iambulus devoted his youth in Greek study, became a merchant when his father died – and was led to the conclusion that Iambulus had been an Nabater that turned out to be a Hellenist and had made a trip to the Arabia Felix.

Chronology

Iambulus was evidently a real person and was perhaps a merchant who had traveled widely himself and was in touch with others who had traveled more widely. The equatorial region is known to the habitable. There is knowledge that in parts of the world the Bears are not visible. The tides are higher than in the Mediterranean. There is knowledge of lakes of fresh water large enough to be seas. There seems to be a vague knowledge of the mass cultivation of cotton, rice, and opium-poppy. There is no understanding of the monsoon – that did not come till later – but the journeys out and back are of equal duration.[12] There is perhaps a vague knowledge of Ceylon – Onesicritus estimated it as 5.000 stadia, i.e., about 6.000 miles in size[13] – and the Borneo islands, but is certainly only vague, as Rohde 1900, has shown.[14]

The terminus a quo is Megasthenes' account of India in about 290. Megasthenes visited the court of Sandrakottos (Chandragupta) at about 300 B.C. as ambassador of Seleucus I several times (Strabo 1917–1932, *Geographica* XV II9 (C. 724); Plutarch 1919, *Alexander*, 62; Clement of Alexandria 1919, *Stromateis* I XV, p. 624, 21–22).[15] The terminus ad quem is the limit of Diodorus' information in the mid-first century B.C.[16] Rose suggested that Iambulus' attribution of a temperate climate to the equator was derived from Poseidonius.[17] Tarn proved that this new of the equatorial climate is found in Eratosthenes, and no doubt goes back to Dalion or the expedition of Alexander (Strabo 1917–1932, *Geographica* II, 3, 2 (C. 97)).[18] The Indian King at Palibothra must be one of the three great Mauryas, Tschungragupta (315–291), Vindusara (291–263), or Asoka (262–226), though this does not preclude the work being later; but it seems unlikely to be appreciably later than 200 B.C.[19] The limited knowledge of eastern plants also suggests a

[12] Ferguson (1975), p. 125.

[13] Brown (1949) [1974], p. 58.

[14] Rohde (1914) [1960], pp. 251–256.

[15] Müller (1878), pp. 397–430.

[16] Ferguson (1975), p. 126; Ehlers (1985), p. 83; Schwarz (1983).

[17] FGrH 87 F78 ap. Cleomedes 1, 6, 31–32. Rose (1939), pp. 9–10.

[18] Tarn (1939), p. 193.

[19] Ferguson (1975), p. 126.

third-century date. But it seems that Iambulus is not familiar with the work of Eratosthenes (c. 235 B.C.).[20] Eratosthenes did know that the Sun was not always overhead at the equator; further, Eratosthenes gave the length of Taprobane as 8.000 stades or about 1.000 miles. It is thus a reasonable presumption that Iambulus was writing between 250 and 255 B.C.[21] He belongs to the constructive period of the Hellenistic thought, and it is significant that with him the sequence of Utopias come to an end.

Influences – Background

Iambulus' real interest concentrated on the analysis of the ethical, economical, and social structure of the society. From this point of view is interesting, as we believe, to research these characteristic features, which are also in common in previous authors, who might have influenced Iambulus.

Character of the Work

The "Sun State" does not belong to the discrimination between "ancient" and "modern or new" utopias, which has been introduced by Finley (1912–1986) and has been adopted since then. According to Finley,[22] the "ancient" utopias have a static, hierarchical, and ascetic character, whereas the "modern" are dynamic and establish the equality. We would like to emphasize that the equality does exist in "Sun State," where there is the hierarchical structure absent; in contrary, the hierarchical structure of the society does appear in Tommasso Campanella's "Civitas

[20] Ferguson (1975), p. 126.

[21] There is no a common view among the authors concerning the date of Iambulus' composition. Ehlers (1985), p. 84 suggests that the work belongs to the end of the fourth century BC. Susemihl (1891) [1965], vol. I, p. 325; Kroll (1914), col. 684; Tarn (1948) [1979], vol. II, p. 411; Altheim and Stiehl (1964), vol. I, pp. 86, 92, suggest that the work belongs to the third century BC. Ferguson (1975), suggests that the work belongs to the period 255–250 BC. Giangrande (1976/77), p. 124, suggests that the work belongs to ca. 240 BC.

Müller (1980), p. 191; Gabba (1981), p. 58 in the middle of the third century. Dawson (1992), p. 172 suggests that the work belongs to the third or second century BC. Baldry (1956), p. 20; Baldassari (1973), p. 474 at the end of the third century or at the beginning of the second century. Salin (1921), p. 280, n. 4, dates it more probably in 200 than 100 BC. Altheim (1948), vol. II, p. 158 suggests that the work has been written at the end of Antiochus' III regency. Schwarz (1970), p. 52 suggests that the work belongs to the end of the Maurya-Dynasty. It has been to underline that all these attempts for the exact dating of composition are subjective and they cannot be proven. Winiarczyk (1997), p. 147.

[22] Finley (1967), pp. 3–20.

Solis" (1602).[23] In Iambulus' "Sun State" is no elite; in principle, this society is completely egaliterian,[24] an idea for which an idealized Sparta may have been the model.[25] The absence of the hierarchical structure in the "Sun State" differentiates this work from other political romances of the Hellenistic times. This characteristic feature does exist in the "Pera" of the Cynic Crates of Thebes[26] and in the description of the land of Mousicanos by the Cynic Onesicritus (Strabo, *Geographica* XV I, 21–24; XV I 34).[27]

In addition, we want to add that the elimination of young children who, during the flight on a great bird, appear to be of inferior physical condition does remind the Spartan custom of exposing weak and disfigured suckling in the Taygetos.[28]

Perhaps a clearer idea of Iambulus' own position and his influence from earlier writers may be gained by separating out the elements in his work that stem from the period before Alexander. Diodorus himself cites a passage from Homer. The notion of a people far away, either in time or place, who lived a happy life in ideal surroundings, was well established in Greek tradition, and the possibilities had already been explored by poets, historians, and philosophers. We have only to remember the Ethiopians of Homer 1919 (*Odyssey* I, 22ff), the happy lot of man before Pandora in Hesiod 1914 (*Work and Days*, 90ff), the idealized Hyperboreans of Herodotus 1920–1924 (*Histories* IV 32ff), the tale of the lost Atlantis in Plato 1929 (*Critias*), and the description of idealized people in Theopompus (Aelian (1997), *Varia Historia* III 48 = FGrH B II 115 F75), to mention only a few familiar examples. The purpose of these idealized descriptions varied with the character of the writer and might range from pure entertainment to an attack on contemporary society.[29] From this point of view, it is interesting, as we believe, to investigate Iambulus' philosophical background, analyzing the socioeconomic characteristics of the work.

---

[23]Noutsos (1979), p. 30.

[24]Mossé (1969), p. 303. Kyztler (1973), p. 67, however, contends that there is a certain hierarchical order because men "have" the wives in common (Diod. Sic. II 58, (1)), because women are not considered apt to rule their group, and because there is the authority that is always exercised by the oldest man in the group. It should, however, be noted that for ancient conceptions legality is very great in Iambulus and that only the modern mind can trace here some remarks of hierarchical structures.

[25]Mossé (1969), p. 304.

[26]On Pera, which is the island, where exists the natural life of the Golden Age, according to the target of the wise, see Aelian, *Varia Historia* 70. Diogenes Laertius 1925, *Vitae Philosophorum* VI 85.

[27]Brown (1949) [1974], pp. 57–59.

[28]Huys (1996), pp. 72–73.

[29]Bichler (1995), pp. 10–15.

Socio-economic Characteristics

The social and economic features of the "Sun State" can be summarized as follows:

(a) The pure type of agricultural economy: The money is absent and the type of barter economy prevails. So, the inhabitants cannot develop "chrematistics."
These features exist in Theopompus' "Meropian Land," where the inhabitants of the city "Eusebes" don't know the money, are living a "natural" life (κατά φύσιν), and there are no diseases (Aelian (1997), *Varia Historia* III 18 (4)=FGrH B II 115F75).[30] There are evidences about the characteristics of Zeno's "Politeia" and the "Pera," the Cynic Crates of Thebes.[31]

(b) Absence of slavery: It is worth noting that there is no reference to the constitution of slavery, a view which is a result of the cosmopolitan ideas of the Hellenistic Times concerning the discrimination between Greeks and barbarians, free men and slaves. Here also the elements of the influence of the Stoic philosophy and the Cynic thought are evident. Megasthenes (350–290 B.C), who idealizes the Indian society, underlines the fact that slavery was nonexistent in the whole of India (Diodorus Siculus 1935, *Biblioteca Historica*, II 39 (5)).

(c) The community of wives that exists in the Islands could have been taken from Plato 1930–35 (*Politeia* V 457C-D; *Laws* V 739C), or from some "nature-people," like Aristotle's "Libyans of the interior" (*Politics* II, 3, 1262a19), Herodotus' descriptions of various "barbarian genres" (cf. Agathyrsoi, Herodotus 1920–1924, *Histories* IV 104; Nasamones in Herodotus 1920–1924, *Histories* IV 172,2; Auseoi in *Histories* IV 180 (5)).

(d) The existence of Homonoia (concord) among the citizens. The friendship and concord are recognized as the two stones in the Stoic city of the "wisemen" and in the cynic thought; both features declare in Iambulus' work, but in the political romancy in general, the presupposition of the internal stability of the city. Connected with the internal stability of the "Sun State" is the organization of labor.

And it is really interesting indeed that the organization of labor in "Sun State" does not seem to have any equal historical preceding. The rotation in labor during the productive process constitutes Iambulus' originality. Thus, Iambulus recognizes the negative attitudes of the division of labor. Filling every office in turn has nothing to do with Stoicism. Iambulus is aware of Aristotle's *Politics* and finds in it useful illustrations; it is presumably from here that the rotation of tasks is taken.[32]

---

[30] Aalders (1975), p. 320.

[31] Cf. Baloglou (1998), pp. 18–36; Baloglou (2002), pp. 85–101 for the Stoic economic philosophy. Baloglou (1999), pp. 132–146; Baloglou (2000b), pp. 258–270 for the economic philosophy of the Cynics.

[32] Aristotle, *Politics* II 2, 1261 a36–37: «ὥσπερ ἂν ἐι μετέβαλλον οἱ σκυτεί0ς καὶ οἱ τέκτονες καὶ μὴ οἱ αὐτοί ἀεί σκυτοτόμοι καὶ τέκτονες ἦσαν».

Sometimes however he seems to be deliberately contradicting Aristotle. He has none of Aristotle's interest in property (Aristotle, *Politics* I 1, 1256a1–5), and whereas Aristotle says "No state is composed of equals" (Aristotle, *Politics* II 2, 1261a24); Iambulus' citizens are equal even physically.

(e) With the recognition of the property system of life as the source for the psychic dissension of the citizens and as consequence of the political society, there is adopted the abolition of the individual property by the introduction of the collective ownership of all the means of production and goods; the appearance of conflict and struggle among the citizens is impossible. Iambulus recognizes that the society, free from the individual property, the social inequality, and oppression, would create the presupposition for a novel development of the science, the astronomy.

A characteristic feature of the "Sun State" that differentiates this work from the previous works of political romancers is the occupation of the inhabitants with astronomy.[33] The occupation of the inhabitants with astronomy, which represents the development of science, has been to study with the introduction of communism. The establishment of communism makes up the prerequisite for the generalization of labor and education, which supports the ideal social structure and brings forward its regular operation.

(f) The existence of the collective ownership is supported by the fundamental principle of "brotherhood," which is declared by the existence of a "true friendship among the citizens."

These features of the "Sun State," which survives Diodorus, seem to be similar with the description of the "golden age" by Hesiod 1914 (*Works and Days*, 109–126), the "Saturnus" human society (Plato 1925, *Statesman* 271E-272A), and the "Meropian Land" by Theopompus (Aelian (1997), *Varia Historia* III 18 (3)–(7)).

The Number Symbolism in Iambulus' Work (7 and 4)

It makes impression that certain numbers in the work appear frequently. The editor attaches great importance to the numbers 7 and 4.[34] Iambulus discovered a group of seven islands similar in size an equidistant from one another (Diodorus Siculus 1935, *Bibliotheca Historica*, II 58 (7)). He lived in the island 7 years (Diodorus Siculus 1935, *Biblioteca Historica*, II 60 (1)). The inhabitants know seven letters (Diodorus Siculus 1935, *Bibliotheca Historica*, II 57 (4)), in which each letter can be represented in four ways ($7 \times 4 = 28$). Iambulus came after a 4-month voyage to the island (Diodorus Siculus 1935, *Bibliotheca Historica*, II 55 (6)) and to India (Diodorus Siculus 1935, *Bibliotheca Historica*, II 60 (1)). The inhabitants are four

[33] Respectively, the inhabitants of the land of Mousicanus described by Onesicritus do occupy with medicine; Strabo 1917–1932, *Geographica* XV I, 34.

[34] Cf. Winiarczyk (1997), pp. 147–148.

cubits in height (Diodorus Siculus 1935, *Bibliotheca Historica*, II 56 (2)) and live together in associations 400 (4 × 100) members each (Diodorus Siculus 1935, *Bibliotheca Historica*, II 58 (2)).

The Role of the "Sun"

According to the deviation of the name with the use of the word "Sun," Iambulus' "Sun state" has similarities with Euhemerus' "Panchaia" (Diodorus Siculus 1935, *Bibliotheca Historica* V 41–46).[35] Iambulus first visits Arabia, and then after various adventures reaches an island set in the ocean far to the south. Euhemerus associated Panchaia with the sun; he had his "City of the Sun" and "Water of the Sun" (Diodorus Siculus 1935, *Bibliotheca Historica* V 41 (4)–42 (2)). Iambulus makes the relation more explicit and is frankly astrological in his approach. Astronomy was the keen interest of some of the so-called gods who resided in early days in Panchaia (Diodorus Siculus 1935, *Bibliotheca Historica* VI 1,4–5; Cicero (1933), *De natura deorum* I, 118–119); it was the most important object of education in the Islands of the Sun.

Furthermore, the existence of the Sun incarnates the justice of the powerful of the earth.[36] It is not without worth to note, as we believe, that the center of the political life in the city of the "Laws" is the temple of Apollon-Sun, where the three controllers of the city are living as priests (Plato 1926a, *Laws* XII 946b–947b). The emperors of the East consider Sun as their symbol.[37]

The utopian conception of a Sun State is widespread during the Hellenistic age when the ancient city–state had started to decline and the political authoritarian structures expanded in larger areas. The utopian conception of a state of equal rights, which takes different forms according to the assessment of each writer, is a thought running throughout antiquity, especially since the social division of labor is developed, which involves individual ownership of the means of production as a frame of the economic act, resulting in the development of unequal income structures inside the state at first and inside the Hellenistic kingdom and the Roman empire later. The reference to a peaceful, with equal rights past, noncharacterized by financial relations, gives a peculiar character to the different utopian structures.[38]

The invocation of the Sun by Iambulus resembles the solar governors of the Orient. Its presence is spread throughout the eastern religions. It is specifically indicative and as we think very important for the evaluation of Iambulus' work, the fact that in the Assyrian and Babylonian tradition and also the Egyptian one, the Sun constitutes the

---

[35]For a collection of all survived testimonies and fragments see Winiarczyk (1991).

[36]Gougoulis, St (1998), pp. 304–305.

[37]Gougoulis (1995/97).

[38]Goodenough (1928), p. 78; Altheim (1948), vol. II, pp. 165–168; Günther (1964), pp. 236–265.

achievement of justice and prosperity among the citizens.[39] For the slaves and poor of all Orient, the Sun-cult promised freedom and a better world. (Artemidorus, *Onirocriticon*, II 36: δούλους δε ελεύθερους ποιεί· ήλιον γαρ και την ελευθερίαν καλούσιν άνθρωποι). Iambulus must have been familiar with this tradition.

We would like to bring into light another relation according to the origin of the name, which has not been mentioned yet by the authors, as far as we know. Alexarchus, a son of Antipater – one of Alexander's generals – was given by his brother Cassander,[40] the ruler of Macedonia from 316 B.C. onwards, a small territory on the Athos peninsula. He founded Uranopolis, the "City of Heaven," and considered this city as a "Cosmopolis" (World-State) in miniature, "a good many years before Zeno appeared".[41] The inhabitants of this city, named "Ouranidai," "Sons of Heaven," used a peculiar vocabulary with archaic diction and compound epithets (Athenaeus (1927–1941), *Deipnosophists* III 98e). He is recorded to have called himself "the Sun" (Clement of Alexandria 1919, *Protrepticus* IV 48), a style that may remind us of Iambulus' "Sun State," meaning a world-ruler. His coins figure the Sun, Moon, and Stars, primarily as being the natural and universal gods (Plato 1926b, *Cratylus*, 397e; Diodorus Siculus 1935, *Bibliotheca Historica* VI I 2; Plutarch, *De Iside et Osiride* 377E), but doubtless they also symbolized himself, his consort, and his citizens, for the stars were obvious by children of Heaven.[42]

Survival-Influences

It has been supported that Iambulus' "Sun State" was the theoretical background of Aristonicus' revolt in Pergamum in 133 B.C. Such an idea is setting up in the abolition of slavery in Aristonicus' movement and in the denomination "Helioupolitai" (Strabo 1917–1932, *Geographica* XIV 1, 38 (C. 646): "εις δε την μεσόγαιαν ανιών ήθροισε δια ταχέων πλήθος απόρων τε ανθρώπων καὶ δούλων επ' ελευθερίᾳ κατακεκλημένων, ους Ηλιοπολίτας εκάλεσε"), which gave Aristonicus to the revolter, who constituted a "politeia," which was supported by the collective ownership.[43] It was further suggested[44] that Aristonicus obtained the name "Ηλιοπολίται (Citizen of the Sun)" and the idea of a Utopian state from the Stoic

[39] Vogt (1965), pp. 43–44; Vogt (1971), pp. 30–31.

[40] Berve (1926), vol. II, p. 21.

[41] Tarn (1948), vol. II, p. 430.

[42] Arnim (1964), vol. III, F. 337.

[43] It was furthered suggested by Pöhlmann (1925), vol. I, p. 404, Cardinali (1910), p. 300; Tarn (1933), p. 11, 34;Tarn (1948), vol. I, pp. 411–412, followed by Lekatsas (1978), pp. 20ff., Barker (1956), pp. 61–62, Hansen (1971), p. 144 that Aristonicus took the name and the idea from Iambulus's work. Cf. Beloch (1901), p. 360; Bidez (1932), p. 49. Heichelheim (1938), p. 642; Ferguson (1975), p. 127.

[44] Pöhlmann (1925), vol. I, p. 406 followed by Bidez (1932), p. 290; Last (1932a, b), p. 104.

philosopher C. Blossius of Cumae. This man was a friend and adviser of Tiberius Gracchus (Cicero (1923), *De Amicita* 37; Valerius Maximus IV 7, 1; Plutarch 1921, *Tiberius Gracchus* 8 (4); 17 (4); 20 (3)), who after Gracchus' death fled to Asia and joined Aristonicus, killing himself after the failure of the rebellion.[45]

With reference to this subject, there are a few things worth mentioning. First, the name does not appear in Diodor's summary nor the name Heliopolitae either, and the inhabitants of the island do not live in one Polis. So it is probable that Iambulus was not able to use such names in his book.[46] Second, it is hard, as Oertel[47] pointed out, to believe that Aristonicus was really planning a movement intended to transform the Pergamene Kingdom into a Utopia. It is, moreover, "far too academic" to "regard the Heliopolis of Aristonicus and his followers as a conception foisted on them by a stoic philosopher from some literary Utopia,"[48] and it is difficult to suppose that the Pergamene Pretender was acquainted with Iambulus' work, if indeed, this work was in existence at the time of his revolt, which is by no means certain.[49] Aristonicus most probably did not mean to create an ideal State. He meant to ascend to the throne of the Attalides, rather.

We also have to stress on another dimension that differentiates Aristonicus' revolt from Iambulus' work. Aristonicus did print between 133 and 131 coins.[50] In the "Sun State," there is no money.

The social meaning of the social theories implicit in Iambulus' "Sun State" was analyzed by von Pőhlmann, who compares Iambulus' "Sun State" to Bebel's socialism, and the system of the specialization of labor in "Sun State" seems to have similarities to modern socialism.[51] Kahrstedt compares the "Sun State" as "die Verwirklichung des + totalen Kommunismus mit vergestellschafteter Produktion."[52] Giangrande characterizes the "Sun State" as a "vision socialiste de la réalité,"[53] whereas Kytzler compares it to "Kolchosen, Kommunen und Kibbuzin."[54]

Trever recognizes that "Iambulus' repudiation of the division of labor in the interest of equality is certainly of the most radical measures ever suggested in the history of communism"[55] and compares it to Ruskin's idea that all should do some

---

[45] Dudley (1941), pp. 94–99.

[46] Winiarczyk (1997), pp. 149–150.

[47] Oertel (1925) in Pöhlmann (1925), vol. II, p. 570, n. 3.

[48] Dudley (1941), p. 98.

[49] Kroll (1914), cols. 681–682; Magie (1950), vol. II, pp. 1040–41, n. 17–18.

[50] Kienast (1977), pp. 250–252; Delplace (1978), pp. 49–51; Adams (1980), pp. 302–314.

[51] Pöhlmann (1925), vol. II, p. 324. von Stern (1921), p. 20 suggested that Iambulus seems to have similarities to the program of Gotha in 1875.

[52] Kahrstedt, Ul (1926), pp. 124–126; Kahrstedt, Ul (1948), p. 264. Cf. the critical notes by Vogt (1965), p. 54.

[53] Giangrande (1976a), p. 29.

[54] Kytzler (1973), p. 63.

[55] Trever (1916) [1975], p. 145.

head and some hand work; Ruskin believes that "workmen ought often to be thinking and thinkers often ought to be working."[56]

As far as our case is concerned, Iambulus attempts to provide with the description of the characteristics of the "Sun State," the connection of the naturality of the primary stage of humanity with his contemporaneous historical reality, which is distinguished for its positive and negative elements. The development and advancement of the scientific research on the one hand, the condemnation of the covetousness, slavery, and "chrematistics" otherwise. The features that are provided in the "Sun State" are the abolition of property and the obligatory labor. The individual property is abolished not only for the purpose of establishing equality among the citizens – as this is achieved through the obligatory labor – not because of its demolishing influence but rather because it endangers the unity of the state. And the attitude towards the family is specified by the longing desire to preserve a united state. The existence of the social justice in that Seven-Island State constitutes a request of the time. Furthermore, this point is significant, and Iambulus' thought reflects the novel trends of the present that comes up as necessary in the sociopolitical framework of its time: the geographical and technical discoveries. The unification of the progress of the technological achievements and the sociopolitical institutions constitute the two axis of the author's work.

Many authors thought that the account is given by Diodorus Siculus 1935 either as the exact description of the island discovered by Iambulus on as a stylistic description of a real island, which was known to Iambulus through accounts given by other authors.

The significance of Iambulus for the utopian imagination was enhanced by his inclusion in Giovanni Battista Rasmusio's mid-sixteenth-century collection of voyages, in which the great Renaissance compiler of travel literature translated the fragments from Diodorus Siculus 1935 into Italian and devoted a rather extended and sophisticated discussion to the authenticity of Iambulus as history.[57] His book[58] enjoyed a great popularity in the sixteenth century a great popularity, as it is proved by the four editions (1550, 1554, 1563, 1588).[59] His book contains an Italian translation of Diodorus' narration and a "Discorso sopra la navigatione di Iambolo mercante antichissimo."[60] In a French translation of the work of the Moorish traveler Leo Africanus published in Lyons in 1556,[61] Iambulus' story and Ramusio 1554 commentary were appended among records of other voyages, thus implying that Iambulus' account could be credited.[62]

[56] Ruskin, *Stones of Venice*, vol. X, p. 201, quoted by Trever (1916) [1975], p. 145.

[57] Manuel and Manuel (1997), pp. 86–87.

[58] Ramusio (1550), quoted by Manuel and Manuel (1997), p. 817, n. 21.

[59] Winiarczyk (1997), p. 139.

[60] Ramusio (1550), f. 190^r–190^v.

[61] Africanus (1556), vol. II, pp. 113–125 quoted by Manuel and Manuel (1997), p. 821, n. 35.

[62] Lucian, *A true Story*, Book I, in Lucian (1921), p. 251, 255.

The above information reinforces the belief that Iambulus' work published by the "Historical Library" of Diodorus Siculus 1935 caused a sensation and was favorably accepted during the Renaissance. The Hellenistic age was a period of lively utopian creation, and there are evident resemblances between this epoch and the Renaissance, which witnessed a similar flowering of the utopian imagination. On one hand, the independent Greek city–states/poleis were being gobbled up by the massive imperial structures of Alexander's successors; on the other hand, the loose, disintegrating framework of feudal society was yielding to new, centralized, dynastic states. In both, there occurred dramatic expansions of the known world to encompass distant lands and peoples. The conquests of Alexander, which pushed the intellectual and artistic horizons of Greece eastward, had their counterpart in the great European explorations of the late fifteenth and early sixteenth centuries, with their far-reaching moral and socioeconomic consequences. Geographical discovery helped to make utopia plausible in both epochs. Authentic narratives about new nations and kingdoms with hitherto unheard-of customs were in themselves so marvelous that they lent verisimilitude to the imaginary utopia, however wild it might be.[63]

From this point of view, Iambulus' work – the last one of the romancers could be compared with that of Campanella. This similarity has been noticed,[64] but it has not been studied in detail.

Campanella's "Civitas Solis"

The Author

Giovanni Campanella was born on 5th September 1568 in Stilo/Calabria, the son of a poor family. At a young age, he became a monk; at the age of 14, he joined the monastic orders of Dominican Friars and changed his name to Tommasso. He was dispatched in 1588 to a theological house of studies at Cosenza. There he knew the rapture of a great illumination when the monks, who used to pass forbidden books among themselves, gave him the works of Bernardino Telesio of Cosenza (1508–1588), a South Italian master. Although Campanella composed an elegy on Telesio's death, he never succeeded in meeting his heroic spiritual mentor, who

[63]Manuel and Manuel (1997), pp. 81–82.

[64]Pöhlmann (1925), vol. II, p. 321, n. 2 underlines the fact that Diodorus's translation in Latin (1472) may have been known to Morus and Campanella and suggests that Iambulus' influence "auf Campanella ist ja ganz unverkennbar." Cf. von Stern (1921), p. 20; Röllig (1967), col. 1309; Kytzler (1973), p. 63; Müller (1977), p. 232; Winiarczyk (1997), p. 153. Bidez (1932), p. 280 suggests that "Iamboulos également que Campanella a emprunté l' idée de sa Cité du Soleil." Morton (1952), p. 19 announces that Benjamin Farrington in his essay on Diodorus Siculus, cites the passage in his "Universal History," which contains an account of the Stoic Utopia, *The Islands of Sun*, a Utopia which certainly influenced Campanella's *City of the Sun* (1623).

drew his truths from the "natura delle cose" and not from the assertions of mere men. The teachers of Scholastic philosophy were troubled by Campanella's infatuation with Telesio, and he was sent off to a retreat.

His life[65] was a constant struggle with the religious authorities, who tried him to make him renounce his beliefs and would often sentence him to imprisonment for a short period of time.

As early as 1593, Campanella had become the prophet of a plan for a universal organization of a society under a new papacy set forth in his treatises "De Monarchia Christianorum" and "De Regimine Ecclesiae," and 2 years later in the "Discorsi ai principi d' Italia" and "Dialogo politico contro Luterani," "Calvinisti ed altri eretici." Campanella was possessed by a vision of reordering humanity, a total reformation of the Church, and a return of mankind to a state of innocence. The time of troubles was upon the world, what with the incursions of the Turks in Calabria, the internecine conflicts within the Church, the religious schisms, the wars of Christian kings, and the strange configurations in the heavens – all signs of the coming great transformation.

In 1599, Campanella was implicated in a conspiracy to oust the Spaniards and establish a republic in Calabria. In this plot to liberate his native province disparate elements converged-libertine monks, freedom-seeking zealots who detested the foreigners, declassed nobles hardly differentiated from bandits. But, Campanella, the utopian visionary, never conceived of the affair as a mere local episode. Everything he touched was set in a universal frame. After the Spanish yoke had been cast off, the reign of a pure religion in the Republic of the Sun would be inaugurated, a faith bolstered by arguments from astrology, history, sacred prophesies – a Babel of foretellings.[66]

At the Naples trial after his arrest on 6th September 1600, Campanella was charged with both heresy and insurrection, and under torture he confessed. During his 27 years stay in the jails of Naples, from 1599 to 1626, Campanella finished the Italian version of the "City of the Sun" (1602), wrote the first version of his "Monarchia Messiae" in Italian,[67] acquired books, received letters, and was allowed to see the visitors.

He was set free in Naples on 23 May 1626 with the intervention of Pope Urban VIII – he who had accused Galileo Galilei – only to be reimprisoned in Rome. On 11 January 1629, he was released once again, but his life was jeopardized by rumors of his complicity in a plot purposely engineered by his disciple Pignatelli, and he was forced to take refuge in a monastery in Frascati. Finally, in 1634, on the advice and with the complicity of the Pope, he escaped from Italy and with the help of the French ambassador clandestinely made his way to France.

---

[65] For Campanella's life, cf. Amabile (1882); Napoli (1947); Cingari (1957); Manuel and Manuel (1997), pp. 261–271; Berneri (1999), pp. 87–92.

[66] In his letter to Cardinal Odoardo Farnese he admitted prophesying the "end of the world" in 1598. Campanella (1927), p. 23, Napoli, August 30th of 1606.

[67] de Mattei (1973). Campanella translated this work in Latin in 1618.

In Paris, he resided in the monastery of Saint Jacobs where he was given a pay. There he was favorably accepted by the King of France Louis XIII, Cardinal Richelieu (1624–1642), who was willing to help him publish his books,[68] though this task was never accomplished because Campanella died in 1639.

Description of the "Civitas Solis"

For some scholars, the first Italian manuscript version of the "Città Del Sole" (1602), a dialogue between a knight Hospitaler of Jerusalem and a Genoese sea captain just returned from Taprobane – an ancient name for Ceylon – remains the most authentic expression of Campanella's thought. The Latin editions of Frankfurt (1623) and Paris (1637), published in his lifetime, and the posthumous text of Utrecht (1643), as well as a variety of manuscripts, present alternatives significant for students of Campanella's deviations, but the core remains unchanged.[69]

Through the report of the Genoese mariner, Campanella presented a city that expands in a circular area, quite far from the foot of the hill. As for its dimensions, the diameter of the city is slightly more than 2 miles and its perimeter approximately 7. The city is divided in big circles, which are named after the seven planets; to pass from one to the other, one has to cross four roads and four gates that are oriented towards the four signs of the horizon. The seven-circled city is built hierarchically and ends at the top of the hill on which there is a very tall and wonderful temple, an architectural miracle, devoted to the worship of the Sun.

On entering the north gate, which is covered with iron and can be moved up and down in an ingenious way, we can see a Fifty-step area between the first and second wall. The beautiful rooms of the houses are separated by thin walls and have windows on both the curved and the hollow side of the building. The hollow wall is eight spans thick, the curved three, while the interior walls are a little thicker than a span.

Description of the Society

The city has a single ruler called Sole, or the Metafisico, who incorporated in himself all power, all knowledge, and all love. Under him were three aides, Pon, Sin, and Mor, or Potesta, Sapienza, and Amore, representing each of the three jurisdictions into

---

[68] de Mattei (1973).

[69] The full title of the work is: F. Thomae Campanellae Calabri O.P., *Realis Philosophiae Epilogisticae Partes Quatuor, Hoc est De Rerum Natura, Hominam Moribus, Politica, (cui Civitas Solis iucta est) & Oeconomica, Cum Adnotationibus Physiologicis*. A Thobia Adami nunc primum editae. Francofurti, Impesis Godefrici Tampachii. Anno MDCXXIII (1623), pp. 415–464, quoted by Winter (1978), pp. 55–57. We refer to the English edition Campanella (1981) and the corresponding Greek translation Campanella (n.d.).

which the city was divided. Thus, Sapienza had supervision over all the sciences and the doctors and teachers of liberal and mechanical arts. Under his direction were as many officials as there were *scienze* – though it was not quite clear from their titles precisely what areas of knowledge they covered. There was an Astrologo, a Cosmografo, a Geometra, a Logico, a Rettorico, a Grammatico, a Medico, a Fisico, a Politico, and a Morale. The categories seem quite traditional, with few innovations.

The fundamental organizational principle of the Solarians was monarchical, and their Metafisico was kept informed of everything that transpired. When the four chiefs, who united in themselves spiritual and temporal power, conferred the Metafisico delivered the final decision. It should be emphasized that Campanella was the first to talk about honors in labor. The hardest labor generally earned the greatest honors, although mechanical arts were not deemed quite so worthy as speculative arts, whose outstanding practitioners became priests. The officials were singled out in early childhood as embodying the virtues of liberality, magnanimity, chastity, gratitude, and pity. Below Sole the rest of the order was hierarchical. He had three subordinates, each of whom had three, to make a total of forty. All except the top four were elected; these major heads remained in office until someone who knew more than they did appeared, whereupon they voluntarily vacated their posts. Each person was rated by the head of his department, and punishments could include exile, death, an eye for an eye, prohibition of the common table, or deprivation of the right to speak to women. The prisoner in the fortified castles of Naples allowed no jails in the City of the Sun.

The educational system was the key to longevity of the ideal city. Elders taught the children to read while they were playing about the walls and began to take cognizance of their special inclinations by visiting the shops of artisans with them. All the Solarians acquired both a general education and an area of special competence. They attributed the development of their keen intelligences to the excellence of their pedagogic methods: Solarian children learnt more in a year that Europeans in ten or fifteen.

From the age of seven, the Solarians spent four hours a day on natural sciences (scienze naturali), an activity that was alternated with physical exercise. Then they turned to mathematics, medicine, and other sciences. There was great competition among the young in their disputations because both in the acquisition of the sciences and in medical knowledge a head who excelled was always recognized – for all Campanella's talk about universal love did not eliminate *concorrenza* (rivalry). The same held for those who worked in the fields, where anyone outstanding was honored as the nobler person.

One of the principal elements in the Solarian system of equality involved a recasting of the very concept of *nobilità*. We, said the Genoese admiral, consider workers ignoble and call the idlers (oziosi) noble, an order reversed in the City of the Sun where the work had been rehabilitated.

Not only was the attempt to popularize scientific knowledge but also the manner of doing so was imaginative. Scientific knowledge was translated into pictures painted on both sides of all seven concentric walls of the circular city and on a globe beneath the cupola of the central temple, where the sphere with its constellations was drawn in the traditional manner.

In the course of the educational process, Solarian brotherhood was fostered within a peer group born under the same constellation. Its members were believed to be related in temperament; they dressed alike and were joined by a special bond. Names were not given by parents but by the Metafisico, who bestowed appellations upon individuals first in accordance with their character and then, as they grew up, in harmony with their performance in the arts and sciences and in war. Honored names awarded in recognition of military victories were highly prized.

Following Plato 1930–35 (*Politeia* V 457b), both men and women were trained in the art of war. The Citta Del Sole was virtually a unisex society, and in the Platonic tradition, men and women performed many of the same functions. There was only a slight difference in battle dress, women wearing their *sopraveste* below the knee, men above. They were fearless in battle because they believed in the immortality of the soul. Warlike exercises were constant to prevent the Solarians from turning into cowards and preparation for the battle became a unifying force in society. Although women did not venture far from the city, they assisted the men. Children on horseback were thrust in the midst of the battle so that, like *lupicini*, they might become accustomed to the taste of blood. The existence of four other kingdoms on the island whose inhabitants were envious of the Solarians kept them on the alert. Sometimes they liberated a city that was being tyrannized, allowing the enemy a brief opportunity to submit voluntarily before they let their troops loose. Ordinarily, Potesta made the military decision, but in matters of great moment, he turned for advice Amore, Sapienza, and Sole, and everyone twenty and over, including women, joined in a grand deliberate assembly. Desertion in the face of the enemy was severely punished, even as extraordinary bravery in helping a comrade was rewarded with a Roman triumph. When the enemy was defeated, the Solarians destroyed the walls immediately and killed his chiefs, the whole procedure taking place in a single day.

Socio-economic Characteristics

The social and economic features of the "Citta Del Sole" can be summarized as follows:

(a) The pure type of agricultural economy.
(b) Trade is condemned and is restricted to the exchange of goods. Gold was despised in "Città Del Sole." The Solarian children laughed when they saw foreign merchants part with their goods for a few coins. The Solarians protected themselves from being infected with the evil customs of foreigners. Foreigners were fed for 3 days, taken on a tour of the city under Solarian guard, and, should they wished to become citizens, were tested for a month in the city. If approved, they were received with great ceremony.

These restricting provisions reveal the influence of the Plato 1926b *Laws* (VIII 847b7–8, 849 b2).

(c) According to Campanella, whose economic thought envisions a limited agricultural community, money does not give value to the merchandise: "Money does not grow in itself but with the labor of those who use it."[70] Consequently, the usurers, traders, and noblemen are not the primary source of production but a public danger: "[...] they are extremely dangerous. We may call them noble but they are actually ignoble."[71]

(d) The existence of concord among the citizens. Friendship and concord are recognized as the two stones in the "Città Del Sole." In Campanella's work, both features declare the presupposition of the internal stability of the city. Connected with the internal stability of the "Città Del Sole" is the organization of labor.

In a rare direct reference to contemporary conditions, Campanella contrasted the Solarians' respect for labor with life in Naples, where only 50,000 of 300,000 persons were employed and the rest of the inhabitants were given over either to impoverished idleness or to luxury.[72] Campanella reduced the length of the working day to four hours.

The Metafisico, or Sole, was the epitome of knowledge of every kind; history, mechanics, mathematics, physics, and astronomy – "tutte le scienze." Sole had to be a metaphysician and a theologian who understood the hierarchical gradations of being and the correspondence among the celestial, terrestrial, and marine things.

(e) With the recognition of the property system of life as the source of the psychic dissension of the citizens and as a consequence of the political society, the abolition of the individual property is established by the introduction of collective ownership of all the means of production and goods; the appearance of conflict and struggle among the Solarians is impossible. Campanella recognizes that the society, free from individual property, social inequality, and oppression, would create the presupposition for a novel development of science.

A characteristic feature of the "Sun State" is the occupation of the Solarians with science. The occupation of the inhabitants with science and scientific research has been to study with the introduction of the communism. The establishment of communism constitutes the prerequisite for the generalization of labor and education, which supports the ideal structure and brings forward its regular operation.

(f) The abolishment of wealth and poverty: Solarian *communita* made everyone at once rich and poor, rich because they had everything they needed and poor because they were not given in to accumulation of goods.

---

[70] Campanella, *Quaestiones oeconomicae* 1619, p. 184.

[71] Campanella, *Quaestiones oeconomicae* 1619, p. 182.

[72] Manuel and Manuel (1997).

The Number Symbolism in "Civitas Solis"

It is worth noting that there are certain numbers that appear more often in "Civitas Solis." Numbers four and seven occupy a distinctive position. The city has a perimeter of seven miles and is divided into seven big circles. To be conquered, the enemy should fight against it seven times. The temple has seven oil lamps, and young men can enter the laboratories at the age of seven.

The communication between the circles can be achieved through four roads and four gates. The administration has been delegated to the Metafisico and the three princes, four men in all. The total number of officials is forty (4 × 10). Teaching in the laboratories is done by four readers for the same subject. A four-h labor is enough to earn a living. The Solarians change clothes four times a year.

The Character of the Work

In his work "De Monarchia Hispania Discursus," the Latin text appeared posthumously in Amsterdam, 1640, Campanella appointed Spain to divine agent for the institution of a universal monarchy that would then be handed over to the papacy for governance in a paradisiacal age.

Campanella's thought is based on a program of a general social transformation. As a matter of fact, Campanella's state is the mirror of a cosmic mechanism in which everything is allowed a place and accomplishes its task as planned, a mechanism of the world, something in between a clock mechanism and a star route, appearing as an island city shown as a world state and thought of as a future State in the chiliastic tradition of the calabrian farmer Joachim von Fiore.

Campanella nevertheless sees the possibility to realize that world state as (a) dominated on one hand the strict organization of the Church, and on the other hand, (b) as given in the beginning of the world monarchy of the Spaniards under Charles the V.

The coincidence of the title of the work with the Sun is not accidental. The Sun is referred to in Plato 1930–35 *Politeia* as the Good's (Agathon) son who looks like his Father (Plato 1930–35, *Politeia* 516c). Not only does the Sun ensure the visibility of the world, but it is the source of birth and growth. Campanella possibly identifies the Sun with the Pope himself who, according to the ideology of the time, is regarded as the Sun, the only one dependent on God and placed on the earth by Him. The title of the work also determines the practical meaning of *Light* that comes to enlighten the *Darkness*, which dominates the society of the era. *Light* means *knowledge*. In this way, not only the divine power and glory but also human knowledge is represented.

The rationale of the work is based on the coincidence of ethics and politics, since the legal perfection of "Città Del Sole" ensures the welfare of its citizens. The common ownership and the governance by philosophers–kings are combined with an idiorythmic dogma of the first Christian era as well as the trend of the revived natural sciences of the time. He does not hesitate to follow Aristotle's proposals for the ideal city with rest and exercise (Aristotle, *Politics* 1334a). The participation of all citizens in the productive process and its exploitation guarantees the welfare of the Solarians and are a prerequisite for its moral behavior. The Solarians live in a logical and philosophical manner. The leader is always elected according to his behavior and not his origin. His qualifications are his broad and deep knowledge of both theological and political issues. The root of a prosperous career is assiduity to eugenism. Furthermore, boys and girls have a common education in which the theoretical and practical direction of the studies is harmoniously linked. In this way, they become acquainted with the total of theoretical studies as well as agricultural works and the art of war.

The establishment of the principle of common ownership eliminates egotism and rivalry. Campanella's economic thought envisions a limited agricultural community, thus condemning the "theoretical life" of feudal lords and the commercial activity of the participants in the urban community.

In such a way, based on strict common ownership and proper education, a solid philanthropic and working community is constructed, which loves science, respects god, and practices virtue.

The communal order of "Civitas Solis" is based on the coincidence of ethics with law. Campanella's "City" distinguishes from other medieval utopias because he considers lack of proper education the main evil. That is why he places the center of balance on rational education, proper and complete physical and mental exercise.

Comparison – Concluding Remarks

From the description of the two Utopian states, there are some common issues that we would like to point out.

(a) Both works have the same name.
(b) Both authors describe a long distance island. Campanella describes the Genoese mariner who arrived in Tabrobane, the island Ceylon. There are some editors[73] of Diodorus' "Historical Library" who suggest that Iambulus arrived in Tabrobane too.[74]

[73] S. Bochart, *Geographiae sacrae pars altera. Chanaan seu De coloniis et sermone Phoenicum*, Cadoni 1646, pp. 768–775 = S. Bochart, *Geographia sacra seu Phaleg et Canaan*, Trajecti ad Rhenum 1707, pp. 691–698, quoted by Winiarczyk (1997), p. 140, n. 38; Diodori Siculi *Bibliothecae historicae libri qui supersunt interprete L.* Rhodomano ad fidem mss. Recensuit P. Wesseling, I., Amstelodami 1745, p. 168, quoted in Winiarczyk (1997), p. 140, n. 39.

[74] Cf. Kroll (1914), col. 682; Ehlers (1985), pp. 79–81; Schwarz (1982), p. 51.

(c) Iambulus and his fellow travelers were captured by robbers. After serving as shepherds for some time, he and one companion were again captured, this time by Ethiopians. The Ethiopians sent the foreigners out to the sea towards the "blessed island."

The Genoese mariner manages to elude the outraged inhabitants of Taprobane and arrives in a big plain from where he is lead to Sun State by armed people.

(d) In both works, we can notice the frequent use of numbers four and seven.

(e) The inhabitants in both works are multilingual and live long.

(f) As far as the familial relations are concerned, the natives of both "States" had no marriages, held women in common and the children, whose parentage was thus unknown, were equally dear to everyone. They were never troubled by civil strife.

(g) There is an absence of slavery, and the natives of both "States" live equally, without social discriminations and without property.

(h) Both economies are based on agriculture. Food was abundant. In Iambulus' "Sun State," money and foreign trade are absent, whereas in "Città Del Sole," the inhabitants recognize the negative consequences of "chrematistics," and the foreign trade is limited.

(i) The absence of slaves creates in both economies the necessity of compulsory labor by the adults. The introduction of collective ownership of all the means of production and goods appears as a presupposition for the obligation of labor and education that supports the ideal society and ensures its harmonious function.

(j) Both authors underline the fact that the time of labor is not very long; Campanella demonstrates this more clearly by referring to a 4-h daily labor.

(k) The occupation of the inhabitants of both "Islands" with astronomy, which represents the development of science, is a common feature in both works.

(l) A feature that differentiates the works is the hierarchical structure of the society in "Città Del Sole," which is absent in the "Sun State."

References

Primary Sources

Aelian (1997), *Historical Miscellany* (*Varia Historia*), trans. by N. Wilson. Cambridge, London: Harvard University Press

Arnim, H. von (1904), *Stoicorum Veterum Fragmenta*, 4 vols. Leipzig:Teubner [repr. Stuttgart: Teubner, 1964]

Artemidorus, *Onirocriticon. Artemidori Daldiani Onirocriticon libri V*, ex recensione R. Hercheri. Lipsiae: Teubner

Athenaeus (1927–1941), *The Deipnosophists*, 7 vols., trans. by Ch. B. Gulick. Cambridge, London: Harvard University Press

Campanella, T. (1981), *The City of the Sun*, trans. by A. M. Elliott and R. Millner. Introduction by A. L. Morton. London: University of California Press

Campanella, T. (1927), *Lettere*, ed. Vincenzo Spampanato. Bari: Laterza
Cicero (1923), *De Amicitia*, trans. by W. A. Falconer. Cambridge, London: Harvard University Press
Cicero (1933), *De Natura Deorum*, trans. by H. Rackham. Cambridge, London: Harvard University Press
Clement of Alexandria (1919), *Stromateis-Protrepticus*, trans. by G. W. Butterworth. Cambridge, London: Harvard University Press
Diodorus Siculus (1935), *Library of History* (*Bibliotheca Historica*), vol. II, trans. by C. H. Oldfather. Cambridge, London: Harvard University Press
Diogenes Laertius (1925), *Lives of Eminent Philosophers*, transl. by R. D. Hicks, 2 vols. Cambridge, London: Harvard University Press
Herodotus (1920–1924), *Histories,* 4 vols, trans. by A. D. Godley. Cambridge, London: Harvard University Press
Hesiod (1914), *Works and Days,* trans. by Hugh G. Evelyn-White. Cambridge, London: Harvard University Press
Homer (1919), *The Odyssey*, 2 vols., trans. by A. T. Murray, revised by G. E. Dimock. Cambridge, London: Harvard University Press
Lucian (1921), *A True Story*, trans. by A. M. Harmon. Cambridge, London: Harvard University Press
More, Th. (1965), *Utopia*, eds. E. Surtz and J. H. Hexter. New Haven: Yale University Press [The Complete Works of St. Thomas More, vol. IV]
Newman, W. L. (1887), Aristotle, *The Politics of Aristotle. With an Introduction, two prefatory essays and notes critical and explanatory*, 4 vols. Oxford: At the Clarendon Press [repr. New York: Oxford University Press]
Plato (1925), *Statesman* (*Politicus*), trans. by H. N. Fowler. Cambridge, London: Harvard University Press
Plato (1926a), *Cratylus*, trans. by H. N. Fowler. Cambridge, London: Harvard University Press
Plato (1926b), *Laws* (*Nomoi*), trans. by R. G. Bury. Cambridge, London: Harvard University Press
Plato (1929), *Critias*, trans. by R. G. Bury. Cambridge, London: Harvard University Press
Plato (1930–1935), *Politeia* (*The Republic*), trans. by P. Shorey. Cambridge, London: Harvard University Press
Plutarch (1919), *The Parallel Lives, vol. VII: Alexander*, trans. by B. Perrin. Cambridge, London: Harvard University Press
Plutarch (1921), *The Parallel Lives, vol. X: Tiberius Gracchus*, trans. by B. Perrin. Cambridge, London: Harvard University Press
Strabo (1917–1932), *Geography* (*Geographica*), 8 vols, trans. by H. L. Jones. Cambridge, London: Harvard University Press

Secondary Literature

Aalders, G. J. D. (1975), *Political Thought in Hellenistic Times*. Amsterdam: A. Hakkert
Adams, J. P. (1980), Aristonikos and the Cistophori, *Historia*, 29, 302–314
Africanus, L. (1556), *Description de l' Afrique, Tierce Partie du Monde*. Lyons
Altheim, F. (1948), *Weltgeschichte Asiens im griechischen Zeitalter*, 2 vols. Halle: M. Niemeyer
Altheim, F. und R. Stiehl (1964), *Die Araber in der alten Welt*, vol. I. Berlin: Duncker & Humblot
Amabile, L. (1882), *Fra Tommasso Campanella: La sua congiura, i suoi processi, e la sua pazzia*. Napoli: Morano
Baldassari, M. (1973), Intorno all' utopia di Giambulo, *Rivista di Filosofia Neo-scolastica* LXV, pp. 303–333, 471–487

Baldry, H. C. (1956), *Ancient Utopias. An Inaugural Lecture*. Southampton

Baloglou, C. (1998), The economic thought of The Early Stoics, *Festschrift "Essays in Economic Analysis" in Honor of Professor R. Theocharis*, edit. by G. Demopoulos, P. Korliras, K. Prodromidis. Athens: Sideris, pp. 18–36

Baloglou, C. (1999), The economic philosophy of the Cynics (in Greek with Summary in French and English), *Mésogeios*, 4, 132–146

Baloglou, C. (2000a), The social and economic organization of Iambulus's "Sun State", *SKEPSIS*, XI, 159–172

Baloglou, C. (2000b), Die ökonomische Philosophie des Kynikers Krates von Theben, *Επετηρις Εταιρείας Βοιωτικών Μελετών*, III (2), 258–270

Baloglou, C. (2002), Economics and Chrematistics in the economic thought of the Stoic Philosophy, *History of Economic Ideas*, X (3), 85–101

Barker, E. (1956), *From Alexander to Constantine. Passages and Documents illustrating the History of Social and Political Ideas from 336 B.C. to AD 337*. Oxford: At the Clarendon Press

Beloch, J. (1901), Socialismus und Kommunismus im Altertum, *Zeitschrift für Sozialwissenschaft*, vol. 4

Berneri, M.-L. (1999), *A Journey through Utopia* (1950), Greek transl. by Bas. Tomanas. Skopelos: Nesides

Berve, H. (1926), *Das Alexanderreich auf prosopographischer Grundlage*, 2 vols. München: C.H. Beck [repr. Salem, New Hampshire: Ayer Company, 1988]

Bichler, R. (1995), *Von der Insel der Seligen zu Platons Staat. Geschichte der antiken Utopie, Teil I*. Wien – Köln – Weimar: Böhlau

Bidez, J. (1932), La cité du monde et la cité du soleil chez des Stoiciens, *Bulletin de L' Académie des Lettres*, V[e] ser., XVIII (7–9), 244–294

Blanchet, L. (1920), *Campanella*. Paris

Braunert, H. (1969), *Utopia. Antworten griechischen Denkens auf die Herausforderung durch soziale Verhältnisse*. Kiel [repr. in H. Braunert, *Politik, Recht und Gesellschaft in der griechisch-römischen Antike. Gesammelte Aufsätze und Reden*, edit. by K. Telschow – M. Zahrnt. Stuttgart 1980, pp. 66–84 [Kieler Historische Studien 26]

Brown, T. S. (1949), *Onesicritus. A Study in Hellenistic Historiography*. Berkeley and Los Angeles: University of California Press [repr. New York, 1974]

Brown, W. E. (1955), Some Hellenistic Utopias, *Classical Weekly* 48 (5), 57–62

Cardinali, G. (1910), La morte di Attalo III a la rivolta di Aristonico, *Saggi di Storia Antica e di Archeologia a G. Beloch*. Roma: Loescher, pp. 269–320

Cingari, G. (1957), *Per una storia della societa calabrese nel XV secolo*. Calabria

Davis, J. C. (1991), "Utopianism", in J. H. Burns and M. Goldie, (eds.), *The Cambridge History of Political Thought 1450–1700*. Cambridge/New York: Cambridge University Press, pp. 329–344

Dawson, D. (1992), *Cities of the Gods. Communist Utopias in Greek Thought*. New York/Oxford: Oxford University Press

Delplace, C. (1978), Le contenu social et économique du soulevement d' Aristonicos: opposition entre riches et pauvres?, *Athenaeum*, 56, 20–53

Dudley, D. R. (1941), Blossius of Cumae, *Journal of Roman Studies*, XXXI, 94–99

Ehlers, W. W. (1985), Mit den Südwestmonsum nach Ceylon. Eine Interpretation der Iambul-Exzerpte Diodors, *Würzburger Jahrbücher für Klassische Philologie*, N.F., 11, 73–84

Ferguson, J. (1975), *Utopias of the Classical World*. London: Thames & Hudson [Aspects of Greek and Roman Life]

Finley, M. I. (1967), Utopianism, Ancient and Modern, in K. H. Wolff and B. Moore Jr. (eds.), *The Critical Spirit. Essays in Honor of Herbert Marcuse*. Boston: Beacon Press, pp. 3–20 [repr. M. I. Finley, *The Use and Abuse of History*. London/New York: Chatto & Windus; The Viking Press, 1975, pp.178–193, 240–242]

Gabba, E. (1981), True History and False History in Classical Antiquity, *Journal of Roman Studies*, LXXI, 50–62

Giangrande, L. (1976), Les utopies hellénistiques, *Cahiers des Études Anciennes*, 5, 17–33
Giangrande, L. (1976/77), Les utopies grecques, *Revue des Études Grecques*, 78/79, 120–128
Goodenough, R. (1928), The political philosophy of Hellenistic Kingship, *Yale Classical Studies*, 1, 55–102
Gougoulis, St. (1995/97), Τα εγκαίνια της Κωνσταντινουπόλεως: η χρονολογία (11 Μαΐου 330) και η σημασία της για την ανανέωση του ρωμαϊκού κράτους (Συμβολή της Εθνλογίας στην Ιστορία), *Βυζαντινός Δόμος*, vol. 8/9
Gougoulis, St. (1998), Οι ψυχές των προγόνων και η οικοδομή της πόλης. Το πλατωνικό υπόβαθρο των εγκαινίων της Κωνσταντινουπόλεως, *Βυζαντιακά*, 18, 287–306
Günther, R. (1964), Der politisch-ideologische Kampf in der römischen Religion in den Letzten zwei Jahrhunderten v.u. Z., *Klio*, 42, 209–297
Hansen, E. V. (1971), *The Attalids of Pergamon*, 2nd edn. Ithaca and London: Cornell University Press [Cornell Studies in Classical Philology XXXVI]
Heichelheim, F. M. (1938), *Wirtschaftsgeschichte des Altertums*. Leiden: Nijthoff
Huys, M. (1996), The Spartan practice of selective infanticide and its parallels in Ancient Utopian Tradition, *Ancient Society*, 27, 47–74
Kaerst, J. (1926), *Geschichte des Hellenismus, vol. II: Das Wesen des Hellenismus*, 2nd edn. Leipzig und Berlin: Teubner [repr. Stuttgart 1969]
Kahrstedt, Ul. (1926), Review: R. von Pöhlmann, Geschichte der sozialen Frage und des Sozialismus in der antiken Welt (1925), *Göttingische Gelehrten Anzeigen*
Kahrstedt, Ul. (1948), *Geschichte des griechisch-römischen Altertums*. München
Kienast, (1977), Eine Silbermünze aus der Zeit des Aristonikoskrieges, *Historia*, XXVI, 250–252
Kroll, W. (1914), Iamb(o)ulos, *Real-Encyclopaedie der classischen Alterthumswissenschaft*, IX (1), 681–683
Kyztler, B. (1973), Utopisches Denken und Handeln in der klassischen Antike, in R. Villgradter und F. Krey (eds), *Der utopische Roman*. Darmstadt: Wissenschaftliche Buchgesellschaft, pp. 45–68
Last, H. (1932a), Tiberius Gracchus, in S. A. Cook, F. E. Adcock, M. P. Charlesworth, eds., *The Cambridge Ancient History*, vol. IX: *The Roman Republic 133–44 B.C.* Cambridge: At the University Press, pp. 1–40
Last, H. (1932b), The Wars of the Age of Marius, in S. A. Cook, F. E. Adcock, M. P. Charlesworth, eds., *The Cambridge Ancient History, vol. IX: The Roman Republic 133–44 B.C.* Cambridge: At the University Press, pp. 102–157
Lekatsas, P. (1978), *Η Πολιτεία του Ηλίου. Η κοινοκτημονική επανάσταση των Δούλων και προλεταρίων της Μικρασίας 133–128 π.Χ.*, 2nd edn., Athens: Kastaniotis
Magie, D. (1950), *Roman Rule in Asia Minor to the end of the third century after Christ, vol. II: Notes*. Princeton: Princeton University Press [repr. 1966]
Manuel F. E. and Fritzie P. Manuel (1997), *Utopian Thought in the Western World*, 7th edn., Cambridge: The Belknap Press of Harvard University Press
Mattei, R. de (1973), Un grande estimatore ed amico Del Campanella in Francia:Pierr de Boissat, *Rendiconti dell' Accademia Nazionale dei Lincei*, ser. VIII, Anno CCCLXX, vol. XXVIII, pp. 3–17
Morton, A. L. (1952), *The English Utopia*. London
Mossé, C. (1969), Les utopies égalitaires à l' époque hellénistique, *Revue Historique*, CCXLI (Avril-Juin), pp. 297–308
Müller, R. (1977), Sozialutopien der Antike, *Das Altertum*, 23 (7), 227–233
Müller, R. (1980), *Menschenbild und Humanismus der Antike. Studien zur Geschichte der Literatur und Philosophie*. Leipzig
Napoli, G. di (1947), *Tommasso Campanella, filosofo della restaurazione cattolica*. Padua
Noutsos, P. (1979), *Ουτοπία και Ιστορία. Ηιστορική διάσταση των ουτοπικών σχεδιασμάτων του T. Campanella και του Fr. Bacon.* Athens: Kedros
Oertel, Fr. (1925), Anhang, in R. von Poehlmann, *Geschichte der sozialen Frage und des Sozialismus in der antiken Welt*, 3rd edn., vol. III. München: C. H. Beck, pp. 509–585

Poehlmann, R. von (1925),*Geschichte der sozialen Frage und des Sozialismus in der antiken Welt*, 3rd. edn., vol. III. München: C. H. Beck [repr. Darmstadt: Wissenschaftliche Gesellschaft, 1984]

Ramusio, G. B. (1554), *Navigationi et viaggi*, 2nd edn., vol. I. Venice

Rohde, E. (1900), *Der griechische Roman und seine Vorläufer*, 2nd edn., Leipzig: Duncker und Humblot

Rohde, E. (1914), *Der griechische Roman und seine Vorläufer*, 3rd edn., Leipzig: Duncker und Humblot [repr. Hildesheim: G. Olms, 1960]

Röllig, W. (1967), Iambulos, *Der Kleine Pauly*, vol. II, cols 1308–1309

Rose, H. J. (1939), The date of Jambulus, *The Classical Quarterly*, 33, 9–10

Salin, Ed. (1921), *Plato und die griechische Utopie*. Munchen und Leipzig: Duncker & Humblot

Schumpeter, J. A. (1994), *History of Economic Analysis*. Edit. from manuscript by Elizabeth Boody Schumpeter and with an Introduction by M. Perlman. London: Routledge

Schwarz, F. F. (1970), Die Griechen und die Maurya-Dynastie, in F. Altheim-R. Stiehl, *Geschichte Mittelasiens im Altertum*. Berlin, pp. 267–316

Schwarz, F. F. (1982), The Itinerary of Iambulus-Utopianism and History, in G.-D. Sontheimer and K. A. Parameswara, eds., *Indology and Law: Studies in Honour of Professor J. Duncan M. Derrett*.Wiesbaden, pp. 18–55 [Beiträge zur Südasienforschung 77]

Schwarz, F. F. (1994), Besprechung: R. Günther und R. Müller, Das goldene Zeitalter. Utopien der hellenistich-römischen Antike. Stuttgart-Berlin-Mainz 1998, *Grazer Beiträge*, 20, 302–308

Stern, E. von (1921), *Sozial- und wirtschaftliche Bewegungen und Theorien in der Antike*. Halle: M. Niemeyer

Susemihl, F. (1891), *Geschichte der griechischen Literatur in der Alexandrinerzeit*, vol. I. Leipzig: Teubner [repr. Hildesheim: G. Olms, 1965]

Tarn, W. W. (1933), Alexander the Great and the Unity of Mankind, *Proceedings of British Academy*, 19, pp. 123–146 [repr. G. T. Griffith, ed., *Alexander the Great. The Main Problems*. Cambridge/New York, 1966, pp. 243–286]

Tarn, W. W. (1939), The Date of Iambulus, *The Classical Quarterly* 33, 193

Tarn, W. W. (1948), *Alexander the Great, vol. II: Sources and Studies*. Cambridge: At the University Press [repr. 1972]

Trever, A. A. (1916), *A History of Greek Economic Thought*, Diss., Chicago [repr. Philadelphia: Porcupine Press, 1975]

Vogt, J. (1965), *Sklaverei und Humanität. Studien zur antiken Sklaverei und ihrer Erforschung*.Wiesbaden: Fr. Steiner [Historia Einzelschriften 8/9]

Vogt, J. (1971), Die Sklaverei im utopischen Denken der Griechen, *Rivista di Storia dell' Antichita*, 1, 19–32

Weinreich, O. (1962), *Der griechische Liebesroman*. Zürich

Winiarczyk, M. (ed.) (1991), *Euhemerus Messenius Reliquiae*. Stuttgart und Leipzig: Teubner [Bibliotheca Scriptorum Graecorum et Romanorum Teubneriana]

Winiarczyk, M. (1997), Das Werk des Jambulos. Forschungsgeschichte (1550–1988) und Interpretationsversuche, *Rheinisches Museum fur Klassische Philologie*, 140, 128–153

Winston, D. (1956), *Iambulus. A Literary Study in Greek Utopianism*. Diss., Columbia University Press

Winter, M. (1979), *Compendium Utopiarum. Typologie und Bibliographie literarischer Utopien*. Stuttgart: Metzler

Zorbas, C. (1997), *Η ανθρωπίνη αξία στις κοινωνικές ουτοπίες* [=The human value in the social utopias]. Katerine: Tertios

Developing Society According to Man's Development

Freedom, Equality, and Solidarity as Guiding Principles for Culture, State, and the Economy, or Decentralizing Society by Means of Steiner's Threefolding

Arno Mong Daastøl and Johannes Michael Hanel

A Gallery of Persons

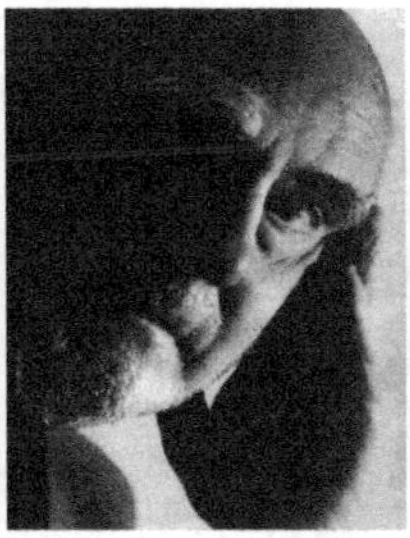

Rudolf Steiner; H. Hegge; Herrmannstorfer; Nicanor Perlas[1]

Preface

Arno Mong Daastøl (Norway) presented the original outline of this article at a student conference in 1991, at Hjalmar Hegge's request – Daastøl's mentor in philosophy. The article was a resume of Hegge's habilitation thesis, which was published in Norwegian and in German. Daastøl focused on the economic aspect,

[1]Picture of Nicanor Perlas from http://www.nicanor-perlas.com/images/stories/idnick.jpg of Udo Herrmannstorfer from http://www.coopera-puk.ch/sammelstiftung_puk/images/stiftungsrat/udo_errmannstorfer.jpg

A.M. Daastøl (✉) and J.M. Hanel (✉)
Institute for Public Economics, University of Erfurt, Thuringia, Germany
e-mail: arno@daastol.com; hanelq@gmail.com

J.G. Backhaus (ed.), *The State as Utopia: Continental Approaches*, The European Heritage in Economics and the Social Sciences 9, DOI 10.1007/978-1-4419-7500-3_12,

and Hegge was present at the presentation.[2] In 2002, Daastøl submitted an elaborated and expanded version for a conference on Law and Economics, which Professor Dr. Jürgen Backhaus has been organizing for many years.[3] Daastøl was unable to polish and edit the article for this publication, since he was busy finishing his own thesis.

Dr. Johannes M. Hanel (Eisenach, Thuringia) has been attending these and other Backhaus conferences for about 20 years. Because he has been studying Rudolf Steiner's social theory and practice since 1974,[4] he was the obvious candidate to edit Arno's papers. He focused on exposing this comprehensive theory called social threefolding, on updating the references and the content. He thereby combines social disciplines such as economics, political science, and sociology in order to present threefolding as social structuring or decentralizing of society as a whole.

Since the authors could not meet, it is not a coproduction in the usual sense. It is a paper by Arno which Johannes edited thoroughly. If there is anything wrong or awkward, the coauthors will discuss who will take the blame. More importantly, we both feel that Steiner's ideas merit active, wide, and thorough discussion; we want to stimulate their adaption to the various societies around the globe. Therefore, the references contain not only works by Steiner and secondary publications on threefolding, but also a few websites that list meetings and study courses on social threefolding. These support putting threefolding into practice, and/or contribute to scientific and political deliberations.

Quite a number of persons have elaborated upon Rudolf Steiner's economic ideas. This article draws on the work and lectures of active and prominent German "three-folders" like Udo Herrmannstorfer, Prof. Dr. Christoph Strawe, and Prof. Dr. Harald Spehl, as well as on those of the late Norwegian philosopher and economist Hjalmar Hegge. He devoted several decades of his life to this task, and his thesis dug well into this fountain well of insights. His and other publications will help us to summarize Rudolf Steiner's socioeconomic ideas, traditionally known as "The *Threefold Commonwealth*."

Since most readers will probably be left with some questions after having read this "taster" on anthroposophical social studies, they can take note of the writings and institutions we refer to or contact the authors. Both in the paper and in the references we mention links and institutions concerned with social threefolding. More important

[2] Hjalmar Hegge was a trained economist from the Norwegian business school in Bergen (NHH) and the secretary of the business organization *Libertas* in the 1960s. In that period Hegge wrote two books: *Håndverkets plass i næringslivet*, 1959 (The role of craft industries in society). *Åndsfrihet og næringsfrihet*, 1965 (Spiritual freedom and free enterprise).

Hegge was the most profound thinker in the Norwegian 'deep-ecology' movement, but charged many ecologists with being reductionists (like Malthus). NHH was also the place where Prof. Leif *Holbæk-Hansen* worked and wrote on three-folding, his collected works are due this year.

[3] Cf. http://daastol.com/ to learn more about the Norwegian author.

[4] Back then, Johannes Hanel started to attend the summer conferences of the Seminary for Liberal Order (Seminar für freiheitliche Ordnung), being still a student at the first Waldorfschool in Stuttgart: www.sffo.de/

than scholarly studies are Steiner's useful methods to reflect, explore, and shape society in ways suited to the complexities of a globalized world.

Introduction

Society changes because we human beings evolve. However, society does not automatically adapt itself to changing consciousness and a new frame of mind. In the early twenty-first century, the fall of communism, the demise of social democracy, and the effects of economic liberalism call for an elaboration of viable and practically feasible alternatives. Without innovative and free thinking, skillful and courageous acting, nature, society, and dignity will continue to be in jeopardy.

Why do we propose Rudolf Steiner's suggestions to stimulate innovation in thinking, feeling, and doing to further social development in the twenty-first century?

- His ideas bridge past and future and make sustainable developments possible.
- They point to self-determined thinking as source for understanding and innovation.
- They allow for our growing sense of autonomy from traditions and for strengthening individuality even in matters of forming and developing groups and institutions.

In short, Steiner's contribution is an obvious candidate for renewed attention if we want to shape our own lives in the socioeconomic sphere as it is unique, timely, and feasible. Steiner's so-called *social threefolding* consists neither of models of what is nor of morals of what should be. It stands out today as it is keenly unique, concerning both the philosophical profoundness and the comprehensiveness of its analysis.

- Firstly, Steiner's ideas explicitly rest upon a firmer philosophical basis than perhaps any socioeconomic strategy.
- Secondly, they represent a rare and balanced view in that they combine an acute sense of proportion with alertness to the complexity of human minds and corresponding social organisms.
- Thirdly, they realistically take into account man's antisocial propensities without which we could neither be free nor individual.[5]

Threefolding the whole of society is timely and realistic because it implies incremental practical solutions without the fanfare and grandeur of revolutionary rhetoric. Steiner's pronounced empirical and practical attitude in a sense epitomizes the German Ethical-Historical School of the period and its ideas concerning "The Social Question." Whereas the Historical School accompanied the German industrial revolution from the 1840s to World War I, Steiner mainly responded to the needs at

[5]Cf. The Steiner lectures of 1918 as edited by A. Neider in 1999 and cited by F. Benesch (1976).

the end of this war, a period of incredible social turmoil. Even while campaigning for a threefold social order in 1919, he cautioned his listeners and readers against generalizing his more concrete proposals to all places and all times.[6]

As frequently, Steiner insists that his threefolding or structuring of the main aspects of society is not a utopia. In the 1920 preface to the fourth German edition to his book on the *Basic Issues of the Social Question*, his conception of a utopian description becomes obvious: "This is not the description of a utopia. I am not saying how things should be arranged, but indicating how people will arrange things for themselves once they activate the type of associative communities which correspond to their own insights and interests."[7] Thus Steiner's "utopia" is that people no longer blame governments, business cycles, the general moral decline, etc. for their situation; they rather take care of themselves and form groups to give self-determination a social dimension. In his lectures and publications, Steiner not only encourages such discussions but also provides helpful themes and a comprehensive foundation. This is what the Nobel Laureate Trygve Haavelmo[8] expects of all mature social scientists:

> The really "grown-up" scientific approach, consists not only in researching existing conditions, but even more in making the practically thinkable alternatives clear.

Haavelmo protests against the dominant nitty-gritty tendencies among economists, which do not help individuals to become free and responsible producers, traders, and consumers.

Although Rudolf Steiner's view is by and large unique, it has been associated with Marxism (see e.g., Strawe), anarchism (cf. A. Daastøl and S. Coiplet 2000), and liberalism, as do many of the authors that publish in the periodical *Fragen der Freiheit*. To what extent Steiner's research agenda and results overlap with other approaches, we cannot discuss in detail in this short exposition of his social thinking. We rather focus on how threefolding is unique in order to stress how it differs from other conceptions of society. However, we do not ignore the numerous points of contact to many political or social views and actions.

Clearly, Steiner proves that the empirical and organic views of society need not be philosophically positivist, mechanistic, deterministic, and materialist. He convincingly combines empirical methods and the integral or organic view of society with the highest forms of idealism in the German or European tradition. His new synthesis sheds light on Johann Gottlieb Fichte's social thoughts a century before. When Fichte (1808) appealed to the unity of the German nation in the last years of the Napoleonic

[6]According to Schmelzer (1991, p. 258) Steiner was pragmatic and principled, both with regard to proposals and to strategies.

[7]We cite *BISQ* or GA 23 (the 23rd volume of Steiner's complete works) usually from the translation by Frank Thomas Smith that is available in http://wn.rsarchive.org/Books/GA023/English/SCR2001/GA023_tnote.html. The original German title is *Kernpunkte der sozialen Frage;* it appeared in April 1919.

[8]Nobel Laureate in economics 1989, specializing in econometrics, born 13 December 1911 in Skedsmo, died in Oslo 28 July 1999.

occupation, he already stressed education and mutual understanding as preconditions for peace. In early 1919, Steiner explained more concretely the needs of the social organism(s) when he addressed himself *To the German People and the Civilized World*. This appeal was signed by personalities from many walks of life.[9]

Already these activities suggest that Steiner is no academic in the derogatory sense of the word. He focused acutely on solving practical matters, as did the younger German Ethical-Historical School or rather the *Verein für Socialpolitik*.[10] Most likely, this focus on social justice or equity is linked to Steiner's personal background, as a man who knew the dire misery of the Social Question firsthand in his own family. Consequently, this contribution looks at Steiner's life and work in general before outlining the history and system of his social thinking. Then we present each of the three social subsystems, their interaction, the international dimension of threefolding, concluding with remarks on the current relevance of decentralizing or threefolding society as a whole, including the economy.

R. Steiner and His Effects for Society in the Last 100 Years

It is little known among economists and other social scientists that Rudolf Steiner (1861–1925) contributed to many aspects of social thinking and practice including economics (Steiner 1922) and even finance (as analyzed by Hardorp[11] and others). He did not systematize existing knowledge, present statistics, or propose models. He was rather preoccupied with enabling human beings to act out of knowledge (Steiner 1894). The core of his ideas is how comprehensive knowledge of man gives us clues to organize social relations and society. What kind of wisdom can guide us toward a social organization and toward actions that match the historical process of individualization? How can each of us be part of creating society when the traditional groups such as classes, parties, ethnic and religious groups, nations, etc. lose their structuring power?

Social theories and practice that are founded on the wisdom of man or, to use a word of Greek origin, anthroposophy, has been helpful for many up to the present

[9]This address or appeal was published in numerous newspapers, and in Steiner 1919 and 1920/1, pp. 428–433; in the English edition of Steiner 1919, p. 141–7 = appendix. In spite of the chaos after the war and the fact that Steiner was not known on the political scene, between 2 February and 5 March 1919, 200 Germans, 100 Austrians, and 20 Swiss signed the appeal. Among them were Hugo Sinsheimer (Social Democrat), Wilhelm von Blume (author of the Württemberg constitution), the historian Walter Goetz (member of the Reichstag 1920–1928), Kurt Wolzendorff who negotiated in Versailles, many teachers, artists, and writers like Hermann Hesse, Jakob Wassermann, and Marie Eugene delle Grazie. Cf. Schmelzer 1919, 132f. for details.

[10]This association was and to some extent still is the most renowned German organization of economists. Although they published a lot on social policy, they seem to have neglected threefolding. Cf Boese 1939, Hanel 1997, and Backhaus & Hanel 1994, especially pp. 62–69.

[11]Cf. the collection of some of his many articles in Hardorp 2008.

as we indicate in the last section of this contribution. For example, the former tutor in philosophy of Arno Daastøl devoted his life to these ideas and published several books on spiritual, social, and commercial freedom. Hjalmar Hegge was originally educated as an economist and was the leading thinker within the early Norwegian liberalist movement "Libertas" in the 1960s, and later within the environmentalist movement.

Why are Hegge and other social scientists and philosophers so interested in Rudolf Steiner's suggestions? The founder of anthroposophy based the examination of society including the economy on wisdom of the human being and condition. Hegge shared Steiner's view that human beings set themselves apart from the rest of the natural world, by thinking or reason, as Aristotle had argued about 2,300 years ago. This specific human characteristic is understood as potential freedom, manifesting itself internally in free thinking and externally in creative producing. Innovating freely is more related to our developing personalities than the free choice we might have on the often mechanical market. Indeed, both the so-called laws of markets and consumption habits are frequently like mental or a biological strait jacket.

For Rudolf Steiner, freedom is primarily a mental activity; markets and other institutions can only be free in as much they are shaped by mentally active individuals. When his pivotal book *The Philosophy of Freedom* (1894) was translated into English, he suggested that it be entitled *Philosophy of Spiritual Activity*; he felt that in English "freedom" usually connotes a passive or given choice rather than the production of the preconditions of such choice. The thesis of Steiner's groundbreaking book is that we can be free in as much as we experience thinking as free activity. From this epistemological starting point, Steiner, Hegge, and others set out to map a dynamic order of an individualizing social world.

In order to better understand this map called social threefolding, it is helpful to look at Rudolf Steiner as a free thinker, fruitful lecturer, and wise advisor, who encompassed most aspects of humanity. Indeed, his anthroposophy is the study of individuality and humanity, or the *conditio humana* (human condition), from our physical nature via society all the way to the dynamic cosmos. As student of Goethe and editor of his scientific writings, Steiner was familiar with Goethe's observation that man is the most interesting object for man.

Because Steiner was a prolific scholar and powerful inspirer of practical life, it is difficult to sum up his life and work in a few lines. The experts for such summaries describe him as follows:

> Rudolf Steiner, born Feb. 27, 1861, Kraljevic,[12] Austria, died March 30, 1925, Dornach, Switzerland
>
> Austrian-born scientist, editor, and founder of anthroposophy, a movement based on the notion that there is a spiritual world comprehensible to pure thought but accessible only to the highest faculties of mental knowledge.

---

[12]More precisely, he was born in Donji Kraljevec, which lies today in northern Croatia, near the border of Hungary and Slovenia: See, http://mercurio.iet.unipi.it/ric/Medjimurje_Pictures.htm and http://www.kotoriba.hr/dkraljev.htm

> Attracted in his youth to the works of Goethe, Steiner edited that poet's scientific works and from 1889 to 1896 worked on the standard edition of his complete works at Weimar.[13] During this period he wrote his *Die Philosophie der Freiheit* (1894; "*The Philosophy of Freedom*"), then moved to Berlin to edit the literary journal *Magazin für Literatur* and to lecture. Coming gradually to believe in spiritual perception independent of the senses, he called the result of his research "anthroposophy," centering on "knowledge produced by the higher self in man." In 1912 he founded the Anthroposophical Society.
>
> Steiner believed that man once participated more fully in spiritual processes of the world through a dreamlike consciousness but had since become restricted by his attachment to material things. The renewed perception of spiritual things required training the human consciousness to rise above attention to matter. The ability to achieve this goal by an exercise of the intellect is theoretically innate in everyone.
>
> In 1913 at Dornach, near Basel, Switz., Steiner built his first Goetheanum, which he characterized as a "school of spiritual science." After a fire in 1922, it was replaced by another building. The Waldorf School movement, derived from his experiments with the Goetheanum, by 1969 had some 80 schools attended by more than 25,000 children in Europe and the United States.[14] Other projects that have grown out of Steiner's work include schools for defective children; a therapeutic clinical center at Arlesheim, Switz.; scientific and mathematical research centers; and schools of drama, speech, painting, and sculpture. Among Steiner's varied writings are *The Philosophy of Spiritual Activity* (1894), *Occult Science: An Outline* (1913), and *Story of My Life* (1924).
>
> Copyright © 1994–2001 *Encyclopædia Britannica*, Inc.

This article contradicts the cited autobiography of Rudolf Steiner (1924) in the phrase "[c]oming gradually to believe in spiritual perception." In fact, Steiner was clairvoyant already as a child.[15] For this essay on threefolding this is only relevant to the extent that the verb "believe" usually contradicts "perceive" and "research." Either Steiner could

---

[13] How can a poet research nature and discuss biological, geological, and physical theories? Johann Wolfgang von Goethe is more accurately described as a "universalist" or polymath who was also politician and manager. This productive man was an eminent public figure who was in touch with over 1,000 contemporaries including Napoleon, Schiller, and Beethoven. Steiner wrote and lectured extensively on Goethe.

[14] In March 2010 there were around 200,000 pupils in 1,027 Waldorf or Steiner schools in 65 countries on all continents, not counting the schools for curative education and special needs. Cf. *Freunde der Erziehungskunst*: http://www.freunde-waldorf.de/fileadmin/dateien/pdfs/PDF_1000–09.pdf and//www.freunde-waldorf.de/info/welt/laenderliste/. – It is not clear what the British "encyclopédistes" mean by "experiments with the Goetheanum" and how these relate to the first Waldorf school in Stuttgart. The owner of the Waldorf Astoria cigarette factory, Emil Molt, organized and financed it after having been inspired by some of Steiner's lectures. They both and many supporters saw threefolding including child-oriented, state-free education as a means to avoid catastrophes like World War I.

[15] "And this is what happened to me always at that time in this manner of my perception of the spiritual world. No one would pay any attention to it. From all directions persons would come with all sorts of spiritistic stuff. With this I in turn would have nothing to do. It was distasteful to me to approach the spiritual in such a way." Steiner 1925 *The Story of my Life,* chapter III about his student life.

perceive spiritual matters or he believed in them. Why does the famous encyclopedia not mention Steiner's social writings or his political activities from around 1917 to 1922? Both issues are for the inclined, thoughtful, and diligent reader to decide.

The History of Social Threefolding

Although the Waldorf- or Steiner Schools are sometimes perceived to be upper-class establishments, the first Waldorf School was for the workers or proletariat of the Waldorf Astoria cigarette factory. Similarly, the anthroposophical society is not known as a lower-class organization. Its founder, however, grew up in a working-class family. A most thorough biographer writes:

"Although he very seldom mentioned his background in poverty, Rudolf Steiner was a child of poor people, ...

He never made a big issue out of the poverty in his paternal home. He normally only mentions incidentally the miserable conditions under which he grew up. But on one occasion, during a discussion in 1919, when a well-known person who only knew poverty through reference and speech, broadcasted the conditions of lower postal employees, Steiner exclaimed: "I have learnt to understand the proletarians through living with them, in that I have myself grown out of the proletariat, in that also I have had to learn to starve with proletarians".[16]

There are many indications that Rudolf Steiner did not live in a vacuum but was in touch with people from many classes, professions, and nations. Although Rudolf Steiner could perceive what we usually call occult, he strongly felt that science should be part of life, including his spiritual science – and even economics (Steiner 1922).

His work in Berlin around the turn of the century brought him into close contact with the working class. For about 5 years he was teaching in socialist schools for workers.[17] There he experienced that the deep longings of most guileless people was not a perennial class struggle and even less the dictatorship of the proletariat. So he indicated the limits of Marxist materialism and class struggle in various ways, thereby exposing the view as ideological that all mental activity is merely ideology.[18] For Rudolf Steiner, on the contrary, mental activity was the

---

[16]See Christoph Lindenberg 1992 and Steiner (1919 Zürich, GA 328); i Sverre Dahls translation, Antropos Forlag 1992, s.7. The Norwegian version reads: "Rudolf Steiner var barn av fattigfolk," skriver Christoph Lindenberg. "Han gjorde aldri noe stort nummer av fattigdommen i sitt foreldrehjem, som regel nevner han bare i forbigående de kummerlige forhold han vokste opp under. Men én gang, i en diskusjon i 1919, da en person som bare kjente fattigdommen av omtale, utbredte seg om hvordan lavere postansatte hadde det, brøt det ut av Steiner: "jeg har lært å forstå proletarene gjennom selv å leve med dem, ved at jeg selv har vokst ut av proletariatet, ved at jeg også måtte lære å sulte med proletarer."

[17]In the Worker's College, he was one of the most successful lecturers with up to 7,000 listeners (Schmelzer 1991, 56). Nevertheless, the leaders tried to get rid of him for ideological reasons.

[18]See the first chapter of *Basic Issues of the Social Question* of 1919.

basis for free deeds including innovative and efficient work. In his books and lectures on esoteric or super-sensible issues he stresses again and again that it is more important to be mentally active than to believe in the results of his clairvoyant research.

Steiner's anthroposophy includes research on how the human body is structured. Around 1917 he found out that our organisms are made up out of three relatively independent subsystems: out of nerves and senses centralized in the head; out of breathing and blood circulation localized in the chest; and out of digesting, reproducing, and moving, radiant from the trunk. This new physiology he published as a sketch in *Riddles of the Soul* (Steiner 1917). He refers to the threefold bodily nature in his social writings and lectures, carefully avoiding misleading analogies.

In quite a few lectures Rudolf Steiner states that social threefolding is not something he conceived abstractly or academically. He therefore "has purposely avoided confining himself to the customary political economic terminology."[19] As mentioned above, Steiner also avoids models and utopias in the sense of merely intellectual constructions. "No one with a sense for the truly practicable will consider what is presented here as utopian. The only arrangements proposed are those which can develop in accordance with contemporary conditions in all walks of life."[20] In which walks of life did Steiner develop his practical sense?[21]

1861, 27 February and later: Rudolf Steiner grows up in a poor, working-class family.

1872–1879: High school pupil at Wiener-Neustadt. When 14 he reads the philosopher I. Kant.

1875–1889: Works as a private teacher, many times to his own classmates, especially in Math and sciences.

1879–1883: As student of physics at Vienna Institute of Technology he lives frugally and studies fast.

1882–1897: Editor of Goethe's scientific works for the J. Kürschner's "*Deutsche National Literatur*" edition (the 5 volumes are in GA 1a–e).

1888: Editor of the "Weekly German Magazine" (*Deutsche Wochenschrift*) (GA 31)

1891: Receives his PhD from Rostock University, published in 1892 as *Truth and Knowledge*.

---

[19] Steiner 1919, only note in the preface signed in April of 1919.

[20] Steiner 1919 (BISQ) *Basic Issues of the Social Question,* English, p.42 in our not-paginated online edition of a total of only 60 pp., drawn from the Rudolf Steiner online archive, §40 of chapter III, i.e., at the end of this chapter. (http://www.rsarchive.org/Books/). In the German edition of 1995, this text is on p.119, §38.

[21] The following list is drawn mainly from V.W. Setzer's chronological biography in http://www.sab.org.br/steiner/biogr-eng.htm, from the Chronology in Steiner (1919 lectures in Dornach and Stuttgart), the Archiv in Dornach (http://www.rudolf-steiner.com/rudolf_steiner/chronik/) and from Schmelzer 1991.

1893: Publishes his *Philosophy of Freedom* (imprint 1894). The first part is a theory of knowledge, the second deals with ethical and practical questions.[22]

1897: Moves to Berlin, where he was the editor (up to 1900) of the "Literature Magazine" (*Magazin für Literatur*) (GA 31), decisively manifesting himself against anti-Semitism, and of the "Drama Journal" (*Dramaturgische Blätter*) with O.E.Hartleben. Activities at the "Free Drama Society," at the Giordano Bruno League, and others.

1899–1904: Instructor at the Berlin "Workers' School of Education" (Arbeiter Bildungsschule), founded by Wilhelm Liebknecht. There he meets leading socialists like Rosa Luxemburg.

1905: Lecturing more and more in the mostly bourgeois *Theosophical Society*.

1905–1906: In his articles on "Anthroposophy and the Social Question," he formulates the "Social Main Law." They appear in his journal *Lucifer-Gnosis*, later in GA34.

1913: Separation from the Theosophic Society and foundation of the *Anthroposophical Society*.

1913–1923: Construction of the first Goetheanum in Dornach, Switzerland, a true work of art in wood.[23]

1914: Marriage with Marie von Sievers (from then on Marie Steiner).

1914–1924: In lectures in Dornach, Berlin and many cities all over Europe, Steiner advices how to renew numerous areas of human activity: art, education, sciences, social life, medicine, pharmacology, therapies, agriculture, architecture, and theology.

1904–1916: Steiner converses with the Chief of Staff Helmuth von Moltke and his wife Eliza.[24] Thus Steiner gets close to the thoughts, feelings, and behavior of European leaders and the reasons for World War I.

1917: "Steiner writes memoranda directed to leading government circles in Germany and Austria."[25] They contain social threefolding in a basic form, focusing on international affairs.

1918: In January, Steiner talks with Max von Baden, from 3 October to 9 November the last chancellor of the Reich. After the abdication of Emperor Wilhelm II and

---

[22]The chapter 14 of the *Philosophy of Freedom* on women emancipation is reprinted in http://www.waldorfanswers.org/RSonIndividualityAndGenus.htm#top

[23]On Steiner as an artist see the exhibition in Wolfsburg until 3 October and in Stuttgart from 5 February 2011; see Wiehl (2010).

[24]cf. Thomas Meyer (1997, 2001), Annika Mombauer (2001), and in German Gundhild Kacer-Bock (no year). See also the note to p.151 in the *Kernpunkte*, Steiner 1919, edition 1996, p. 180.

[25]Cf. Chapter IV, note 13 to p. 137 in Steiner 1919 = *Basic Issues of the Social Question;* in the German edition of 1996, unnumbered note to p.152 on p. 181, referring to chapter IV, § 9. The memoranda are published in *Aufsätze über die Dreigliederung des sozialen Organimus.* GA 24, Steiner 1919–22.

the Revolution of 9 November, Steiner lectures to workers, their new councils, and all looking for new ideas.

1919, January 25–27: Steiner discusses and formulates the Call to the German People and the Civilized World signed by prominent people in Central Europe. Intensive activities as a writer and lecturer on his ideas on social renewal, the *Threefold Commonwealth* (GA 23, 328–341) mainly in Southern Germany. In autumn, foundation of the Free Waldorf School (Freie Waldorfschule) in Stuttgart (GA 293–295), directed by him up to his death; this school still exists, at the Hausmann street on the Uhlandshöhe with around 900 pupils. It was closed by the Nazis from 1938 to 1945.

1920: March foundation of the holding companies "Der Kommende Tag" in Germany and "Futura AG" in Switzerland, for enterprises dedicated to threefolding; ongoing lecturing and consulting activities.

1921: Appeal to find a solution for Oberschlesien (Upper Silesia, now Polish *Górny Śląsk)* through threefolding. Founding of the weekly *Das Goetheanum and* of the first Anthroposophic Clinic, in Arlesheim, next to Dornach, by Steiner's coworker Ita Wegman; this clinic continues its operation as the Ita Wegman Klinik.

1922: Summer, lectures on World Economics (WE). Founding of the now global pharmaceutical enterprise Weleda on 21 November. New Year's Eve, the wooden Goetheanum is criminally set afire. On the following day, Steiner continues lecturing.

1923: Beginning of the design and gypsum modeling of the 2nd Goetheanum, to be built after his death, from 1925 to 1928, in reinforced concrete. During the Christmas Conference of 1923, foundation of the new General Anthroposophical Society.

1924: Course on agriculture in Koberwitz (GA 327), founding of bio-dynamic farming. Course on Curative Education (GA 317), originating this field of application of Anthroposophy. After intensive activity of lectures and courses in the last months, and his last lecture on 9 September to members of the Society, beginning of his fatal disease.

1925: Death in Dornach on 30 March. Publication of lectures from shorthand notes up to the present. His published work, including lecture cycles, comprises more than 350 titles.

Organizing and giving around 6,000 lectures, sometimes several a day without much academic or other institutional support requires a keen understanding of the available means of communication and transportation. Consequently, Steiner was a contemporary in a very comprehensive way. Thus, he was an example for the teachers of his Waldorf School of whom he asked to be contemporaries.

The above chronology does not yet explain what social threefolding is, whether it suits our time, and how we can bring it about. To present threefolding, we use mainly these few "basic ideas" and publications although Rudolf Steiner provides a wealth of both of them:

1898 "Sociological Basic Law" in "Freedom and Society": first the individual was part of communities, later she emancipated herself from corporations in order to develop her personality.[26]

1905–1906 "Social Main Law" in articles on "Theosophy and the Social Question," (GA 34)[27]: "The welfare of a unity of people working together is all the greater, the less the individual claims for herself the products of her own achievements …."

1919 *BISQ: Basic Issues of the Social Question*[28]: This is the basic book of social threefolding. There Steiner reconciles the individualistic sociological law of 1898 with the communal social law of 1905–1906.

1921: Lecture in Oslo (Christiana) called "The Cardinal Question of Business Life" (Steiner 1921).

1922 WE: This course on *World Economics* stimulates a new foundation for economics as a social science explaining price formation and supporting the economic or market associations suggested in *BISQ*.[29]

The Three Realms of Society and Their Guiding Principles

Commonly, Steiner's social threefolding is associated with Plato's Ideal State in his *Politeia*. For this reason, let us first clarify how Plato's conception of a tripartite society differs from that of Steiner. In his habilitation thesis, Hegge analyzed carefully what is common between Plato and Steiner and how they differ.[30]

[26]"Die Menschheit strebt im Anfange der Kulturzustände nach Entstehung sozialer Verbände; dem Interesse dieser Verbände wird zunächst das Interesse des Individuums geopfert; die weitere Entwicklung führt zur Befreiung des Individuums von dem Interesse der Verbände und zur freien Entfaltung der Bedürfnisse und Kräfte des Einzelnen." Rudolf Steiner (1898, GA 31, pp. 255–6), Freiheit und Gesellschaft.

[27]«Das Heil einer Gesamtheit von zusammenarbeitenden Menschen ist um so größer, je weniger der einzelne die Erträgnisse seiner Leistungen für sich beansprucht, das heißt, je mehr er von diesen Erträgnissen an seine Mitarbeiter abgibt, und je mehr seine eigenen Bedürfnisse nicht aus seinen Leistungen, sondern aus den Leistungen der anderen befriedigt werden.» Steiner 1905–1906, reprinted in GA 34, p.213. The first word in the German title changed: *Theosophie/Anthroposophie/Geisteswissenschaft und soziale Frage.*

[28]Other translations call this book "*The Threefold Commonwealth*" ("TC"); originally *Die Kernpunkte der sozialen Frage* was translated as T*he Cardinal Points of the Social Question, see references.*

[29]These 14 lectures and six discussions held between 24 July and 6 August at the Goetheanum in Dornach for students of economics were translated with various titles; now they are usually called "*World Economy*." *The Formation of a Science of World-Economics"* ("WE," originally called *Course in National Economics*). See Steiner 1922. The late Prof. Leif Holbæk-Hanssen wrote in his 1975 preface to WE that the thought content of these courses will paradoxically be most difficult for those who feel most at home within today's economic theory. Holbæk-Hanssen was professor of economics at the national business school in Bergen, Norway.

[30]Hegge (1992), pp. 304f., and especially, pp. 285–6: "*Erstens* denkt Platon die verschiedenen Bereiche nicht als gleichrangig im Hinblick auf ihre Funktionen, indem die beiden letzteren dem ersten untergeordnet werden: 'Die Philosophen sollen regieren'…." In Plato's state individuality is not important. It is an elitist, class or corporative state.

Plato and Steiner agree that the economy can be separated from the state, at least analytically. Up to the nineteenth century, it was common to inquire about the estate of a person before employing, marrying, or even socializing with her or him. For Steiner, however, modern individuals are not limited to live and act mainly in one field, class, estate, or caste of society. His threefolding is structural, not personal: "Through this formation man will be able to be truly man. The formation will enable him to participate in all three social sectors. He will have a professional interest in the sector which includes his occupation; and he will have vital connections with the others, necessitated by the nature of their institutions. The external social organism which forms the foundation for human life will be tripartite; each individual will constitute a binding element for its three sectors."[31] Clearly, the individual is in control of society and its organization as Steiner's sociological basic law of 1898 is realized.

Just as little as self-determination means that we can change our physiology, freedom means that we change or even remove all rules of living in society. These social rules and structures do not limit our freedom but make it possible because freedom and chaos are as different as individuality and egotism. Since we have a body, we need an economy, since we feel dignity we need a state that protects it, and since we have questions and other spiritual needs we need culture including education, science, arts, and religion.

Life is complex, indeed, but if it is simplified artificially for the sake of modeling, quantification, or power concentration, it becomes unsustainable, as already World War I showed. Steiner questions both the belief in a "unitary state" that bails out banks, runs schools, etc. and in an economic system called "capitalism" that reduces human beings and natural resources to commodities. But how can society avoid falling into pieces if the all encompassing market or state do not hold individuals together? Individuals can become aware of their limitations and therefore find it helpful to associate with others to make life freer, more pleasant and meaningful in various ways. This implies that we not only explore our limits but also our potentials in order to come to know what we are in reality.

In order to expose the nature of human beings, Steiner often refers to the history of mentality, as the German philosopher Jürgen Habermas does. Why have we grown increasingly fond of freedom, equality, and solidarity since the eighteenth century? Looking at the French Revolution, Steiner points out how difficult it has been to strive for these three archetypes of equity at the same time. During the nineteenth century, many found these three ideals contradictory but still all necessary for a just society. The famous dictum by the Russian Anarchist, Count Michael Bakunin reveals this struggle for the guiding principles of a just society with regard to two ideals:

> Liberty without socialism is privilege, injustice;
>
> Socialism without liberty is slavery and brutality.
>
> Michael Bakunin

[31] Steiner 1919, last paragraph of chapter III in *BISQ*.

But how can we strive for freedom, equality, and solidarity[32] at the same time? Steiner could solve these intricacies by assigning these ideals to different fields of society:

> These contradictions exist because the true social meaning of these three ideals only becomes evident through an understanding of the necessary triformation of the social organism. The three members are not to be united and centralized in some abstract, theoretical parliamentary body. Each of the three members is to be centralized within itself, and then, through their mutual cooperation, the unity of the overall social organism can come about. In real life, the apparent contradictions act as a unifying element. An apprehension of the living social organism can be attained when one is able to observe the true formation of this organism with respect to fraternity, equality and liberty. It will then be evident that human cooperation in economic life must be based on the fraternity which is inherent in associations. In the second member, the civil rights system, which is concerned with purely human, person-to-person relations, it is necessary to strive for the realization of the ideal of equality. And in the relatively independent spiritual sector of the social organism it is necessary to freely strive for the ideal of freedom. Seen in this light, the real worth of these three ideals becomes clear. They cannot be realized in a chaotic society, but only in a healthy, threefold social organism. No abstract, centralized social structure is able to realize the ideals of liberty, equality and fraternity in such disarrangement; but each of the three sectors of the social organism can draw strength from one of these impulses and cooperate in a positive manner with the other sectors.[33]

From the quote we can derive the first two columns of this table:

Social subsystem	Guiding ideal	Financing or funding
Culture, civil society	Freedom of the individual	Voluntary funding
State, governments	Equality between individuals	Taxes
Economy, world market	Solidarity by division of labor	Profits

Illegitimate overextension of one principle into another sphere creates malfunctions, and eventually hits back on the legitimate social sphere, distorting relations there as well. Rudolf Steiner discusses in particular the overextension of freedom and equality, and of markets and governments with regard to capitalist countries. Looking at Russia, he warns of the overextension of brotherhood. When it is forced, solidarity becomes socialism and by excluding liberalism, despotism. Already in 1919 Steiner observed that Lenin and his staff did not oppose tsarism; their system "is the whole essence of tsarism, only extended for another class, that is, tsarism continued in a worse manner."[34]

[32]"Liberté, egalité, fraternité" are still the motto of the French republic and therefore present in public discourse, e.g., "freedom and equality truly form an indivisible couple, the progeny of which could well be brotherhood. The three terms, in their tension, in their future, express that community of people who all acknowledge themselves as free agents associated together in the responsibility for the *res publica* and construction of a common humanity. That's exactly what Jaurès meant when he wrote that Humanity is yet to come." Ulrich 2009.

[33]Steiner 1919, §48 or next to last paragraph of chapter II, p. 88 in the German edition of 1996, §44. In the USA, Beuys made these interrelations between ideals and structures somewhat popular, see http://en.wikipedia.org/wiki/Social_sculpture

[34]Steiner 1919 October in Zurich, p. 114, edited and published by Pietro Archiati in 2006.

Freedom is not a helpful principle for the economy because we are neither free to produce nor consume whatever we want. Our skills, the natural resources, and our income limit us in the market place. Even renewable energies will not change this because our planet and our abilities are limited. More and more people become aware that we have to overcome our growth habit.[35] Obviously, the principle of equality is no more helpful to satisfy our needs, be it as professionals or as consumers. I do not want to have the same food or medicine as my neighbor but that which satisfies my needs.

No one is accorded the freedom to use money or talent to cheat or bribe someone into a contract or vote. It is also not helpful to vote for someone because we pity him or her. Before the law and in contractual relations we are all equal. Then our sense of justice is satisfied. However, just as we are not equal in our needs and wants, we are not equal in our talents and capabilities. How can we unfold our talents and satisfy our physical and mental needs? This question points to an efficient economy that is not an end in itself.

Global Division of Labor as Objective Solidarity

If anything, assigning solidarity to a market economy seems utopian or unreal. However, Rudolf Steiner characterizes the world economy and the ideal of brotherhood in such a way that egotism becomes uneconomical, irrelevant, and inefficient both for analysis and life. Thereby he distinguishes work for income from work for the production of goods.

> Much has been said about the modern division of labor, about its time-saving effects, its contribution to perfecting the production process and the exchange of commodities, etc., but little attention has been paid to how it influences the individual's relation to his work performance. Whoever works in a social organism which is based on the division of labor never really earns his income by himself; he earns it through the work of all the participants in the social organism.[36]

The better I satisfy other people's needs, the better I can satisfy my own needs; the social standing of all involved in that kind of market exchanges will thus increase. The less I produce for myself, the better a group of people, a nation, or the world is. My income depends on whether I satisfy other persons' needs. Since in mass production I have to think first about others, altruism is primary. Economies of scale imply thinking of the needs of others. Consequently, I can satisfy my needs only to the extent I satisfy my neighbors' demands as long as we live in an economy with a global division of labor.

---

[35] See Dennis Gabor (1976) and Jonathan Foley (2010) and Bill McKibben (2010).

[36] This is the beginning of the long §50 in the 3rd chapter of *Basic Issues of the Social Question,* in the translation of Frank Thomas Smith; pp.133–5 in the German edition of 1996.

How interest in others (Steiner 1918 as edited by Neider) makes the economy more efficient Steiner demonstrates with the tailor that became rather famous through his lectures and discussions in his course *World Economics* of 1922 (pp. I 44–46). Each little bit of self-sufficiency makes commodities a bit dearer. When the students in Dornach at the Goetheanum challenged this, Steiner pointed out that a single suit hardly changes the price level. Yet he insisted that: "Products become cheaper through division of labor. When you work, under division of labor, for a community your own products will also become cheaper than they would be if you were to work for yourself."[37] That is why the more I produce for others, the more efficient the economy becomes. For most people and commodities, factory outlets are more expensive than shops as soon as full transport costs are included. Although common prejudice still has it that salespeople make things more expensive, this is certainly not the case. In fact, Great Britain became a world power through the economies of trade and trade capital.[38]

Does Steiner's objective solidarity correspond to Adam Smith's invisible hand that harmonizes egotistical acts? In the framework of threefolding, objective altruism can become subjective altruism that still enhances efficiency if

(a) The economy is not imperialistic but no more and no less than one autonomous sector of society besides the state and culture or civil society.[39]
(b) People really think through why they do what, all those working together in an enterprise, the policy makers, and trade unionists. Consumers, salespeople, and producers realize that they can produce sound judgments on prices and innovations only together. That is the task of the associations so basic to threefolding.[40]
(c) Fair and sustainable prices require that money becomes a reliable equivalent for commodities. Otherwise the worldwide division of labor will be distorted and inefficient. To be equivalent to reproducible goods, "purchasing money" needs not to lose value

[37] The translation of WE includes only discussion of the tailor example from the six seminaries with the students that followed some of the 14 lectures of the *Course on World Economics*. The original reads: "Wenn man unter dem Einfluss der Arbeitsteilung für eine Gemeinschaft arbeitet, so kommen einem auch die eigenen Produkte billiger zu stehen, als wenn man für sich selber arbeitet. Darin besteht eben gerade das wirklich Verbilligende der Arbeitsteilung." Steiner 1922, 2 August, *Seminary*, p. 42 of the German edition.

[38] "In England, for example, Trade Capital was transformed gradually into Industrial Capital. For in England industrialism evolved out of trade, and it evolved far more slowly than in Germany. …" More generally: "Circulating Capital is more or less covered by these three categories: Trade Capital, Loaned Capital and Industrial Capital. Moreover, these three are contained in the economic process in the most varied ways." Steiner 1922, 1 August, Lecture IX.

[39] On how economics can be imperialistic see Cooter (1981–2) and the references, e.g., to Gary S. Becker in http://en.wikipedia.org/wiki/Economic_imperialism_%28economics%29

[40] On associations of consumers, traders, and producers to find the right prices see Lecture X, pp. 152–3 in the German edition of *World Economy*. How these price-finding associations transcend the market mechanism is an ongoing debate we cannot summarize or enter here.

> through inflation but to transform into "loan or entrepreneur money" and then "gift money."[41]

To what extent these conditions have been part of reality for the last 100 years thinkers can find out for themselves. This inquiry is all the more possible for those having clear concepts of what is part of the economy and of Man. Then they can avoid what can be called the fallacy of the dualistic or split image of Man: I am thinking and acting altruistically, but most other people just think about themselves. In fact, we all feel anti- and sympathically, we act at times altruistically and in other instances egotistically since we know good and evil, since we feel pain and have to work on earth.

Having left paradise, we need an economy and produce, trade, and consume those reproducible goods we call commodities because we are partly tied to nature through our physical body. "The entire homogeneous entity consisting of processes which begin with man's relation to nature and continue through his activities in transforming the products of nature into consumable goods, all these processes, and only these, comprise the economic member of a healthy social organism."[42] As Man is not completely tied to nature, he can transform nature. Therefore, the economy is as much determined by all kinds of work as by nature. In as much as work is transformed by human ingenuity, it can produce not only commodities but also capital.

Work or labor is not part of the economy because economic institutions are set up to deal with the production and exchange of commodities. These are goods that are valuable in as much as they are consumed. We do not consume labor; Man has an absolute or intrinsic value.

If it is not an economic good (commodity), what kind of good is labor then?

> The economy, within the circumference of which the production, inter-change and consumption of commodities belong, should be considered without preconceptions. The essential difference between the person-to-person relationship in which one produces commodities for the other, and the rights relationship as such will be evident. Careful consideration will lead to the conviction and the practical requirement that in the social organism legal rights must be completely separated from the economic sector.[43]

---

[41] In the 12th lecture of 4 August 1922 Steiner indicates his conception of money: "Now, when for the purposes of pure exchange we use money as an equivalent, we must admit that, as against articles which decay, money is an unfair competitor. For, in normal circumstances, nowadays, money does not *seem* to decay." In reality, such purchasing money becomes lending money and eventually disappears either into the ground as pseudo or unreal real estate value or becomes "donation money." On this, see the GLS-Bank (Gemeinschaftsbank für Leihen und Schenken), the Bank for Loans and Donations, as mentioned in the last section of this contribution. Herrmannstorfer, Schweppenhäuser (1971) and Suhr elaborated on Steiner's monetary theory. Cf. also Helmut Creutz and Kennedy on Gesell's similar conception of neutral money that is a true equivalent of "aging" commodities.

[42] *BISQ*, chapter II, §17; p. 66 in the German edition of 1996.

[43] *BISQ*, chapter II, §18, S.67 of German *edition*.

It is the sphere or realm of the state that is in charge of protecting the human rights, as Steiner mentions in the paragraph from which the above quote is taken. How can the states be structured if their principles derive not from economic purposes? What are the limits and what is the scope of governments and legislatures if the essence of the state is the protection and maybe development of human rights? How can we deal with commodities without compromising our dignity? How can we school our talents and efficiency without becoming more equal than others? To address such questions the following section will deal with the peculiarities of the states and human rights policies. These also determine labor as human resources just as nature limits natural resources. The economy receives these two kinds of resources as inputs. How can the democratic process determine how labor is inputted into the economic process?

The Limits and Scope of Equality and of States

Since Steiner writes even less detailed on governments and laws than on the economy and culture, he leaves here even more to the committed citizen to work out than regarding the other fields of the *Threefold Commonwealth*.[44] Steiner's key concept to describe just policies and delimit the actions of legislatures, executives, and jurisdictions is **equal dignity**. "Whereas the economy is concerned with all aspects of man's natural needs and the production, circulation and consumption of commodities, this second member of the social organism can only concern itself with all aspects of the relations between human beings which derive from purely human sources." If we feel respected, we tend to be peaceful and encouraged to engage in all aspects of society. Then we feel as being equal among equals even if we have less talents or wealth than somebody else.

The democratic state strives for equality as is evident for example by the increasing nondiscrimination legislation in many states. If it is not overacted, such legislation allows for discrimination according to abilities and purchasing power. Consequently, the state can take care of all those issues that can be dealt with by the common sense of all people prepared to engage in a debate and where equality is just. Most everybody agrees that we should all be equal before the law. Hardly anybody believes that we should have all the same religion, the same favorite art or artist, be all doctors, teachers, or managers, etc. Nevertheless, a judge should treat a doctor just as a junky, a manager just as an unemployed.

This characterization excludes cultural and economic subsidies and administration from the business of governments. Does it reduce the state to a laissez-faire regimen? Because equality implies equal opportunities, Steiner assigns some aspects

[44] This is the title of another translation of *Kernpunkte der sozialen Frage*. Here we use mainly the translation entitled *Basic Issues of the Social Question*.

of labor and capital to the realm of the state. How can the principle of equality further the dignity in work, and individual abilities in capital employment?

Consciously, Steiner avoids concrete recommendations for institutional setups. He insists that even in times of distress and turmoil we better base institutional decisions on basic insights into human and social developments. Therefore, it is difficult to say, for example, whether Steiner would be in favor of basic income or oppose it.[45]

It is clear, however, that the division of labor implies a **separation of labor and income**. This is one aspect of Steiner's fundamental social law of 1905:

> The well-being of a community working together will be greater, the less the individual claims the proceeds of his work for himself, i.e., the more of these proceeds he hands over to his fellow-workers, the more his own needs are satisfied, not out of his own work but out of the work done by others. Every arrangement in a community that is contrary to this law will inevitably engender distress and want somewhere. [...] The important point here is that working for other people and obtaining a certain income should be two completely separate things.[46]

Elsewhere, Steiner explains: "What matters here is that the concept of work should not be related to the concept of income in an arbitrary way, as it so often is today. A person receives an income not just for eating and drinking, or for otherwise satisfying his physical or spiritual needs, but because he works for other people."[47] Taking these two statements together it seems that a citizen's income on the level of the minimum subsistence level (MSL) and the usual varying compensations for work goes along with threefolding.

Our physical needs are very similar. Most of us need around 10, 000 Euros, Pounds Sterling, or US Dollars a year in order not to starve and freeze.[48] If we want to satisfy our other needs, we can ask for wages or donations depending on whether we work gainfully or in a not-for-profit sector. When we cannot work at all, we depend on philanthropy or some kind of aid for those needs that are above the breadline or subsistence minimum.

---

[45]"Amongst the small number of anthroposophists who are interested in the social matters, most consider a citizen's income to be the realisation of Rudolf Steiner's 1905 formulation of the 'fundamental social law.' However, anyone who studies the fundamental social law in depth would have to reject this assumption. An unconditional basic income for all would be anything but social." This is the conclusion of Coiplet who runs the *Institute for Social Threefolding* in Berlin. See http://www.threefolding.org/essays/2007–04–100.html Maurice Le Guerrannic (2009) concludes similarly.

[46]Cf. Steiner 1905–6; Usher analyzed this social law in his 1993 essay. See note 26 for the German text.

[47]Both translations are taken from http://www.threefolding.org/essays/2007–04–100.html

[48]We simplify the complex discussion around the various subsistence levels: physiological, socioeconomical, what remains income tax-free, etc. According to the German law of obligations this minimum level has been €930 net, or about €1,300 gross a month for a single person since 1 July 2007. In the USA, the poverty threshold for a single person under 65 was US$11,161. For the percentages of inhabitants living below the poverty line see https://www.cia.gov/library/publications/the-world-factbook/fields/2046.html?countryName=&countryCode=&regionCode=%C5%B8

By guaranteeing a living wage for all citizens, whether they are children or senior citizens, ill or out of work, the governments make it possible for all people to work less. This also reduces involuntary unemployment which is as undeserving as compulsory work. The governments need also to reduce working hours and raise more indirect than direct taxes in order to allow a balance in what is commonly called the labor market. Once we are neither forced to work nor forced to stay out of work, our dignity is safeguarded.

Unfolding our talents often involves **capital**: a college of teachers needs a school building, engineers need machines, inventors need laboratories, etc. Often we need further education, various advice, or access to recent discoveries. All this is hard to get if laws protect indefinitely the financial and other property without stipulating a process according to which those who use it have the best abilities to use and develop real and financial capital.

The traditional concept of property rights is a remnant of Roman law, which functioned in a relatively static, stationary society. Accordingly, this judicial system is static and thing-oriented, in a way that rights are seen as rights to things – property. Today's society is precisely not characterized by the individual's stable relations to her soil, but by the individual's changing functions in society. Our time is distinguished by rapid changes both in skills and structures and should accordingly have a concept of rights adapted to this. In many cases, a dynamic concept of property rights oriented toward the functions required in a globalized economy can be realized as tenure by lease or user rights.

Would such limited **property rights** jeopardize individual liberty in the economic area? As mentioned, within threefolding freedom cannot be a guiding principle within a globalized economy. In this light, property rights guarantee the development and display of the individual's abilities. Accordingly, the type of property is to correspond to individual abilities if both the development of the individual and of the economy are to be optimized. In principle, this precludes transfer of property by inheritance or auctions (market transactions), since these cannot guarantee that the receiver or acquirer has the necessary qualifications to utilize the capital in the best possible way.

How these user rights can be institutionalized, Steiner does not indicate in detail because this he leaves to the democratic process. He suggests, however, that capital can be allotted to the able individual(s) by qualified institutions. This does not mean the political authorities, but rather those professionally qualified within the relevant area of production. Such institutions he calls **associations**; they also include the consumers (cf. footnote 39).

In many ways social development has moved in the direction of user rights. Usually, the owners of a firm appoint able managers that in a sense have the user right for some period. There are also allodial possession and various arrangements concerning licenses and concessions.

Even when he talked to socialists Steiner insisted on how important (limited) property rights are. Since his thoughts can de-emotionalize the debate on property rights, we cite here extensively from the middle of the chapter on "Capitalism and Social Ideas. (Capital, Human Labor)":

> The human being relates to what he produces, alone or together with others, as he relates to the dexterity of his own limbs. The undermining of free disposition over the means of production is equivalent to crippling the free application of dexterity in his limbs.
>
> Private ownership is, however, nothing other than the medium for this free disposition. As far as the social organism is concerned, the only significance of ownership is that the owner has the right of disposition over the property through his own free initiative. One sees that in society two things are bound together which have quite different significance for the social organism: The free disposition over the capital base of social production, and the legal relationship through which he who exercises this disposition, by means of his right of disposition, precludes others from the free utilization of this capital base.
>
> It is not the original free disposition which leads to social damage, but only the prolongation of the right of disposition when the appropriate conditions which connect individual human abilities to this disposition have ceased to exist.[49]

For a hint as to how Steiner would curtail the overextension of private property we cite his thoughts on the copyright laws: "We do have a facility in our times which partially fulfills this requirement [of limited property] in respect of so-called intellectual property. At a certain time after its creator's death it becomes community property. This corresponds to a truly social way of thinking. Closely as the creation of a purely intellectual property is bound to an individual's talents, it is at the same time a product of human society and must, at the right moment, be handed over to this society. It is in no way different with respect to other property."[50] Handling the institution of property correctly will be much easier once society is threefolded. "The people, united in the social organism, act as a totality through the rights-state. The exercise of individual abilities pertains to the spiritual organization."[51]

Consequently, the states can regulate the economy and the other aspects of society adequately only to the extent people are inspired by an independent, inspiring, and active cultural life. "It is only necessary to decide once and for all that the rights-state must gradually relinquish its control over spiritual life and the economy, and not to offer resistance when what should happen really happens: that private educational institutions arise and the economy becomes self-sustaining. The state-owned schools and economic enterprises do not have to be eliminated overnight; but the gradual dismantling of the state educational and economic apparatus could well develop from small beginnings. Above all, it is necessary for those who are thoroughly convinced of the correctness of these or similar social ideas to provide for their dissemination." To disseminate threefolding is part of the free spiritual life ("freies Geistesleben") as

[49]These are paragraphs 28 to the beginning of 30 of chapter III in *BISQ, in* the German edition (1996) § 26 to 28 on p. 109, entitled *Die Kernpunkte der Sozialen Frage.*

[50]Chapter III, § 31 of *BISQ* or §29 on p. 110 in the German edition of 1996.

[51]Here, in *BISQ* §32 "rights-state" stands for "Rechtsstaat." Usually this common German term is rendered as "constitutional state/democracy" or "state (under the rule) of law."

we can testify. We are not paid for writing this chapter; rare are individuals and even rarer institutions that remunerate such basic research.

How is it possible then to establish a third sector of society next to the state and the economy? Is the civil society not just a kind of pastime of those bored with screens, drugs, or avarice? These questions point to the subject of the next chapter.

Free Culture, Stimulating Civil Society or the Individual in Charge of Social Development

What we now call civil society was Rudolf Steiner's main field of action. With approximately 6,000 lectures[52] and around 30 treatises and collections of articles and essays, he stimulated the field he called "free spiritual life" ("freies Geistesleben"). Already about 1 year after the first edition of *Basic Issues of the Social Question* Steiner writes a preface to the 41st to the 80th thousand. In this preface he emphasizes the importance of individual insights based on the free spiritual life. "This book must assume the unpopular task of showing that the chaotic condition of our public life derives from the dependence of spiritual life on the political state and economic interests. It must also show that the liberation of spiritual life and culture from this dependence constitutes an important element of the burning social question."[53]

This task of freeing culture from political and economic constraints and administration has become unpopular since the bourgeoisie consolidated itself after the World War. Indeed, this imprint of the second 40,000 copies sold much slower than the first 40,000 of the book *Die Kernpunkte der sozialen Frage*. Social threefolding is still considered quaint by many who are in charge, be it in the economy, in governments, and even in culture. Most people take serious only the economy or the state. We often hear economists or other social scientists talk about government or market failure, but not about culture failure. In fact, this is Rudolf Steiner's contribution to social analysis: He attributes the social chaos of his time to the failure of culture and consequently of individual development. As long as they are in the clutches of governments and markets, dignity remains a utopian value.

The German constitution states the basic values as follows in its first two articles:

Art. 1: (1) Human dignity shall be inviolable. To respect and protect it shall be the duty of all state authority.

[52] In 1888, Rudolf Steiner gave his first lecture, in 1910 he gave 200, and in 1923, 461 lectures.

[53] This is §9 of the preface to the German edition of 1920 which is called the fourth edition in the English translation by Frank Thomas Smith.

Art. 2: (1) Every person shall have the right to free development of his personality insofar as he does not violate the rights of others or offend against the constitutional order or the moral law.

These rights imply free culture that for Rudolf Steiner consists mainly of four activities:

i. Artistic creativity and appreciation of all arts, including the art of creating groups of individuals and institutions.[54] Steiner is still known as architect of the Goetheanum, writer of four plays, and inventor of eurythmy.[55]
ii. Religious service,[56] morality, ethics[57];
iii. Research, truth, and science[58];
iv. Education as an art (Howard) in free schools, families, etc.[59]

Instead of going here into these fields and their institutions, we make some indications in the footnotes, the last section, and the references. The three branches of spiritual life can be the basis of education as an art once they are enlivened or part of life. To relate art, religion, and science to life and society is a major task of anthroposophy.[60]

---

[54] Probably the most famous and original proponent of Steiner's concept of social art was Joseph Beuys. His "formulation of the concept of **social sculpture**, in which society as a whole was to be regarded as one great work of art (the Wagnerian Gesamtkunstwerk)" is recorded in the video "Willoughby SHARP, *Joseph Beuys, Public Dialogues* (1974/120 min)," a record of Beuy's first major public discussion in the USA. See http://en.wikipedia.org/wiki/Social_sculpture. In the UK, social art is developed in the Social Sculpture Research Unit of Oxford Brookes University, Oxford, UK, OX3 0BP.

[55] "In 1912 Frau Smits, the mother of a young girl who loved movement, asked Rudolf Steiner the question, *Was it possible to find new sources from which an art of movement could be developed?* In answer to this question posed by Frau Smits, Rudolf Steiner went into an entirely different direction than changes happening in the field of dance. As described in 'About Eurythmy,' human sound is a bridge between the two dimensions of life, inner and outer, spiritual and material. … [Beside the stage art] Two other professional applications of eurythmy developed shortly afterward." http://www.eurythmy.org/history1.htm on 9 May 10.

[56] "The Christian Community was established in 1922 under the leadership of Friedrich Rittelmeyer. Rudolf Steiner played an indispensable part in establishing its constitution and forms of service. … Congregations are sustained by the financial support and practical care of their members." http://www.thechristiancommunity.co.uk/ 9 May 10.

[57] The second part of Steiner's *Philosophy of Freedom* of 1894 is devoted to ethics; the first to a comprehensive theory of knowledge as we observed on page 9.

[58] See the preceding note. The 11 sections of the School of Spiritual Science in Dornach, Switzerland, are listed in http://www.goetheanum.org/hochschule.html?&L=1 9 May 10. One task of the Section for the Social Sciences is to provide space for exchange between the people active in anthroposophical institutions, as in educational, medical, special needs education, commercial and agricultural organizations. Zimmermann (2007) describes the "School of Spiritual Science" in general.

[59] See especially Gary Lamb (2004) on the *Social Mission of Waldorf Education.*

[60] Many anthroposophical institutions include in their philosophy the dictum Steiner pronounced when he opened the first Waldorf School in Stuttgart in September 1919: "«Lebendig werdende Wissenschaft,/Lebendig werdende Kunst,/Lebendig werdende Religion,/das ist schließlich Erziehung, das ist schließlich Unterricht.» Diese ebenso umfassende wie begeisternde Aufgabe wurde von Rudolf Steiner bei der Eröffnung der ersten Waldorfschule 1919 den Lehrern übergeben." http://www.schoolofnature.org/uploads/media/WN_10_2007.pdf

When Steiner characterizes the development of this fourfold field it seems to overlap with what we now call civil society. "Everything which occurs in the social organization due to economic activity and rights-awareness is influenced by what emanates from a third source: the individual abilities of each human being." (*BISQ*, chapter II, §38) This also answers the question as to the source of innovation. How can we overcome traditions and routines in order to create new products, institutions, and ideas?

How can we develop individual abilities as the wellspring of the new? This requires free institutions; consequently, anthroposophical institutions are frequently called "free" or "independent" when they are part of culture: Free Waldorf schools, Frije School,[61] Free College,[62] etc. The principle of freedom is always paired with responsibility and opposed to the arbitrary. The Free Culture is not just for free or spare time, but essential for a dynamic, evolving society. As long as the economy or the states organize research and education, they are more oriented toward stabilizing existing institutions than to develop abilities and innovations.

But how can cultural activities be financed and organized without government involvement? "Free receptivity, the only suitable means, is paralyzed when the social integration of these efforts and achievements is directly conditioned by economic life or organized by the state. There is only one possible healthy form of development for spiritual life: what it produces shall be the result of its own impulses and a relationship of mutual understanding shall exist between itself and the recipients of its achievements."[63] When the individual is autonomous, neither states nor the economy can force or induce people to attend concerts, religious services, or research. To this increasing freedom corresponds growing voluntary financing of cultural activities.

Of course, it is convenient to have state- or enterprise-funded schools and research institutions. But this kind of funding makes us sluggish and blind for conflicts and collisions of interests.

> People think that the state can provide the educational facilities and that the teachers who occupy them can develop culture and spiritual life "freely" in them. This opinion ignores how closely related the content of spiritual life is to the innermost essence of the human being in which it is developing, and how this development can only be free when it is introduced into the social organism through the impulses which originate in spiritual life itself, and through no others. Through fusion with the state, not only the administration of

[61]For a current list of such schools see http://www.vrijescholen.nl/index.php?ac=[Portaal]%20 Schools.

[62]Of course, the attribute "free" or "frei" does not always mean independent in the sense of free cultural life. For example, the Freie Universität Berlin is run by the state of Berlin and gets €290 million in subsidies; in some contexts "free" means "'without tuition." A truly free institution of higher learning is the http://www.freie-hochschule-stuttgart.de/. There students can follow courses in threefolding.

[63]*BISQ*, §38 of chapter II; in the German edition of 1996 p. 80f. and §35.

> science and the part of spiritual life connected with it has been determined, but the content as well. (*BISQ* Ch. II, §36)

This fusion was and is different in America than in Europe. However, it is not possible here to go into what is sometimes discussed by the sociology of science.[64]

For some time we have agreed that religious institutions should not be run or influenced by the state. How can we liberate all kinds of schools, from kindergartens to colleges, artistic and research institutions from economic and legal interests and administration? Steiner not only hoped for donations but set up a network of businesses that might give part of their profits to these free institutions. He was active in fund-raising as well, especially for a World School Association (cf. Lamb 2004).

Since children cannot ask the public for support, Steiner suggests that parents could get an educational supplement to their earnings: "Children will have the right to education; the working head of a family will have a higher income than a single person. The "more" will come to him through arrangements established by agreement of all three social organizations."[65] As the Waldorf Astoria cigarette factory did in 1919ff., some enterprises today pay part of the fees for the children of their employees. However, these payments are usually earmarked for attending a certain school. Much freer would be voucher systems because then even the children of unemployed parents could attend the school that best suits the family.[66]

Although most people are quite aware of whether an institution is financed by taxes or profits, there is still little awareness for the peculiarities of institutions relying consciously on free contributions. However, to provide commodities against freezing and hunger, to formulate or administer laws, provide security or advance international relations differs obviously from boosting new ideas and developing personalities. Why do so few people realize this and act accordingly?

It seems that the more we talk about innovation in general, the less we understand how the new comes into the world. This seems to be related to the fact that most schools are run by the state. Therefore, neither teachers nor parents or pupils at large can fully appreciate free institutions, individuality, and conscious development or society. This renders an understanding of threefolding more difficult. Curiously, the objections Steiner had to face are still similar today:

---

[64] For the influence of business and government on US schools see Lamb (2004); on German schools in 1889 see Schmelzer 1991, p.26: The emperor William II wanted to use schools against communist and socialist ideas. Schools should also teach the fear of God and the love for the nation. Just these days a study proved (again) that the enterprise financing a study influences its outcome: see Gisela Schott, Henry Pachl, Ulrich Limbach, Ursula Gundert-Remy, Klaus Lieb, and Wolf-D. Ludwig (2010).

[65] *BISQ*, ch. III, §45. Since Steiner insists that his concrete proposals are valid only for the time after World War I in southwest Germany, we go beyond it here and assume that around 2010 he might have supported vouchers. Clearly, more important than a particular way of financing free schools, was and is their establishment, if threefolding is to be brought about consciously.

[66] See Behrens 1995 and Maurer 1994 on reasons for and models of educational voucher systems.

(a) Why do we need to establish threefolding since the tendencies are here already? For example, more and more schools are independent, economic activities of the states are privatized, and human rights play an increasing role in international relations.
(b) People are not ready to contribute voluntarily to cultural institutions. Therefore, they have to be tax financed. Furthermore, governmental and economic institutions have to work closely together; otherwise nations do not grow economically or lose in global competition.
(c) The interactions between the three realms and between nations are getting too complicated.

Since the first two objections contradict each other, we will focus on the third one in the following two sections.

International Relations or the Ambiguous Concept of "Nation"

Most people tend to assume that the political issues of the twenty-first century are quite different from about 100 years ago. However, if we scrutinize Steiner's description of what went wrong between 1866 and 1923, we can much better understand some of the current problems, e.g.,

i. Why Ireland, the USSR, and Yugoslavia fell apart
ii. Why cultures, religions, or East and West clash
iii. Why the EU as a supranational institution and the Euro as a transnational currency are not popular

Rudolf Steiner very rarely presents himself as an academic and so he hardly ever spends time to define terms. This is also true for the terms "nation" or "people." He rather describes what notions of "nation" are obsolete, respectively promising or progressive. From what follows it is clear in what sense "nation" is still meaningful and in what senses it blurs necessary distinctions and developments.

Still today, many politicians hardly hesitate to be salespersons of companies based within their territories even though these companies are often multinationals that minimize taxes, social involvement, and environmental obligations. On 31 May 2010 the German president Köhler resigned because he was criticized for suggesting on 22 May that a nation as dependent as Germany on foreign trade could use military force to protect her trade. However, gunboat diplomacy is not covered by the German constitution. Nevertheless, ex-president Köhler (too) honestly described what is happening in many parts of the world, whether it is legal or not.

Politicians are even less hesitant to tell schools what and how to teach, to set research agendas, in short, to attach strings to all kinds of subsidies, be they cultural or economic. They feel to be in charge not only of the state but of the nation in the wide sense of the word, including the economy and the cultural activities of the legislative territory.

Whoever observes life attentively will rarely find that human rights, economic and cultural interests are congruent. Human rights and cultural identities are as little for sale as can the production of goods and services be legislated. Although this is self-evident, only few people try to sort out this mingling of social realms systematically. Why is it infrequently seen as the cause for the aggravation of the competition for natural resources at decreasing prices, the arms race, the clash of cultures,[67] and other twenty-first-century problems? Of course, threefolding will not eliminate conflicts; it will, however, make their nonviolent solution easier, be it between nations, institutions, or individuals.[68]

For the peaceful settlement of disputes it is as important to separate economic from political relations as the autonomy of cultural institutions including their international relations.

> The spiritual/cultural organizations of the various countries will be able to enter into mutual relations which derive exclusively from the common spiritual life of mankind. The self-sustaining spiritual sector, independent of the state, will develop conditions which are impossible to attain when recognition of spiritual activities is dependent on the rights-state instead of the spiritual organism's administration. In this respect there is no difference between scientific activities, which are obviously international, and other spiritual activities. A people's own language and everything related to it also constitute a spiritual area. National awareness itself belongs to this area. The people of one language region do not come into unnatural conflict with the people of another if political organizations and economic power are not used to assert their cultures. (*BISQ*, ch. 4, §2)

Obviously, this means that states, political parties, and the security forces stay neutral with regard to national conflicts in the proper sense of the word. These legal institutions strive toward equality, i.e., they maintain in speeches, through police, and courts that all people and peoples are of equal worth. According to Art. 7 of the UN declaration of Human Rights we all agreed: "All are equal before the law and are entitled without any discrimination to equal protection of the law. All are entitled to equal protection against any discrimination in violation of this Declaration and against any incitement to such discrimination." This ideal was universally proclaimed on 10 December 1948. Just as liberty, equality has been a prevailing ideal since the eighteenth century.[69]

Living, studying, and then lecturing frequently in Austria-Hungary in the years from before the Austro-Prussian war in 1866 to the end of the Hapsburg Empire in 1918, Rudolf Steiner observed a longing and need for new developments during this time.

---

[67]The virtual world simulation website http://www.aclashofcultures.com/ wants to teach conflict resolution and decrease violence in society without a comprehensive view of society. But this game might be a beginning ....

[68]See for example, the UNESCO study "Best Practices of Non-Violent Conflict Resolution" in http://www.unicef.org/violencestudy/pdf/Non-violent%20conflict%20resolution%20-%20 schools.pdf

[69]See for example, *The Ideal of Equality, edited by* Matthew Clayton and Andrew Williams (2000, eds.) and *A Historical Sketch of Liberty and Equality by Maitland* (*1875*).

> Its spiritual life, with roots in a multiplicity of ethnic communities, required the development of a form for which the obsolete uniform state was a hindrance. The Serb-Austrian conflict, which was the starting-point of the world-war catastrophe, is the most valid proof that, as of a certain time, the political borders of this uniform state should not have constituted the borders for its ethnic life as well. [Note 9] Had the possibility existed for a self-sustaining spiritual life, independent of the political state and its borders, to develop beyond these borders in harmony with the goals of the ethnic groups, then the conflict, which had its roots in the spiritual sector, would not have exploded in a political catastrophe. (*BISQ*, ch.4, §10)

This holds true also for the armed conflicts in former Yugoslavia and within the territory of the former USSR. These and other wars prove how outdated that kind of nationalism is that is supported by and furthers militarization. Around 1919, intelligent people would agree with that even more after World War II. Nevertheless, only few speak up for a conscious threefolding. On the contrary, the uniform state tends to become either a plutocracy or a theocracy, and sometimes both. Even Europe is all but developing democracy. Only due to a nongovernmental organization the right for people's initiatives is part of the Lisbon constitution.[70]

We began this contribution by indicating why Steiner does not want to be considered a utopian. Now we can understand why he considers the statesmen of his time as utopians in the sense of being far from reality. In the spring of 1914, the so-called competent political and many other leaders believed

> that peace in Europe, as far as could be humanly foreseen, was secure thanks to the efforts of governments. These 'statesmen' had no idea that their words and deeds no longer had any relation whatsoever to the real course of events. But they were the 'experts'. Those who had been developing contrary views during the last decades, such as those expressed by the author months before the outbreak of war and, finally, to a small audience in Vienna (a larger audience would only have been derisive) were considered to be "eccentric." (*BISQ*, ch. IV, §7)

Frequently, Rudolf Steiner points out how important it is to be attentive and thereby develop a sense for reality. Sometimes he encourages altruism and fair trade, he speaks up against commercialism and egotism. However, more important are deeds based on insights into what really goes on in the world and within us. Then the three sectors of society can be both autonomous and harmonious.

The Concurrence of Culture, State, and Economy

People usually ignore social threefolding not because they are martial or ignorant, but because they fear too complicated structures if society is not centralized any longer. Just as people like to think of the human body as a computer with the brain

[70] See the European Constitution, Article I-47 on "The principle of participatory democracy" that was introduced thanks to the *Mehr Demokratie* and similar organizations in favor of direct democracy; see Michael Efler/Gerald Häfner/Roman Huber/Percy Vogel (2009) *Europe: not without the people* and *Direkte Demokratie 1789–1989*. Flensburger Hefte; 24 (1989); 240 pp. DM 14,80.

as the CPU (central processing unit), they expect of a president or government to rule a country in all its major parts. History showed, however, that even such popular leaders as M. Gorbachev or B. Obama cannot avoid military conflicts, government and market failures.

Even though some parties promise it and some voters expect it, politics cannot enhance morality, science, language, or education. But what exactly furthers peace, democracy, and innovations in modern times? How can the economy, the state, religions, arts, sciences, and education of different regions and countries interact if they are decentralized and self-governed?

> Each of the three sectors will have an independent relation to the corresponding sector of another social organism. Economic relations between countries will exist without being directly influenced by the relations between their respective rights-states.* Conversely, the relations between rights-states will develop, within certain limits, completely independent of economic relations. Through this independence of development, the relations will act upon each other in a conciliatory way in cases of conflict. The resulting complex of mutual interests among the individual social organisms will make national frontiers seem inconsequential for human coexistence. (*BISQ* chapter IV, §1)

In the footnote Steiner indicates a research program for the *law and economics discipline*: "* To object that rights and economic relations really constitute a whole and cannot be separated is to misunderstand what is meant here concerning social formation. In the overall commercial process both kinds of relation of course act as a whole. There is, however, a difference if rights are established according to economic requirements, or if they are established according to the elementary sense of human rights and then are applied to economic affairs." To talk about "markets" and "governments" is justified when human dignity is clearly more important than profits or elections. As soon as the individual is exploited, he or she revolts and causes social tensions. These will explode if the constitutional state and economic arbitration are not strong enough to settle these disputes fairly and expeditiously.

The disturbing financial crises underscore in yet another way how important it is to decide who is in charge of money. What could be the role of the "equalizer" called state or law, of the "co-operator" called economy or market, or of the "liberator" culture or free spiritual life with regard to a healthy world monetary system or even a world currency? Helmut Creutz discusses *29 errors regarding money*; Schweppenhäuser believes that we have *Sick Money*. This is not to say that bankers, finance ministers, or other so-called experts or practitioners are stupid. However, they often do not consider the mindset of people, the whole of society and its structure in their decisions and policies.

Consequently, who is in charge need not be in touch with reality. To write about social threefolding in a volume about the state as utopia sheds a special light on this title. It is indeed a utopia in the sense of a figment of the brain that the state or the financial sector is all of society. The state can only exist if it can tax a strong, because autonomous, economy and because it can recruit states-people, members of parliament, and security people that are freely educated. By being independent of government administration, schools and universities can supply the state and the economy with innovative people that know how to assert their dignity over and against political power and economic exploitation.

Understanding threefolding means not only to model society as a tripartite entity. It also implies holding together the three sectors or realms of society. For these tasks it takes individuals who freely engage in learning, who accept democratic decisions where they are justified, and who relate consciously to the solidarity embedded in a global economy. As we cited above before footnote 30: "The external social organism which forms the foundation for human life will be tripartite; each individual will constitute a binding element for its three sectors."[71] Thus, threefolding implies that humans are political beings; Aristotle coined the term "zoon politicon" (ζ ον πολιτικ ν).

Whereas in Plato's time society was determining most individuals to a large degree, it is now each woman or man that can organize social life. This will bring about independent schools, hospitals, and theaters, but also presupposes freely educated, healthy, and creative individuals ready to shape families, firms, and other institutions. As already some individuals and organizations show: Yes, we can implement threefolding! Economic, legal, and cultural life can work together without a centralized state if we as individuals take on responsibility.

Epilogue: Threefolding in Practice Today

Since the demise of the emperors on 9 November 1918, it is easier for wise and active women and men to develop society and lead democratically. This is why Rudolf Steiner started to become politically active around this time. As mentioned, in February 1919 he and his supporters circulated his appeal "To the German People and the Civilized World." It is now the last chapter of his seminal book on social threefolding from which we quoted extensively.

In the appeal he outlines succinctly how society develops if knowledgeable and observing individuals are in charge. We are thankful that the editor of this volume asked us to include this introduction to Steiner's social research because:

[T]oday the public must bring to it what it could not have brought a short time ago: understanding men and women who want to work for what it advocates – if it is worth being understood and being put into practice. What should come about now is only possible through the activity of such people.[72]

Those individuals who try to understand the foundations of social change are frequently active in institutions that practice or analyze threefolding in the light of Rudolf Steiner's indications[73]:

I. Active primarily in the **economic field** are:

---

[71] Steiner 1919, last paragraph of chapter III.

[72] *Basic Issues of the Social Question*, last sentences of chapter IV, §18 of the English and §14 of the German edition of 1996, here on p. 156.

[73] A rich source of institutions is the *Adressenverzeichnis Anthroposophie 2006/2007*; Frankfurt/Main: Info3, 2006; 768 p. ISBN10: 3–723–51224–0.

1. Banks like the GLS Gemeinschaftsbank in Bochum/Germany, the Dutch Triodos bank, now in several countries of Europe. They are part of the Global Alliance for Banking on Values and of the Institute for Social banking that sponsors a third International Summer School on Ethical or Social Banking from 18th to 23rd of July 2010.[74]
2. Foundations: Software AG Stiftung, Mahle Stiftung, Waldorfstiftung
3. Associations as in Luxembourg, around Stuttgart, etc. Community supported agriculture in Scotland, USA, etc.
4. Publishers like the Verlag Freies Geistesleben, Verlag Urachhaus, *Info3*, and the FIU-Verlag[75] in Germany; the Rudolf Steiner Verlag and the Verlag am Goetheanum in Switzerland.
5. Bio-dynamic farming instigated by Steiner 1924 all over the world.[76]
6. Health food and other trade establishments.[77]
7. Pharmaceutical companies like Wala and Weleda[78]

II. Active mainly in the **political area** are:

1. *The Omnibus for Direct Democracy* to introduce a federal referendum law in Germany based on Art. 20 of the German constitution or "Basic Law." *More Democracy* as "the driving force for referenda and a better electoral law." Some members support threefolding.[79]
2. Some politicians, e.g., Otto Schily (in Steiner 1996), Gerald Häfner,[80] member of the European Parliament, and Nicanor Perlas, running for president in the Philippines in the 10 May elections of 2010.[81]

---

[74]Cf. http://www.gls.de/ (about 1,3 billion €) http://de.wikipedia.org/wiki/Triodos_Bank (almost 5 billion €), http://www.social-banking.org/. This Institute for Social Banking was founded by 12 ethical banks from central and northern Europe in 2006. The Global Alliance for Banking on Values unites banks working according to the highest standards in ethical banking with 7 million customers in 20 countries.

[75]"FIU" stands for Free International University founded by Beuys in 1973. The publisher and author Rainer Rappmann founded the publishing company in Wangen im Allgäu in 1991.

[76]For an overview over the farms that cultivate the land bio-dynamically see http://www.demeter.net/. For a vivid description of how to do this in an Egyptian dessert see Abouleish (2001) on Sekem.

[77]Alnatura seeks to cooperate with all firms that are dedicated to social development and sustainability, see http://alnatura.de/de/was-wir-wollen, similarly http://www.dm-drogeriemarkt.de/dmDHomepage/generator/dmD/Homepage/Unternehmen/Portrait/Portr_C3_A4t.html and http://www.tegut.com/

[78]http://www.dr.hauschka.de/english/wala/ and http://www.weleda.de/Unternehmen/Philosophie/Leitbild. Founded in 1921 as one of Steiner's activities for threefolding, Weleda does still not consider wages as costs. All incomes are part of the Economic Value Added (EVA).

[79]See http://www.omnibus.org/english_information.html and http://www.mehr-demokratie.de/english-information.html. 23 to 25 March 2007 *Mehr Demokratie* staged a congress together with the *Netzwerk Dreigliederung* (network for threefolding) to compensate the European democracy deficit with proposals that are now published in Efler, etc. (2009).

[80]Personal communication in a break during the Annual General Meeting of *Mehr Demokratie* in Eisenach 8 May 2010.

[81]Cf. http://www.nickperlas.com/?page_id=91 and http://www.globenet3.org/index.shtml. Perlas writes in 2009 on the strategic weaknesses of the civil society and on alternatives to neoliberalism.

(c) Some individuals and groups supporting a so-called unconditional basic income, e.g., the founder of the drug-store chain "dm," Götz Werner.[82] He is in charge of an entrepreneurial institute and of www.unternimm-die-zukunft.de. Undertaking the future implies financing the government mainly through expenditure taxes according to Dr. B. Hardorp's (2008) research.

III. Among the institutions in the *cultural sphere* are:

1. Waldorfschools and Waldorf kindergartens,[83] Camphill and other places for handicapped children and adults,[84] etc.
2. Around a dozen institutes and foundations have been established around the world in the pursuit of elaborating Steiner's ideas on the *Threefold Commonwealth*.[85] Some universities like the University Witten/Herdecke and the Alanus Hochschule near Bonn find it helpful to address legal, economic, and cultural matters in their own light before bringing them together in the decision-making process or in a general theory of society.
3. There are at least two study courses on threefolding: the *Study Course for Social Development*, taking place for the third time from February 2010 to January 2012, and an American self-taught course.[86]
4. Various social scientists including economists have elaborated on Steiner's social ideas: the late professor in economics in Freiburg, Folkert Wilken (books in English 1969 and 1982), Hans Georg Schweppenhäuser, Bernard Lievegoed (in English 1969), Udo Hermannstorfer (1991, in English 2009), Georg F. von Canal, Theodor Beltle, Herbert Witzenmann, Claus von Scharmer, Prof. Dr. Dieter Suhr of the University of Augsburg, Helmut Creutz, Rolf Henrich (1989), Hjalmar Hegge, as well as the late Norwegian professor in economics Leif Holbæk-Hanssen and Peter Normann Waage.[87]
5. Artists like Ninette Sombart, the youngest child of the economist Werner Sombart,[88] and of course Joseph Beuys, who inspired some of his students, e.g., Johannes Stüttgen (Cf. Mayer, Thomas/Stüttgen, J. (2004)).

[82] Prof. Götz W. Werner is in charge of the *Interfakultatives Institut für Entrepreneurship*, Engesserstraße 13, D-76131 Karlsruhe, +49 (0)721/608 – 8960; cf. http://www.iep.uni-karlsruhe.de/

[83] Cf. http://www.dreigliederung.de/waldorfschule/ with further references.

[84] The *Council for Curative Education and Social Therapy* lists 533 curative education centers, 62 training centers, 31 national, professional, and parents' associations in 40 countries, see http://www.khsdornach.org/en/home-en/list-of-centres/

[85] A wealth of information can be found in http://www.sozialimpulse.de/forsch.htm. The English texts are available in http://www.threefolding.net/. Find more institutes and links in the References below.

[86] Studiengang für Sozialentwicklung, cf. www.sozialimpulse.de/studiengang.htm

[87] Waage's *Manpower and the Market* was published in German in 2003, English translation pending.

[88] On Werner Sombart and threefolding see Hanel (2008), on N. Sombart see Harlan (2005).

6. The Christian Community that usually pays its priests according to need.
7. Nursing homes, hospitals like the Filderklinik and the Gemeinschaftskrankenhaus Herdecke, therapists, and quite a few anthroposophical physicians.[89] A patients' organization stands for a corresponding health policy.[90]
8. Consultancies like Trigon, Ways to Quality, etc. (see links in references).

Some of these individuals and organizations are associated with the threefolding network that is based in Stuttgart.[91] An exhaustive list is less important than the question whether the mentioned personalities and institutions can contribute toward a humane social development. In light of this task we want to conclude with the motto of the American Rudolf Steiner Institute:

"Transforming Ourselves for the Sake of the World."[92]

References for Steiner's Social Threefolding

Periodicals, links, and titles by Rudolf Steiner are at the end of this Bibliography

* = digitalized

GA = Gesamtausgabe or Complete Works of Steiner's oeuvre, mainly edited by the Rudolf Steiner archive (http://www.rudolf-steiner.com/) and published by the Rudolf Steiner Verlag in Dornach, Switzerland. It comprises around 350 volumes plus documents and reproductions of Steiner's artistic work. Some English translations can be found in http://www.rsarchive.org.

CW = Collected Works by Steiner. Recently, SteinerBooks, 610 Main Street, Great Barrington, MA 01230; Fax: 413.528.8826 started to edit this English version of the GA.

BISQ = Steiner (1919) Basic Issues of the Social Question; for other titles see below

WE = Steiner (1922) World Economy, see below in the bibliography

Steiner's and others' works on the threefold social organism can be found in http://www.dreigliederung.de/bibliographie/einleitung.html. This bibliography by Erwin Haas is also available in print and counts currently 3929 entries with publications dating from 1919 to 2005. (Maybe this one will be the 4,000th if funding can be found to continue the bibliography.)

Titles Not by Steiner

Abouleish, Ibrahim (2001) *Die Sekem Vision – Eine Begegnung von Orient und Okzident verändert Ägypten.* Stuttgart, Berlin: Mayer, 2004²; 224 pp. (ISBN 3–932386–77–9) (http://en.wikipedia.org/wiki/Ibrahim_Abouleish);

– in French (2007) *Sekem: une communauté durable dans le désert égyptien.* La Boissière en Thelle: Aethera

Arenson, Adolf (1930) *Leitfaden durch 50 Vortragszyklen Rudolf Steiners.* Stuttgart: Verlag Freies Geistesleben, 1991; 1023 pp. €51.--

[89] A list of anthroposophical medicine can be found in http://www.damid.de/medizin/index.html.

[90] http://www.gesundheitaktiv-heilkunst.de/index.php

[91] http://www.sozialimpulse.de/netzwerk.htm

[92] On the many activities of this training institute cf. http://www.steinerinstitute.org/index.aspx

Backhaus, Jürgen and Hanel, Johannes (1994) *Die Nachfolge. Ein Versuch über Heinrich Herkner, den Volkswirt.* Mit einer Bibliographie und einem Porträt Herkners. Festgabe für Herrn Professor Dr. Kurt G.A. Jeserich zum neunzigsten Geburtstage am 5. Februar 1994. Marburg: Metropolis; 227 pp. (Beiträge zur Geschichte der deutschsprachigen Ökonomie; 6)

Bakunin, Michael (1866) Revolutionary Catechism. No place: Publ. by "Black Panther", c. 1971. Also in Bakunin on Anarchy. Selected works by the activist-founder of world anarchism. Edited, translated, and with an introduction by Sam Dolgoff; preface by Paul Avrich. London: George Allen and Unwin 1973; xxvii, 405, vii p. ISBN 43210120

Becker, Gary S. (1993) "Economic Imperialism", Interview now in http://www.acton.org/publications/randl/rl_interview_76.php

Behrens, Eckhard (1993) "Gliederung des Sozialen Organismus" pp. 3–4 in *Fragen der Freiheit,* Heft 225, November/Dezember 1993: *Überwindung des Zentralismus*

Behrens, Eckhard (1995) "Der Bildungsgutschein. Die Finanzierung des Bildungswesens wird auf Autonomie und Wettbewerb ausgerichtet." Diskussionsbeitrag von Eckhard Behrens, Reg.Dir. a.D. 3. Juni 1995 in *Fragen der Freiheit* and http://www.sffo.de/fdf.htm

Beltle, Theodor (1987) *Die menschenwürdige Gesellschaft.* Frankfurt/Main: Fischer-TB.-Vlg. 159 pp. ISBN-10: 359625549X [ex libris JHhanel]

Benesch, Friedrich (1976) *Pfingsten heute. Gemeinschaft im Zeichen des Individualismus.* Stuttgart: Urachhaus, 1981²; 48 pp. (Vorträge 12)

Boese, Franz (1939) *Geschichte des Verein für Socialpolitik 1872–1932. Im Auftrag des Liquidationsausschusses verfaßt vom Schriftführer Dr. Franz Boese.* Berlin: Duncker and Humblot; 322 pp. + zweiseitiger "Letzter Bericht … von C. v. Dietze". It includes a bibliography of this *Verein* in the last volume 188.

Beuys, Joseph (1990) *Energy Plan for the Western Man. Joseph Beuys in America,* Compiled by Carin Kuoni. New York: Four Walls Eight Windows; XI, 274 pp. $18.95.--

Bos, Lex (1994) "Organisationsentwicklung und Mesodreigliederung (Interview)" in http://www.dreigliederung.de/essays/1994–06–007.html

Bos, Lex (1996) *Christus-Wirken im Sozialen.* Dornach: Verlag am Goetheanum; 40 pp. (Geisteswissenschaftliche Vorträge) [ex libris JHanel]

Carr, William A. (1969) *A History of Germany 1815–1990.* London: Edward Arnold; 4th ed. 1991, repr. 1994 by Hodder education; 430 p. *1815–2002* Oxford University Press 2008

Cassirer, Ernst (1946) *The Myth of the State.* New Haven: Yale University Press; (Gesammelte Werke; 25. Hamburg: Meiner, 2007; VI, 327 p. edited by Maureen Lukay)

Clayton, Matthew and Andrew Williams (2000, eds) *The Ideal of Equality.* Houndmills, Basingstoke, Hampshire: Macmillan Press; New York: St. Martin s Press, 2000. As paperback Palgrave Macmillan; 240 pages, ISBN: 978–0–333–97119–2, ISBN10: 0–333–97119–1

Coiplet, Silvain (2000) Anarchismus und soziale Dreigliederung, ein Vergleich, cf. http://www.dreigliederung.de/publish/anarchismusprobe.html (see also Perlas 2009)

Coiplet, Silvain (2008) *Steiner-CD Soziale Dreigliederung. Grundwerke, Textsammlungen, Stichwortregister.* Berlin: Selbstverlag € 40.-- (Mit freundlicher Genehmigung der Rudolf Steiner-Nachlassverwaltung) (www.dreigliederung.de)

Cooter, Robert D. (1981–2) Law and the Imperialism of Economics. An Introduction to the Economic Analysis of Law and a Review of the Major Books. in *UCLA Law Review*, pp.1260 ff.

Creutz, Helmut (2003) *Das Geld-Syndrom. Wege zu einer krisenfreien Marktwirtschaft.* Frankfurt/Main, Berlin: Ullstein; 627 p. (5 Aufl. Nachdr.) ISBN 3–928493–46–9.

Creutz, Helmut (2008) *Die 29 Irrtümer rund ums Geld.* München: Signum Wirtschaftsverlag; 304 pp. As audio *book*: Daun TechniSat Digital, Div. Radioropa-Hörbuch 2006.

Creutz, Helmut (2008a French) *Le syndrome de la monnaie: Vers une économie de marché sans crise.* Paris: Economica; 456 p.: graph., tabl., ISBN 978–2–7178–5457–2 € 37.

Creutz, Helmut (2008b English) *The Money Syndrome: Towards a Market Economy Free From crises.* Munich: Publ. ed.: GVM Krishna (R. Mittelstaedt); 626 pp. [Transl. from German by Y. Aruna]

Daastøl, Arno Mong (2007) "Anthroposophy and Anarcho-Syndicalism" paper not yet published, partly used to write this one; available from the authors.

Dalin, Bo (2010) "*Steiner* Waldorf education, Social Three-Folding and Civil Society: Education as cultural power" in *RoSE – Research on Steiner Education*, Vol 1, No 1 (2010), cf. http://www.rosejourn.com/index.php/rose/article/view/8

Direkte Demokratie 1789–1989. Flensburger Hefte; 24 (1989); 240 pp. DM 14,80

Dolgoff, Sam (1974, ed.) *The Anarchist Collectives. Workers' Self-management in the Spanish Revolution 1936–1939*. Introduction by Murray Bookchin. New York: Free Life Ed. 1974; XXXIX, 192 p.

Efler, Michael/Häfner, Gerald/Huber, Roman/Vogel, Percy (2009) *Europe: Not Without the People! The Dismal State of Democracy in the European Union and How to Mend It*. Published online by *Mehr Demokratie* (more democracy), see http://www.mehr-demokratie.de/english-information.html (pdf, 540 kB, 159 pp.)

Eucken, Walter (1950) *The Foundations of Economics. History and Theory in the Analysis of Economic Reality*. Berlin: Springer; VIII, 358 S. (ISBN: 978–3–540–55189–8; 133,70 € bound)

Foley, Jonathan (April 2010) Boundaries for a Healthy Planet, in *Scientific American*, pp. 38–41.

Frei, Dieter W. (1988) *Menschengemässe Politik: die soziale Herausforderung*. Dornach: Verlag am Goetheanum; 223 pp. 3–7235–0476–0 DM 28.-- [ex libris Jhanel]

Gabor, Dennis/Colombo, Umberto/King, Alexander/Galli, Riccardo (1976) Das Ende der Verschwendung. Zur materiellen Lage der Menschheit. Ein Tatsachenbericht an den Club of Rome. Mit Beiträgen von Eduard Pestel. Stuttgart: Deutsche Verlags-Anstalt; 252 pp. (original title: *Beyond the Age of Waste….*)

Gide, Charles and Charles Rist (1909) *Histoire des doctrines economiques depuis les physiocrates jusqu'à nos jours*. Paris, Sirey, 1909; Royal octavo. pp. xix, 766. Index. *History of Economic Doctrines. From the Time of the Physiocrats to the Present Day*, translation from the French original, 2nd English edition, London: George G. Harrap, 1948; 800 pp.

Habermas, Jürgen (1968) *Vitenskap som ideologi*, Oslo, Gyldendal, 1969, translated from the original *Technik und Wissenschaft als "Ideologie"*, Frankfurt a.M.: Surkamp (translated to English as *Technology and Science as Ideology*)

Hanel, Albert (2004) *Rudolf Steiner - Adolf Hitler. Versuch einer Gegenüberstellung*. Frankfurt/Main: R.G. Fischer; 156 pp. [ex libris JHanel]

Hanel, Johannes M. (1997):Statistical Regularities, Freedom, and Social Policy: Wagner and Schmoller on Freedom under the Statistical Law of Large Numbers. Or: Why Moral Statistics Precede their Association for Social Reform, 513–594 in Backhaus, Jürgen G. (1997, Ed.): *Essays on Social Security and Taxation*. Marburg: Metropolis; 656 pp.

Hanel, Johannes M. (2008) *Assessing Induced Technology. Sombart's Understanding of Technical Change in the History of Economics*. Göttingen: Cuvillier; 384 pp. €28,80. – (Technology and Society 1; Dissertation at the University of Maastricht)

Hansen, Oskar Borgman (1979) *Antroposofi Rudolf Steiners bidrag til videnskab, kunst og religion*, Copenhagen: Berlingske Forlag; 259 pp.

Hansen, Oskar Borgman (1979) *En vej til samfundets fornyelse* (*A Road to the Renewal of Society*) Copenhagen: Berlingske Forlag

Hardorp, Benedictus (1986) *Anthroposophie und Dreigliederung*. Stuttgart: Freies Geistesleben; 172 pp. ISBN: 3772508731

Hardorp, Benedictus (2008) *Arbeit und Kapital als schöpferische Kräfte: Einkommensbildung und Besteuerung als gesellschaftliches Teilungsverfahren*. Karlsruhe: KIT Scientific Publishing; 214 pp. €28,50

Harlan, Volker (2004) *Alles Sichtbare haftet am Unsichtbaren – Werk und Leben von Ninetta Sombart*. Stuttgart: Urachhaus Verlag; 208 pp. 90 full-page color images, bound 42 €

Hegge, Hjalmar (1978) *Menneske og Naturen. Naturforståelsen gjennom tidene – med særlig henblikk på vår tids miljøkrise*. Oslo: Universitetsforlaget, 2nd revised edition, Oslo: Antropos, 1993 (translated: *Man and Nature. The Image of Nature through the Times – with Particular Focus on the Present Environmental Crisis*.)

Hegge, Hjalmar (1988) *Freiheit, Individualität und Gesellschaft. Eine philosophische Studie zur menschlichen Existenz*, Stuttgart: Verlag Freies Geistesleben, 1992; 445 pp. (LOGOI. Philosophie, Literatur, Geschichte. Hg. Von Manfred Krüger; 10) Translation by Stephan Rotthaus and Gabriele Sperlich-Rotthaus [ex libris JHanel] of the Norwegian original *Frihet, individualitet og samtunn. En moralfllosofisk, erkjennelsesteoretisk og sosialfilosofisk studie i menneskelig eksistens*. Oslo: Universitetsforlaget. (commentary in http://www.dreigliederung.de/bibliographie/3441.html)

Hegge, Hjalmar (1988a) *Erkjennelse og virkelighet*, ('Knowledge and Reality') a reworked edition of his Masters Thesis with the same title, 1957), Oslo: Antropos forlag, 2002

Hegge, Hjalmar. (1988). *Frihet, individualitet og samtunn. En moralfllosofisk, erkjennelsesteoretisk og sosialfilosofisk studie i menneskelig eksistens*, Oslo: Universitetsforlaget, new print: Oslo: Antropos forlag, 2002

Herrmannstorfer, Udo (1990) *Individualität und Staat. Dreigliederung des sozialen Organismus: eine aktuelle Zeitforderung*. Bad Liebenzell-Unterlengenhardt: Verein für ein erweitertes Heilwesen; 32 pp. (Merkblätter für eine bewußte Lebensführung in Gesundheit und Krankheit; 138)

Herrmannstorfer, Udo (1991) *Scheinmarktwirtschaft. Arbeit, Boden, Kapital und die Globalisierung der Wirtschaft*. Stuttgart: Freies Geistesleben, 1997[3]; 229 pp. ISBN: 978–3–7725–1206–3 €10,50 (Praxis Anthroposophie)

Herrmannstorfer, Udo (2009) *Pseudo Market Economy. Labour, Land, Capital and the Globalisation of the Economy*. This English edition published by: Institut für soziale Gegenwartsfragen e.V. Stuttgart, edited by Dr. Christoph Strawe. Translation: Carol Bergin, Julia Kramer, Prof. Dr. Hellmut Fischmeister, Johannes Lauterbach and Ulrich Morgenthaler © Verlag Freies Geistesleben Stuttgart. The German original appeared first in 1991.

Holbæk-Hanssen, Leif (1976) *Metoder og modeller i markedsføringen, I-III, part III: Planlegging, budsjettering og styringssystemer, chapter 4: Det selvstyrte samfunn som fremtidsbilde*. Oslo: Tanum-Norli

Holbæk-Hanssen, Leif (1984) *Et samfunn for menneskelig utvikling. Bidrag til tenkingen om alternativ framtid*. Oslo: Tanum-Norli

Howard, Michael (without year) "Education as an Art: The Role of Art in Human Development." *A project sponsored by the Waldorf Education Research Institute*. In http://www.waldorflibrary.org/Journal_Articles/RB6106.pdf 9 May 2010.

Kacer-Bock, Gundhild (no year) Hellmuth von Moltke in http://biographien.kulturimpuls.org/detail.php?&id=1159 on 5 June 2010

Kennedy, Margrit (1990) *Geld ohne Zinsen und Inflation: Ein Tauschmittel, das jedem dient*. München: Goldmann, 2006; 268 pp.

Kimpfler, Anton (1980) *Kulturgestaltung aus dem Wesen des Menschen*: als Gabe für d. Zukunft. Freiburg/Br.: Verlag Die Kommenden; 71 pp.

Lamb, Gary (2004) *The Social Mission of Waldorf Education, Independent, Privately Founded, accessible to all*. Fair Oaks/CA: The Association of Waldorf Schools of North America; 133 pp.

Le Guerrannic, Maurice (2009) *Grundeinkommen im Lichte der sozialen Dreigliederung*. Basel: Triskel, 2009; 169 pp. contains the chapter "Kapitalismus und soziale Ideen" aus "Die Kernpunkte der sozialen Frage" by Rudolf Steiner ISBN 978–3–905893–19–9

Leinhas, Emil (1946) *Zur Dreigliederung des sozialen Organismus*. Lorch – Stuttgart: Bürger-Verlag Alfons Bürger; 57 pp.

Lievegoed, Bernardus C.J. (1965) *Dem einundzwanzigsten Jahrhundert entgegen. Acht Vorträge gehalten in Spring Valley 1965*. Frankfurt/Main: Info 3 Verlag; 107 pp.

Lindenberg, Christoph (1992) *Rudolf Steiner mit Selbstzeugnissen und Bilddokumenten*. D-21465 Reinbek: Rowohlt Taschenbuch Verlag; 1959pp. ISBN: 3499505002; i Sverre Dahls translation, Antropos Forlag 1992

Lindenberg, Christoph (1997) *Rudolf Steiner. Eine Biographie*, Band 1: 1861–1910, Band 2: 1911–1925. Stuttgart: Freies Geistesleben, ISBN 3–7725–1551–7

Mäder, Ingo/Peter Schilinski (1997) *Liebe ist Interesse am Anderen*: Erfahrungsberichte und Aufsätze. Wasserburg: Jedermensch

Maitland, Frederic William (1875) *A Historical Sketch of Liberty and Equality: As Ideals of English Political Philosophy from the Time of Hobbes to the Time of Coleridge.* Indianapolis: Liberty Fund, 2001; 208 pages, €16,99.-- $20.--

Mayer, Thomas/Stüttgen, Johannes (2004) *Kunstwerk Volksabstimmung: die spirituelle und künstlerische Dimension der direkten Demokratie*/Mit einem Beitr. von Joseph Beuys. Wangen/ Allgäu: FIU-Verlag; 127 pp.

Marcuse, Herbert (1968*) *Der eindimensionale Mensch*, Neuwied/Berlin: Luchterhand; 282 p. Now volume 7 in the collected works: 2004; 282 p. – English: *One-Dimensional Man.*

Maurer, Mathias (1994) *Der Bildungsgutschein.* Stuttgart: Freies Geistesleben; 104 pages.

McKibben, Bill (April 2010) Breaking the Growth Habit. in *Scientific American*, pp. 45–51.

Meyer, Thomas (1997, ed.) *Helmuth von Moltke, Light for the new millennium: Rudolf Steiner's association with Helmuth and Eliza von Moltke: letters, documents and after-death communications.* London: Rudolf Steiner Press. 1997. ISBN 1–85584051–0.

Meyer, Thomas (Sept. 2001) Kampf gegen die Wahrheit über ein Kernstück europäischer Geschichte. Annika Mombauers Buch über Helmuth von Moltke und den Ersten Weltkrieg in *Der Europäer*, 5, 7–15, 2001.

Mises, Ludwig von (1922) *Socialism. An Economic and Sociological Analysis*, 569 p. original in German: *Die Gemeinwirtschaft. Untersuchungen uber den Sozialismus.* Stuttgart, Gustav Fischer Verlag, 1981. First English translation: London: Jonathan Cape Ltd, 1936; text in www.mises.org

Mises, Ludwig von (1949) *Human Action. A Treatise on Economics.* New Haven: Yale University Press, revised 1963, 1966 and 1996; 912 p. $20.-- cf. www.mises.org

Moltke, Hellmuth von (1914) *Die "Schuld"am Kriege – Betrachtungen und Erinnerungen des Generalstabschefs H. v. Moltke über die Vorgänge vom Juli 1914 bis November 1914.* Stuttgart 1919 (eingestampfte Broschüre mit einem Vorwort R. Steiners = pulped brochure with a preface by R. Steiner), interpreted in Schmelzer 1991.

Mombauer, Annika (2001) *Helmuth von Moltke and the Origins of the First World War.* Cambridge University Press; 325 pp. 0–521–79101–4

Nisbet, Robert A. (1989) *The Present Age: Progress and Anarchy in Modern America.* New York: Harper & Row; XII, 145 pp. ISBN: 0–06–091578–1

Nisbet, Robert A. (1967) *The Sociological Tradition*, New Brunswick, NJ.: Transaction Publishers 1993; XIX, 349 pp.

Perlas, Nicanor (2003) *Shaping Globalization. Civil Society, Cultural Power, and Threefolding.* Gabriola Islands/BC, Canada: New Society Publishers; 300 pp.

Perlas, Nicanor (2009) *Zivilgesellschaft und Soziale Dreigliederung.* Edited and introduced by Matthias Schmelzer, with an essay by S. Coiplet. 2 vols. Berlin: Institut für soziale Dreigliederung; 33 and 37 pp.

Rappmann, Rainer (1996 ed.) *Denker, Künstler, Revolutionäre: Beuys, Dutschke, Schilinski, Schmundt; vier Leben für Freiheit, Demokratie und Sozialismus*/mit Beitr. von Joseph Beuys, Heinrich Böll, Wilfried Heidt, Karlheinz Flau, Henning Köhler, Walter Kugler, Rainer Rappmann, Ulrich Rösch, Peter Schilinski, Wilhelm Schmundt, Johannes Stüttgen und Ulle Weber. Wangen: FIU-Verlag; 175 pp. ISBN 3–928780–13–1 ca. € 19.--

Rechtsleben und soziale Zukunftsimpulse. Von der Dreigliederungsidee Rudolf Steiners zur Volksgesetzgebung. Flensburger Hefte; 25 (Sommer 1989); 243 pp. DM 16,80

Rocker, Rudolf (1938) *Anarcho-Syndicalism: Theory and Practice. An Introduction to a Subject Which the Spanish War Has Brought into Overwhelming Prominence.* First edition by Secker and Warburg, London, 158 pp. Second expanded edition by Modern Publishers, Indore City, India, 1947, 202 pages.

Scharmer, Otto (2010, Mai) "Kapitalismus 3.0. Die sieben Akupunkturpunkte des sozialen Organismus" *Info 3*, Mai 2010; pp. 10–20.

Schilinski, Peter (1997) *Soziale Dreigliederung. Eine Einführung.* Wasserburg/Bodensee: jedermensch Verlag; 85pp. Aufsätze, Zeitschriftenartikel und frühe 'Kommentare' zusammengestellt und überarbeitet von Ingo Mäder und hg. vom Modell Wasserburg e.V.) ISBN 3–9931615–03–0.

Schmelzer, Albert (1991) *Die Dreigliederungsbewegung 1919. Rudolf Steiners Einsatz für den Selbstverwaltungsimpuls*. Stuttgart: Freies Geistesleben; 312 pp. (Edition Hardenberg) 36 DM.

Schmundt, Wilhelm (1973) *Revolution und Evolution: auf d. Weg zu e. Elementarlehre d. sozialen Organismus*. Hrsg. u. mit e. Vorw. vers. von Wilfried Heidt u. Ulrich Rösch. Ausführung d. Bildtaf.: Peter Schata Achberg: Verlag Edition 3. Weg; 163 pp. (Reihe Wissenschaft; 3) see also Rappmann (ed.)

Schott, Gisela, Pachl, Henry, Limbach, Ulrich, Gundert-Remy, Ursula, Lieb, Klaus, Ludwig, and Wolf-Dieter (2010) "The Financing of Drug Trials by Pharmaceutical Companies and Its Consequences: Part 2. A Qualitative, Systematic Review of the Literature on Possible Influences on Authorship, Access to Trial Date, and Trial Registration and Publication." The English version of this article is available online www.aerzteblatt-international.de. Original German: "Finanzierung von Arzneimittelstudien durch pharmazeutische Unternehmen und die Folgen" in *Deutsches Ärzteblatt* Int 2010; 107(17): 295–301; DOI: 10.328/aerztebl.2010.0295; 30 April 2010; www.Aerzteblatt.de/lit1710

Schumpeter, Joseph A. (1954) *History of Economic Analysis*. New York: Oxford University Press; 1260 pp.

Schweppenhäuser, Hans Georg (1967) *Die Teilung Deutschlands als soziale Herausforderung. Neue Ideen für neue Wege*. Freiburg, Bücher der Kommenden; bound edition.

Schweppenhäuser, Hans Georg (1970) *Macht des Eigentums – Auf dem Weg in eine neue Soziale Zukunft*. Stuttgart: Radius; 95 pp.

Schweppenhäuser, Hans Georg (1971) *Das Kranke Geld. Vorschläge für eine organische Geldordnung von morgen*. (The Sick Money. Proposals for a future organic monetary order). (Stuttgart: Radius) Frankfurt, Fischer Taschenbuchverlag, 1982; 1989.

Schweppenhäuser, Hans Georg (1977) *Das Drama der modernen Industriegesellschaft und seine Hauptakteure Adam Smith und Karl Marx*.Freiburg: Institut für soziale Gegenwartsfragen; 144 pp.

Setzer, V.W. (6 May 2010) *Rudolf Steiner. Chronological Biography*. Version 1.8 Translated from the original in Portuguese, published in www.ime.usp.br/~vwsetzer.

Strawe, Christoph (1986) *Marxismus und Anthroposophie*. Stuttgart: Klett-Cotta; XVI, 347 p.

Strawe, Christoph (1987ff.) *Studientexte zur Dreigliederung des sozialen Organismus und zur Zeitlage*. Vorbemerkung: Es handelt sich um Texte, die der Autor in den Jahren seit 1987 geschrieben hat - die meisten für verschiedene Zeitschriften. Sie werden hiermit nun - manchmal geringfügig überarbeitet - als Studienmaterial zur Verfügung gestellt. Die Sammlung wird laufend ergänzt.* http://www.sozialimpulse.de/studientexte.htm

Suhr, Dieter (1989) *The capitalistic cost-benefit structure of money: an analysis of money's structural non-neutrality and its effects on the economy* [With a contribution by Hans R. L. Cohrssen]. Berlin, Heidelberg, New York, London, Paris, Tokyo: Springer; X, 136 pp.

Taylor, Charles (1979) *Hegel and modern society*. Cambridge: Cambridge University Press, 2003. (Modern European philosophy). Translated into Swedish as *Hegel och det moderna samhället*, Göteborg: Röda Bokförlaget, 1988.

Ulrich, Mauric (2009) "Equality and Freedom" in *L'Humanité*, Monday 13 July 2009, online in http://www.truthout.org/071409G

Usher, Stephen E. (1993) The Fundamental Social Law, *The Threefold Review*, Summer/Fall 1993 (Issue No. 9)

Usher, Stephen E. (2009) "The Threefold Social Organism: An Introduction" in http://www.rudolfsteinerweb.com/Rudolf_Steiner_and_Economics.php

Verhulst, Jos/Nijeboer, Arjen (2008) *Direct Democracy. Facts and Arguments about the Introduction of Initiative and Referendum*. With a contribution by Paul Carline. Published as PDF in http://wissen.mehr-demokratie.de/buch-direkte-demokratie.html by *Mehr Demokratie*

Waage, Peter Normann (2002) *Mennesket, makten og markedet. Rudolf Steiners sosiale ideer i møte med globaliseringen*. Oslo: Pax Forlag

Waage, Peter Normann (2003) *Mensch, Markt, Macht. Rudolf Steiners Sozialimpuls im Spannungsfeld der Globalisierung*. Dornach: Pforte Verlag; 263 pp. Aus dem Norwegischen von Jürgen Vater. 978–3–85636–150–1; € 20.00

Werner, Götz W. (2007) *Einkommen für alle. Der dm-Chef über die Machbarkeit des bedingungslosen Grundeinkommens.* Unter Mitarbeit von Enrik Lauer, Berlin und Regine Möller, Düsseldorf. Bergisch-Gladbach: Lübbe, 2008; 239 pp. €8,95.--

Wiehl, Angelika (2010) "Durchbruch: Zeitgenossenschaft" in *Info 3,* June 10: 56–61, referring to the catalogs of the exhibitions in Wolfsburg.

Witzenmann, Herbert (1995) *Geldordnung als Bewusstseinsfrage*. Dornach: Gideon Spicker Verlag; 80 pp. ISBN: 978–3–85704–227–0. EAN: 9783857042270 (more of his titles in http://www.witzenmannzentrum.ch/werke.html

Zimmermann, Heinz (2007) School of Spiritual Science. Analyses and Outlook of the present situation, part I. *Journal of the Pedagogical Section at the Goetheanum*, Christmas, 32, 34–38.

Zumdick, Wolfgang (2001²) *Der Tod hält mich wach. Joseph Beuys – Rudolf Steiner, Grundzüge ihres Denkens.*Dornach: Pforte Verlag; 192 pp.

Zumdick, Wolfgang (2007) *Exchange values [Medienkombination]: images of invisible lives; Soziale Skulptur heute/Shelley Sacks. Kongress Ursache Zukunft, Goetheanum, Dornach, 2007.* Wangen/Allgäu: Fiu-Verlag; 59 pp. English and German, book and CD ISBN 978–3–928780–66–7; 3–928780–66–2 EAN 9783928780667 EUR 16.00.

Institutions, Periodicals and Links (See http)

Adressenverzeichnis Anthroposophie 2006/2007. Frankfurt: Verlag Info3, 2006; 768 p.

Alanus-Hochschule in Alfter near Bonn: This College for Art and Business strives to qualify its students in social art, see http://www.alanus.edu/alanus-hochschule-philosophie.html

Anthromedia contains many links, e.g., to the Forum on Social Sciences in Berlin, 22 May 2010 http://www.anthromedia.com/

Associative economics institute: http://www.ae-institute.com/

Banks: http://rsfsocialfinance.org/ in San Francisco; http://prometheus.co.nz/ in New Zealand, http://en.wikipedia.org/wiki/Triodos_Bank is based in the Netherlands with branches in the United Kingdom, Germany, Spain, and Belgium; http://www.gls.de/die-gls-bank/ueber-uns/gls-bank/english-portrait.html. This German bank for lending and donating was just voted to be the Bank of the Year by n-tv and Boerse online, issue 23/10 (June 2010); http://www.lanef.com/ in Villeurbanne near Lyon in France; the http://www.gabv.org/ or Global Alliance for Banking on Values in Zeist, NL, provides further information.

Betriebliche Altersversorgung: see Pension funds and insurance companies

Consultancies: http://www.trigon.at/, http://www.wegezurqualitaet.info/index.php?id=56, Lex Bos (1994)

Die Drei. Zeitschrift für Anthroposophie in Wissenschaft, Kunst und sozialem Leben. 77. Jahrgang 2007. Herausgegeben für die Anthroposophische Gesellschaft in Deutschland von Karl-Martin Dietz. Redaktion: Dr. Stephan Stockmar (Verantwortlicher im Sinne vom § 10 Abs. 3 MDStV) unter Mitarbeit von Angelika Sandtmann und Ralf Sonnenberg Die Verantwortung für den Inhalt der Beiträge tragen die Autoren. Anschrift der Redaktion: Alt-Niederursel 45, 60439 Frankfurt am Main, Telefon (069) 95 77 61 21 Telefax 58 23 58

Donau-Universität Krems, has offered a Masters in Waldorf education since 2007. http://www.donau-uni.ac.at/de/index.php

Dreigliederung des sozialen Organismus, Steiner's articles are reprinted on pp 11–126 in Steiner 1919–22.

Fragen der Freiheit. Beiträge zur freiheitlichen Ordnung von Kultur, Staat und Wirtschaft. Edited by: Seminar für freiheitliche Ordnung e.V. Badstr. 35, D - 73087 Boll Tel.: 07164 - 35 73; Fax: - 70 34; order: eMail: info@sffo.de | Internet: www.sffo.de. Redaktion: Fritz Andres, Dhauner Str. 180, D - 55606 Kirn/Nahe; eMail: fritz.andres@gmx.de

Freie Hochschule Stuttgart offers usually a course in threefolding for future teachers: http://www.freie-hochschule-stuttgart.de/

Freunde der Erziehungskunst: http://www.freunde-waldorf.de/die-freunde/GlobNet3. Global Network for Social Threefolding. See http://globenet3.org/threefold.shtml

Herbert Witzenmann Zentrum, Rüttiweg 8, CH 4143 Dornach. The activities of this center are part of the Johannes Kreyenbühl Akademie, cf. www.witzenmannzentrum.ch/kurse.html

http://anthroposophie.byu.edu/soziologie.html

http://www.anthromedia.com/

http://www.anthromedia.net/pressemeldungen-und-news/veranstaltungskalender/kalender-detail/?tx_ttnews[tt_news]=1342&tx_ttnews[backPid]=2&cHash=36aa0e19bf contains e.g., *Die Eigentumsfrage im Kapitalismus 3.0*, 20 May 2010.

http://www.anthroposophie.net/soziales/soziales_dreigliederung.htm

http://www.anthroposophy.com/ contains a wealth of informations and links.

http://www.eulenspiegel-wasserburg.de/ Here people meet who publish in *jedermensch.*

http://www.flensburgerhefte.de/neu/suchen.html; cf. Direkte *Demokratie* and *Rechtsleben.*

http://www.gesundheitaktiv-heilkunst.de/index.php This organization for patients interested in anthroposophical medicine and pluralistic health care publishes broshures, books etc. They are best known for their *Merkblätter für eine bewußte Lebensführung in Gesundheit und Krankheit,* of which Hermannstorfer 1990 is # 138. Until around the year 2000 what is now 'gesundheit aktiv' was the 'Verein für ein erweitertes Heilwesen'.

http://www.globenet3.org/threefold.shtml

http://www.kulturzentrum-achberg.de/ This cultural center shows e.g., "Money in the Social Organism"until 31st May 2010.

http://www.lebensgemeinschaft.org/English/index.html deal with capital in practice.

http://www.rudolfsteinerweb.com/Rudolf_Steiner_Works.php

http://www.top-saarbruecken.de/ consulting in the light of social threefolding.

Info3. Anthroposophie im Dialog. Das unabhängige Monatsmagazin zu den Ideen Rudolf Steiners im Dialog mit giestigen Gegenwartsströmungen. 35. Jahrgang 2010. Info3-Verlag, Kirchgartenstr. 1, 60439 Frankfurt; vertrieb@info3.de (ed. Heisterkamp).

Initiative Netzwerk Dreigliederung. Libanonstr. 3, D-70184 Stuttgart, Tel.: (0711) 2368950, Fax: 2360218, E-Mail: netzwerk@sozialimpulse.de English http://www.threefolding.net/

Institut für soziale Dreigliederung. This Berlin Institute has an English site: http://www.threefolding.org/

Institut für soziale Gegenwartsfragen e.V. Stuttgart; cf. http://www.sozialimpulse.de/institut.htm; English http://www.threefolding.net/

Institute for Social Renewal, Loma Mar/CA and Ghent/NY: http://www.socialrenewal.com/

Jedermensch: Freiheit im Geistesleben – Gleichheit im Rechtsleben – Zusammenarbeit im Wirtschaftsleben: www.jedermensch.net See also Schilinski.

Johannes Kreyenbühl Akademie zur Synergie von Natur- und Geisteswissenschaft, Im Boge 10, CH-8332 Russikon/ZH. Ihr Sie versteht sich als eine Institution des freien Geisteslebens. Ihr wirtschaftlicher Träger ist die Johannes Kreyenbühl Stiftung. Ihr Zweck gemäss Handelsregister ist die Förderung der Synthese und Synergie der Natur- und Geisteswissenschaften im Sinne des Lebenswerkes von Johannes Kreyenbühl (1846 - 1929), Rudolf Steiner (1861 - 1925), Albert Steffen (1884 - 1963), Herbert Witzenmann (1905 - 1988) u.a.

Netzwerk Dreigliederung, cf. Institut für soziale Gegenwartsfragen e.V. Stuttgart.

New Trinity and Unity is the motto of the website of http://www.wilfried-heidt.de/. W. Heidt is the director of the Achberger Instituts für Zeitgeschichte und Sozialforschung.

Pension Funds in CH-Ittigen: http://www.coopera-puk.ch/sammelstiftung_puk/images/stiftung-srat/udo_errmannstorfer.jpg. Here is the founder's photo.

http://www.hannoversche-kassen.de/

Plymouth University offers degrees in Waldorf education: http://www.plymouth.ac.uk/research-cover/rcp.asp?pagetype=G&page=322

Praxis für soziale Ordnung, Practice for Social Order (PSO)

Seminar für freiheitliche Ordnung, Bad Boll: http://www.sffo.de/

Sozialimpulse. Hg. von der Initiative Netzwerk Dreigliederung, Libanonstr. 3, 70184 Stuttgart, Tel.: 0711–2368950, Fax 2360218, E-Mail Netzwerk@sozialimpulse.de. Erscheint 4mal jährlich. Redaktion Dr. Christoph Strawe. ISSN 1863–0480. Bezug gegen Selbstkostenbeteiligung (Richtsatz € 20,-/CHF 35,- pro Jahr)

Sozialwissenschaftliche Sektion der Hochschule für Geisteswissenschaft in Dornach: http://www.goetheanum.org/59.html

Universität Witten/Herdecke is consciously a free institution not run by a government: http://www.uni-wh.de/die-uwh/profil/?L=0

Waldorf Researchers and Educators Network: http://www.ecswe.net/wren/index.html. See also http://www.steinerwaldorf.org/index.html

Works by Rudolf Steiner

The Wikipedia articles on social threefolding or Soziale Dreigliederung list the most popular works on Steiner's social ideas. Other websites are more comprehensive, like www.threefolding.org/net, www.Dreigliederung.de; see at Links. On Steiner and his anthroposophy in general see http://www.rudolf-steiner-haus-stuttgart.de/rudolf_steiner_haus/bibliothek/ueber.php?pageid=4 and http://www.steinerverlag.com/. Especially the titles of the lectures can vary from edition to edition because frequently they were not by Steiner. On his life see Steiner (1925), section 3 above, and http://www.rudolf-steiner.com/rudolf_steiner/chronik/

Steiner, Rudolf (1894) *Die Philosophie der Freiheit – Grundzüge einer modernen Weltanschauung, Seelische Beobachtungsresultate nach naturwissenschaftlicher Methode.* Berlin: Felber. Now Dornach: Rudolf Steiner Verlag, 1984; 224 pp. (66th to 75th thousend) (Rudolf Steiner Taschenbücher aus dem Gesamtwerk; 627) (Ungekürzte Ausgabe nach dem gleichnamigen Band der Rudolf Steiner Gesamtausgabe GA 4, 1978[14]).

English: Steiner, Rudolf (1894) *The Philosophy of Freedom. (The Philosophy of Spiritual Activity). The Basis for a Modern World Conception*, in German first 1894, second German edition, revised and enlarged by the author, Berlin, 1918; First English edition, *The Philosophy of Freedom*, London, 1916; Second English edition, revised and enlarged*,London, 1922, Third English edition*, London, 1932; Fourth English edition, revised translation*, London, 1939; Fifth English edition*, London, 1940; Sixth English edition*, London, 1949; American edition, new translation*, New York, 1963; Seventh English edition, thoroughly revised translation, London, 1964. This translation, based on the 12th German edition, 1962, is published by permission of Rudolf Steiner-Nachlassverwaltung, Dornach, Switzerland. – *English translations of this book from 1922 to 1963 were published with the title *The Philosophy of Spiritual Activity*

Norwegian: Steiner, Rudolf (1894) *Frihetens filosofi. Grunntrekk av en moderne verdensanskuelse.* Oslo: Antropos, 1978.

Steiner, Rudolf (1898) *Freiheit und Gesellschaft*. GA 31 (contains on pp. 255–6 the sociological basic law, cf. http://www.anthroposophie.net/steiner/bib_steiner_freiheit_gesellschaft.htm) and http://www.rsarchive.org/Links/out_frame.php?PHPSESSID=37bkphvbqm29f0kiikro9e0r20&ID=685. First publication in: *Magazin für Literatur*, 67. Jg., Nr. 29 und 30, 23. und 30. Juli 1898 (GA 31, S. 251–262).

Steiner, Rudolf (1905–06) *Geisteswissenschaft und soziale Frage* (1st edition:*Theosophie und soziale Frage*, later: *Antroposophie und soziale Frage*), Dornach: Rudolf Steiner Verlag, 1989; 48 pp. (from GA 34).

Norwegian: RS (1905–06). *Åndsvitenskapen og det sociale spørsmål.* Copenhagen, 1978.

Steiner, Rudolf (1915–21) *Aufsätze über die Dreigliederung des sozialen Organismus und zur Zeitlage 1915–1921.* Dornach: Rudolf Steiner Verlag; 496 pp. bound 43€

Steiner, Rudolf (1917 GA21) *Von Seelenrätseln. Anthropologie und Anthroposophie, Max Dessoir über Anthroposophie, Franz Brentano (Ein v). Skizzenhafte Erweiterungen.* Dornach: Rudolf Steiner Verlag; 182 pp. Cloth 978–3–7274–0210–4 € 26.--

English (1917, CW21) *Riddles of the Soul. The Case for Anthroposophy.* New York: Anthroposophic Press/Steiner Books, 2009; 190 pp. ISBN: 9780880106245 (Paperback) (SteinerBooks, The Collected Works of Rudolf Steiner 21) $25.00.

Steiner, Rudolf (1917a) *Menschliche und menschheitliche Entwicklungswahrheiten. Das Karma des Materialismus.* 17 Vorträge, Berlin vom 29. Mai - 25. September 1917 Dornach: Rudolf Steiner

Verlag, 1982; 392 pp. Rudolf Steiner Gesamtausgabe GA 176; ISBN 978–3–7274–1760–3 [Nach vom Vortragenden nicht durchges. Nachschr. hrsg. von d. Rudolf-Steiner-Nachlassverwaltung. Die Hrsg. besorgten Margrit Schmid u. Hans W. Zbinden].

English: *Aspects of human evolution*. Eight lectures given between May and July of 1917 in Berlin. Hudson, N.Y.: Anthroposophic Press; London: R. Steiner Press, 1987; 186 pp. -- (Translation of: *Menschliche und menschheitliche Entwicklungswahrheiten*.) ISBN 0–88010–251–9($20.00); 0–88010–252–7($9.95).

French: *Vérités de l'évolution de l'homme et de l'humanité. Le karma du matérialisme.* 17 conférences faites à Berlin du 29 mai au 25 septembre 1917. Trad. de l'allemand par Geneviève Bideau. Montesson: Ed. Novalis, 2004; 344 pp. (Collection Horizons d'aujourd'hui; 18) (Einheitssachtitel *Menschliche und menschheitliche Entwicklungswahrheiten* <franz.> ISBN 2–910112–45–4 -- EUR 30.00.

Steiner, Rudolf (1918, 22 Jan – 6. Aug.) *Erdensterben und Weltenleben. Anthroposophische Lebensgaben. Bewußtseins-Notwendigkeiten für Gegenwart und Zukunft*. 21 Vorträge, gehalten in Berlin vom 22. Januar bis 6. August 1918. Dornach/Schweiz: Rudolf Steiner Verlag, 1991; 480 pp. [ex libris Bäumler].

Steiner, Rudolf (1918a) *Die soziale Grundforderung unserer Zeit. In geänderter Zeitlage.*Zwölf Vorträge, gehalten in Dornach und Bern vom 29. November bis 21. Dezember 1918. Dornach/Schweiz: Rudolf Steiner Verlag, 1979; 330 pp. (1st edition 1963, combined out of Zyklus 51 and 52 published in 1921) [ex libris JHanel].

Steiner, Rudolf (1918b, 26 October–12 December) *Interesse für den anderen Menschen*. Herausgegeben, eingeleitet und mit einem Nachwort versehen von Andreas Neider. Stuttgart: Verlag Freies Geistesleben, 1989; 120 pp. (From GA185 *Geschichtliche Symptomatologie*; GA 186: *Die sozialen Grundforderungen unserer Zeit. In geänderter Zeitlage*.) [ex libris Bäumler].

*Steiner, Rudolf (1919) Die Kernpunkte der sozialen Frage in den Lebensnotwendigkeiten der Gegenwart und Zukunft, Dornach Verlag des "Goetheanum". In Kommission bei Rudolf Geering, Buch-Antiquar*iatshandlung Basel, 1919; VIII, 180 pp. [ex libris Jhanel].

1919 31st tp 40th thousend. Stuttgart: Greiner & Pfeiffer; VII, 128 pp. (Hrsg. von d. Treuhandgesellsch. d. Goetheaneum Dornach).

1920, With a preface and introduction to the 41st to 80th thousend. Stuttgart: Der Kommende Tag, A.G. 113 pp. (Internationale Bücherei für Sozial- und Geisteswissenschaften) [ex libris Jhanel].

1996 – Mit einem Nachwort von Otto Schily (pp.165–176). Dornach/Schweiz: Rudolf Steiner Verlag, 1996; 189 pp. (Edition Rudolf Steiner, 1st to 3rd thousend) [ex libris Jhanel].

1976^{6} GA 23 = Rudolf Steiner Gesamtausgabe (CW). Dornach: Rudolf Steiner Verlag, 1976^{6}; 166 pp. Bound 978–3–7274–0230–2.

English: *Basic Issues of the Social Question. Relevant to the Necessities of Life in the Present and Future*. In www.SouthernCrossReview.org (Translated by Frank Thomas Smith who writes an introduction. Cited as *BISQ*) This translation first published as *Towards Social Renewal: Basic Issues of the Social Question.* Third revised edition. London: Rudolf Steiner Press, 1977^{3}; 151 pp. ISBN-13: 978–0854403110 now also available with the title *Towards Social Renewal. Rethinking the Basis of Society.* Written 1919 (CW 23) Translated by Matthew Barton. ISBN: 1–85584–072–3 London: Rudolf Steiner Press, 1999; IX, 134 pp. £ 9.95; in US $19.95 1–85584–072–3 earlier versions: *The Threefold Commonwealth*, London: Anthroposophical Publishing Company, First published in English 1923, Second Edition revised and abridged by F. C. Heckel entitled *The Threefold Social Order*, Anthroposophic Press Inc., New York, 1966, Reprinted 1972 (available concurrently with the Third Edition), (Vol. No. 23 in the Bibliographical Survey, 1961). The English edition is published in agreement with the Rudolf Steiner-Nachlassverwaltung, Dornach, Switzerland.

French: *Eléments fondamentaux pour la solution du problème social: 13 articles commentaires (*trad. française [par un groupe d'étude (Eléments fondamentaux), G. Klockenbring (13 articles commentaires)]) 2e éd. Genève: Editions antroposophiques romandes, 1991; 247 pp.

Netherlandish: *De kernpunten van het sociale vraagstuk* (vert. uit het Duits en bew. door Mouringh Boeke) Zeist: Vrij Geestesleven, 1988; 143 pp.

Norwegian: *Kjernepunktene i det sosiale spørsmål. Livsnødvendigheter I nåtid og fremtid, fritt selvforvaltende åndsliv, demokratisk rettsystem, assosiativt selvstyrende næringsliv.* Bergen: Forlaget de tre funksjoner, c/o Paul Jebsen, 1969. This is a translation of *Die Kernpunkte der Sozialen Frage,* Steiner 1919), 1977.

Russian: Kaligula, 1992, available in http://opac-online.de/opac/de/qsel_frm.html.S

Spanish: *Los puntos esenciales de la cuestión social en las necesidades vitales de la época actual y venidera* (Trad. del alemán: Jaime Vergara Antuña) Madrid (España): Ed. Rudolf Steiner, 1996; 139 pp.

Steiner, Rudolf (1919a GA193) *Der innere Aspekt des sozialen Rätsels. Luziferische Vergangenheit und ahrimanische Zukunft.* 10 Vorträge in verschiedenen Städten. Dornach: Rudolf Steiner Verlag; 227 pp. 978–3–7274–1930–0 € 30.--

English (1919) *The Inner Aspect of the Social Question.* Three lectures given in Zürich, 4 & 11 Feb., 9 March, 1919. London: Rudolf Steiner Press, 1974. ISBN 0–85440–050–8.

Steiner, Rudolf (1919a = GA 296) *Die Erziehungsfrage als soziale Frage. Die spirituellen, kulturgeschichtlichen und sozialen Hintergründe der Waldorfschul-Pädagogik.* 6 Vorträge, Dornach 1919. Rudolf Steiner Gesamtausgabe GA 296. Dornach: Rudolf Steiner Verlag; 128, cloth 978–3–7274–2960–6 € 26.--

Steiner, Rudolf (1919b GA 330–1) *Neugestaltung des sozialen Organismus. Freiheit im Geistesleben – Gleichheit im Rechtsleben – Brüderlichkeit im Wirtschaftsleben.14 öffentliche Vorträge, gehalten in Stuttgart zwischen dem 22. April und dem 30. Juli.* Dornach/Schweiz: Rudolf Steiner Verlag, 1971; 431 pp. (1st edition in the GA 1993).

Steiner, Rudolf (1919c English GA296, 192, 330/1) *Education as a Force for Social Change.* Herndon, VA 20172–0960: Anthroposophic Press, 1997 (selection of lectures translated from GA 296, GA 192, and 330/1).

Steiner, Rudolf (1919d Zürich = GA 328) *Die soziale Frage.* 6 lectures. Dornach: Rudolf Steiner Verlag; 198 pp. 978–3–7274–3280–4 € 30.--

Steiner, Rudolf (1919e) *Barometer des Fortschritts. Gesetze des sozialen Lebens.* Dornach: Rudolf Steiner Verlag; CXC, 190 pp.; ISBN:978–3–7274–5390–8 12€ (introduction by Rösch, Ulrich/Kugler, Walter).

Steiner, Rudolf (1919f GA 332a Ocotober) *Soziale Zukunft.* 6 Vorträge mit Fragenbeantwortungen, Zürich 1919: Die soziale Frage als Geistes-, Rechts- und Wirtschaftsfrage/Das Wirtschaften auf assoziativer Grundlage/Rechtsfragen. Aufgaben und Grenzen der Demokratie/Geistesfragen. Kunst, Wissenschaft, Religion. Erziehungswesen. Soziale Kunst/Das nationale und internationale Leben im dreigegliederten sozialen Organismus. Rudolf Steiner Gesamtausgabe GA 332a. Dornach: Rudolf Steiner Verlag; 238 pp., cloth, 978–3–7274–3325–2 €36,50.--

English (1919g Ocotober, GA 332a) The *Social Future.* Six lectures, Zürich, October 24–30 1919. Trans. H. B. Monges. Anthroposophic Press, New York, 1972. GA 332a.

Steiner, Rudolf (1919h, Oct. in Zurich, similar as 332a) *Dreigliederung von Geist, Recht und Wirtschaft.* Ein Grundkurs in Sozialwissenschaft. Bad Liebenzell: Archiati Verlag; 354 pp. ISBN: 978–3–938650–50–9 (Grundkurse; this basic course countains five lectures and a discussion pp. 333–350; index) 12€ (same lectures as *Social Future*, CW 332a, edited by Archiatti) [ex libris JHanel].

Steiner, Rudolf (1919i English 4Oct19) *Social Understanding Through Spiritual Scientific Knowledge.* Trans: unknown. 1 lecture, Dornach, 4 Oct 1919, GA 191. Anthroposophic Press, New York. 20 pp. ISBN 0 88010–075–3.

Steiner, Rudolf (1919j = GA 331) *Betriebsräte und Sozialisierung -- Diskussionsabende mit den Arbeiterausschüssen der großen Betriebe Stuttgarts*, 1919, 1. Aufl. 1989, GA-Nr. 331. Dornach, Switzerland: Rudolf Steiner Verlag; 320 pp. €41.--

Steiner, Rudolf (1919k = GA 192) *Geisteswissenschaftliche Behandlung sozialer und Pädagogischer Fragen.* 17 Vorträge, gehalten in Stuttgart zwischen dem 21. April und 28. September 1919, darunter 'Drei Vorträge über Volkspädagogigk') GA-Nr. 192. Dornach, Switzerland: Rudolf Steiner Verlag, 1991; 320 pp. [ex libris Jhanel] (1964[1])

Steiner, Rudolf (1919l = 25. April 1919 or audio) *Mut zur Freiheit und zur sozialen Gerechtigkeit.* Ein Vortrag vor Arbeitern der Dailmer-Werke. Gehalten in Stuttgart am 25. April 1919. Bad Liebenzell: Archiati Verlag, 54 p. or running time (Gesamtlaufzeit) ca. 96 min.

Steiner, Rudolf (1919m = 26. May – 30 December 1919) *Gedankenfreiheit und soziale Kräfte. Die sozialen Forderungen der Gegenwart und ihre praktische Verwirklichung.* Sechs öffentliche Vorträge, mit einem Schlußwort, gehalten zwischen dem 26. Mai und 30. Dezember 1919 in Ulm, Berlin und Stuttgart. Dornach, Switzerland: Rudolf Steiner Verlag, 1986; 185 pp. (GA 333) [ex libris Albert Hanel]

Steiner, Rudolf (1919–1920 GA 24) *In Ausführung der Dreigliederung des sozialen Organismus.* Stuttgart 1920. This collection of articles from the periodical *Dreigliederung des sozialen Organismus* is reprinted on pp 11–126 in Steiner 1919–22.

English *The Renewal of the Social Organism.* 24 essays written during 1919 and 1920. (GA 24) Translated by E. Bowen-Wedgewood and Ruth Mariott. New York: SteinerBooks, Anthroposophic Press, 1985; 174 pp. $10.95; ISBN: 9780880101257

Norwegian *De tre funksjoner og systemer - i den Sosiale Organisme og deres Livsbetingelser*, Bergen: Forlaget DE TRE FUNKSJONER A/S, 1968, printed as articles in the weekly «Dreigliederung des sozialen Organismus», Stuttgart, 1919/1920

Steiner, Rudolf (1919/20 GA 337a Stgt) *Soziale Ideen - Soziale Wirklichkeit - Soziale Praxis. Frage- und Studienabende des Bundes für Dreigliederung des sozialen Organismus in Stuttgart, 1919/1920* [Volume 1] Dornach: Rudolf Steiner Verlag; 416 pp. 14 S. Faks. v. Notizbucheintr. (ISBN: 978–3–7274–3371–9) € 47,50 – GA 337b Schweiz) *Soziale Ideen – Soziale Wirklichkeit – Soziale Praxis. Diskussionsabende des Schweizer Bundes für Dreigliederung des sozialen Organismus sowie Seminar- und Frageabende zur Dreigliederung im Zusammenhang mit wissenschaftlichen Fachkursen, Dornach 1920/21.* [Volume 2] Dornach: Rudolf Steiner Verlag; 365 pp. 8 pp. Faks. v. Notizbucheintr. €43

Steiner, Rudolf (1919–20b CW 34) *Anthroposophy and the Social Question.* Three articles (from GA 34). New York: Mercury Press, 1982. ISBN 0–936132–42–6.

Steiner, Rudolf (1919–21) *Staatspolitik und Menschheitspolitik.* Aufsätze über die Dreigliederung des sozialen Organismus 1919–1921. Dornach: Rudolf Steiner Verlag; 217 pp. (ISBN:978–3–7274–6670–0).

Steiner, Rudolf (1920 GA 334) *Vom Einheitsstaat zum dreigliedrigen sozialen Organismus.* 11 öffentliche Vorträge, Basel, Zürich und Dornach 1920. R. Steiner Gesamtausgabe GA 334, Dornach: Rudolf Steiner Verlag; 312 pp. Cloth, 978–3–7274–3340–5; EUR 41.00.

Steiner, Rudolf (1920a English) *Social Issues, Meditative Thinking and the Threefold Social Order.* 11 lectures, various cities, Jan 5 - May 6 1920. Anthroposophic Press, New York. 200 pp. ISBN 0–88010–359–0 h/b, 0–88010–358–2 p/b.

Steiner, Rudolf (1920b) *Füreinander in Freiheit. Im Spannungsfeld zwischen Individuum und Gemeinschaft.* Bad Liebenzell: Archiati Verlag; 106 pp. ISBN:978–3–938650–48–6. 8€ bound.

Steiner, Rudolf (1920c English) *Spiritual Science as a Foundation for Social Forms.* 18 lectures, Dornach 6–29 Aug. 3–11 Sept, Berlin 17 and 18 Sept 1920, GA 199. Trans: M. St Goar, ed. A. Howard. Anthroposophic Press, New York. 309 pp. ISBN 0 85440 045 1 h/b, 085440–035 4.

Steiner, Rudolf (1920d) *Fragen der Seele und Fragen des Lebens. Wer darf gegen den Untergang des Abendlandes reden? Die großen Aufgaben von heute im Geistesleben, Rechtsleben und Wirtschaftsleben.* Drei Gegenwartsreden gehalten in Stuttgart am 15. Juni, 29. Juli und 20. September. Dornach/Schweiz: Im Selbstverlag der Rudolf Steiner – Nachlassverwaltung, 1952; 100 pp. (edited by Dr. Hans Erhard Lauer) [ex libris JHanel].

Steiner, Rudolf (1921 Oslo 30 Nov.) *Die Kardinalfrage des Wirtschaftslebens.* Dornach/Schweiz: Rudolf Steiner Verlag, 1984²; 48 pp. (also in Steiner 1921a = GA 79).

Steiner, Rudolf (1921a = GA79) *Die Wirklichkeit der höheren Welten.* Dornach/Schweiz: Rudolf Steiner Verlag, 1988²; 288 pp. (contains Steiner 1921).

Steiner, Rudolf (1921 audio) *Mit dem Mut der Liebe zu einer Wirtschaft der freien Menschen.* Bad Liebenzell: Archiati Verlag; 53 pp. or 78Min. (ISBN:978–3–938650–42–4) running time 78 Min.

Steiner, Rudolf (1922 = GA 340–1) *Nationalökonomischer Kurs*. Vierzehn Vorträge, gehalten in Dornach vom 24. Juli bis 6. August 1922 für Studenten der Nationalökonomie. *Nationalökonomisches Seminar.* Sechs Besprechungen mit den Teilnehmern am Nationalökonomischen Kurs in Dornach vom 31. Juli bis 5. August 1922. Dornach/Schweiz: Rudolf Steiner Verlag, 1996; 335 pp. GA 340 and 341 (first published in Dornach (Schweiz) by Anthropos. Verlag) in 1933. English: World Economy = WE (Aufgaben einer neuen Wirtschaftswissenschaft) [ex libris JHanel]

English: *World Economy – The Formation of a Science of World Economics*. 14 lectures, Dornach, 24 July - 6 August 1922. Trans: A. O. Barfield. T. G. Jones. GA 340. London: Rudolf Steiner Press, 1972. ISBN 0–85440–266–7 p/b. – First English Edition 1936/37, Second (revised) Edition 1949, Third Edition (clothbound and paperback) 1972. Translated from shorthand reports unrevised by the lecturer. The original texts of the lectures were published in German under the title *Nationalökonomischer Kurs*. (No. 340 in the Bibliographical Survey, 1961, of the *Complete Edition* of the works of Rudolf Steiner.)"

Norwegian: Steiner, Rudolf (1922) *Samfundsøkonomi*, Oslo: Private printing, 1975, translated from the original in German: *National-ökonomischer Kurs*

Steiner, Rudolf (1922a = GA 341) *Nationalökonomisches Seminar.* Sechs Besprechungen mit den Teilnehmern am Nationalökonomischen Kurs in Dornach vom 31. Juli bis 5. August 1922. Dornach/Schweiz: Rudolf Steiner Verlag, 1973; 110 pp. GA 341 (edited by Folkert Wilken and Wolfram Groddeck) [ex libris JHanel].

Steiner, Rudolf (1922b) *Der große soziale Reformator*. Wie Steiner in England über den 'Christus' spricht. Ein Vortrag gehalten in London am 18. November 1922. Bad Liebenzell: Archiati Verlag; 40p. Heft Nr. 46: Ein Geschenk für Menschen, die innere Selbständigkeit suchen. [ex libris JHanel].

Steiner, Rudolf (1924, 1 March - 25 June) *Die Geschichte der Menschheit und die Weltanschauungen der Kulturvölker.* 17 Vorträge, gehalten für die Arbeiter am Goetheanumbau in Dornach vom 1. März bis 25. Juni 1924. Dornach/Schweiz: Rudolf Steiner Verlag, 1992; 335 (GA 353; Rudolf Steiner Taschenbücher aus dem Gesamtwerk; #727) [ex libris Bäumler].

Steiner, Rudolf (1925) *Mein Lebensgang*. Stuttgart: Freies Geistesleben, 1967; 357 p. (Rudolf Steiner Taschenbuch-Ausgaben; 13).

Englisch: *The Story of my Life*. Complete works = GA 28. London: The Anthroposophical Publishing Company, 1928; since 1999 in http://wn.rsarchive.org/Books/GA028/TSoML/GA028_index.html. The German original is in http://www.anthroposophie.net/steiner/Lebensgang/bib_steiner_lebensgang3.htm#Geistwelt

The Utopian Element in the Formation of Doctrines on the State in German "Staatswissenschaft"

Karl-Heinz Schmidt

The Problem: Utopia or Models of the State?

The term "utopia," translated as "nowhere," is to designate ethical–practical–political ways of thinking (Diehl 1926, 578 f). It is applied in European literature and sciences since the sixteenth century (Thomas Morus 1516). In its antique and classical form, utopia should expose a well-functioning social order based on the principle of justice (Baloglou 2009). But, such order is not found in reality; therefore, utopia is used as a normative term, to think and identify an organizational form of life, which can be applied to evaluate the concrete performance of social life. This is the static or vertical type of utopia (Table 1).

In contrast to it, a dynamic or horizontal type of utopia may be distinguished. It is understood to expose the result of a long-term process of social development, the process of realization of the targeted order of society. Consequently, not only the aims but also the instruments and means to realize the aims are highly important. Dynamic utopias are to identify the adequate ways and means to progress from a given social order to the utopian "better" form of the state and social life (Pieper 1989, Sp. 578).

In economic and social sciences, yet, models of the state and of public policies are widely applied. The models are based on specific assumptions and functional relations of variables. They may be of static or dynamic character, and they are formulated in mathematical terms – at a growing extent. Instead, Utopia are exposed in verbal terms, and they are of normative character more often than models of the state. The problem therefore is to distinguish long-term models and dynamic utopia of the state. Some examples of investigations on the state in different economic systems will be pointed out in the following paragraphs (Table 2).

K.-H. Schmidt (✉)
University of Paderborn, Faculty of Economics, Paderborn, Germany
e-mail: Karl-Heinz_Schmidt@notes.uni-paderborn.de

J.G. Backhaus (ed.), *The State as Utopia: Continental Approaches*, The European Heritage in Economics and the Social Sciences 9, DOI 10.1007/978-1-4419-7500-3_13,

Table 1 Definitions of "Utopia"

a) Literary definition of "Utopia":	
Utopia =	Writings, by which the authors expose the preferred future status of a society, demonstrated by a state written in poetry.
(Diehl, K.: Art. Sozialismus und Kommunismus, HdSt,VII, 1926, 578 – 612, esp. 586)	
Former Exemples:	Platon: Kritias oder Athen und Atlantis Thomas Morus, 1516 Campanella: Civitas solis, 1602 Harrington: Oceana, 1656 Vairasse d'Allais: Histoire des Sévarambes, 1677/79 F. Bacon: NovaAtlantis, 1683
b) Modern Definition:	
Utopia =	Design for a complete order of the society, based on justice and focused on a critical program contrasting to the existing society and to be applied to correct the status and development of the society.
(Pieper, A.: Art. Utopie, Staatslexikon 5/1989, Sp.576– 580, esp. 577)	
c) General definition (Pieper, A., 1989, 577):	
Utopia =	normative term with an ethicalpractical intention, by which a form of life is exposed as a comparative measure (Maßstabfunktion).

Guidelines and Definitions

Starting from the translation of "utopia" as "nowhere," two guidelines of interpreting this term may be exposed: one following the static character and another following the dynamic character of "utopia."

The static utopia demonstrates a form of social life that is understood to function as a measure to calculate the divergence between the existing real society and a virtual society.

The dynamic utopia concerns the process of development from the existing to the projected future society. This type of utopia may be recognized in the writings of Karl Marx and Friedrich Engels (Pieper 1989, Sp. 578).

Further guidelines of this article should be recognized in the assumed structure and long-term development of property rights, especially of private property, and of

Table 2 Types of "Utopia"

"Utopia"

Static utopia:	Dynamic utopia
Exposed form of life functioning as comparative measure ("nowhere") = vertical utopia (basic model: Platon's "State": up-and-down-movement of social groups; also: Campanella's "Civitas solis").	(Time-oriented u.) = horizontal utopia ("anytime"); not to be applied as comparative measure, but as result of a process of social development focussing on the final objective, the realized utopia.
↓	↓
Emphasis on the imagination of a new society, not burdened by any tradition or convention.	Emphasis on the measures to transform the existing into the programmed society.
	↓
	Critical time utopia (Anti-utopia)

Dystopia:	Eutopia:
frightening visions of the final phase of technical society. A technical society was already exposed by F. Bacon (1638): technical apparatus are developed by monchs to repeat the divine creation of the world.	positive (idealistic) exposition of the process to a future society.

Source: See Pieper, A., 1989, 557 f.

the state. The development of the society is split in two paths: either towards the end of private property or towards a combination of private property and public property. While the end of private property means the performance of a social order on the grounds of collective property, the combination of private and public property covers different structures of private, cooperative, and public property. The role of the state also differs according to the structure and development of the property rights. For example, Marx and Engels tried to demonstrate that the end of private property will mean that the state will become superfluous and will be substituted by a well-functioning society of free individuals (Pieper 1989, Sp. 578).

The criticism of Marxian utopia brought about different types of anti-utopia, demonstrating the impossibility to separate a normative demand (for a better social order) from the empirical prognosis and complaining about a deficit of ethics, which is not focused on a perfect, but on a sufficiently functioning ("erträgliche") order of social life (Pieper 1989, Sp. 578).

Another type of criticism is designated as "dystopia"; it aims at demonstrating frightening visions of hell, to be expected as the final stage of a highly technological society, the members of which are manipulated to make them function as automata. An early example of this type of critical utopia may be acknowledged in Francis Bacon's Work on "Nova Atlantis" (1638); it concerns a state, which is governed by friars (Ordensbrüder) acting as scientists simultaneously to research on nature by application of sophisticated technological apparatus. Therefore, Bacon was even called a forerunner of science–fiction–literature. As examples of anti-utopia from modern time may be mentioned George Orwell's famous books "Nineteen-eighty-four" (1949) and "Animal Farm."

Summarizing, all types of utopia turn out to be focused on two functions: (1) to expose social criticism, (2) to demonstrate an ethical purpose of politics. Thus, the state is included in the institutional framework of the existing and the future society being designed by the specific type of utopia (Pieper 1989, S. 579 f; Erzgräber 1980; Manuel and Manuel 1979).

Utopian Ideas in the Concepts of the State in German "Staatswissenschaft"

From Feudalism to Individualism

The "State" as a national unit has been organized during a long-term process of social and economic development. The European national states resulted from the activities of absolute sovereigns, including cultivation of land and economic development of the countries. To realize their aims, they needed human beings and money (Table 3). Human labour was demanded to have the land cultivated and settlements being founded. Money was needed, because official clerks, administrators, and soldiers could no more be salaried by lending agricultural ground, but by paying them in monetary terms. Therefore, the former feudal armies had to be substituted by armies of salaried soldiers and later by national armies. The sovereigns and their political chancellors aimed at both pillars of political power: growth of the population and growth of monetary fiscal revenues. The idea of the performance of public power was based on three basic assumptions: (1) Human actions, focused on human interests, in individual and in political life; individual interests are assumed to be orientated to the satisfaction of private wants and needs, political interests to be focused on privileges and political power. (2) The interests in political and social

Table 3 From Feudalism to Industrialism

Absolute Sovereign

↓

Performance of public power

based on

↙ ↓ ↘

Human actions (Population)

Conflicting interests; harmony of interests by a strong state

Mechanical-materialistic view of the state: power by public revenues and disposal on resources

Conclusion of German Cameralists:

(Caspar Klock, 1583– 1655;

Johann Joachim Becher, 1625 – 1682)

The power of the state is based on the treasure of the state

↓

The utopian aspect of the concept of the state:

Idea of the enlighted Sovereign:

Objectives (Interests)

↙ ↘

Increase of the well-being of "his" people in "his" state

Increase of the power of "his" state

↙ ↘

to levy higher taxes

to finance bureaucracy, court and wars

life are assumed to be conflicting, but external political pressure tends to increase the harmony of interests inside a country; therefore, a strong state is demanded. (3) A vision of history following from a mechanical–materialistic view: the state is understood to govern other people the more intensively, the more power and external commodities are at disposal of the state.

Following from these basic assumptions, it becomes clear why sovereigns and bureaucrats of the late absolutism were strictly interested to increase the public revenues and to accumulate public wealth: to strengthen the performance of the state, to organize the military force, and to stabilize the economy (Schäfer 1987, 276 f). The power of the state is based on the treasure of state. This was the core information of German Cameralists of the sixteenth and seventeenth century, for example of Caspar Klock (1583–1655) and Johann Joachim Becher (1625–1682). Fritz Karl Mann pointed out these determinant factors of political power at the stage of late absolutism and early industrialism in his earlier study on the ideals of tax policy (Mann 1937, 2–7).

The utopian aspect of the related concept of the state becomes apparent in the idea of the sovereign interested to increase the well being of "his" people in "his" state. Political economy revealed the underlying basic interests of the sovereign and of "his" administrating bureaucrats: the German cameralist Capspar Klock exposed a principle of limited rights of the state to levy burdensome taxes from the citizens and to demand the right of the citizens to deny the payment of the taxes (Mann 1937, 123; Tautscher 1956, 463, 466). Also, other cameralists of the eighteenth century pointed out limits of the public taxation and expenditures, f.e. Wilhelm Freiherr von Schröder (1721). In fact, the former basic idea of the absolute sovereign was set out to rational criticism. The demand of the people for reduced taxes and less expenditure by the sovereign and the administration of the state was increased and sustained by liberal ideas. The sovereign was no more accepted as the "absolute" ruler, based on transcendental power. The economic development towards industrialism intensified the demand for individual freedom and private property.

The "State" in the Concepts of Natural and Positive Order

During the eighteenth century, the views of mercantilistic authors on the interrelations between "State" and economy were undermined by the criticism of the state by authors of political economy in European countries. Their writings were focused on the effects of the division of labour and of technological change, on the functions of market prices and on the effects of taxes and expenditures carried out by the princes and bureaucrats.

An early author of the transition from mercantilism to new ideas on economic systems was the German Ernst Ludwig Carl (1682–1743). His basic publication, «Traité de la richesse des princes et de leurs états ...» (1722/23) was based on three central ideas on the impact of the state: (1) the idea of "natural order" of the society: the state is imagined to be part of the "natural order"; (2) the idea of the "active state", setting up a legislation focused on the harmony of the economic interests in the society. Both ideas considered (3) the idea, which gained increasing importance in the eighteenth century, mainly in France: the idea of "Physiocracy": agriculture was taken to be the most productive sector of the economy (Table 4). But how did

Table 4 Physiocratic system and the State

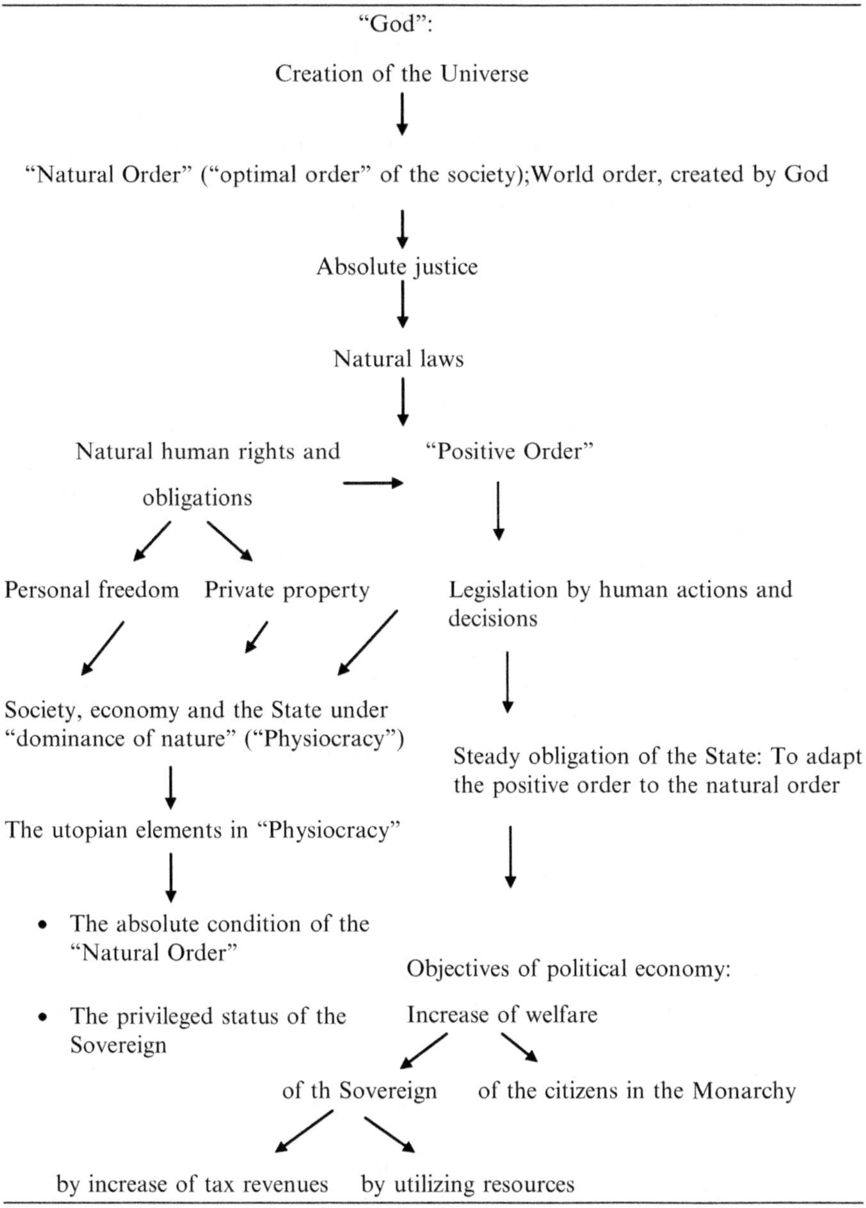

the "natural order" come about? According to François Quesnay (1694–1774), the concept of natural rights would determine that continuously valid, optimal laws are the basis of all social facts and development. The society only needs to follow the "natural laws," because they were understood to be created by God, when God created the Universe. The laws instead set up by human legislation form the "positive order," the impact of which was understood to realize the general principles of the "natural order." According to these principles, the "natural order" is valid for all social phenomena, including the production of commodities and the supply of services (Stavenhagen 1969, 36).

The utopian element in the physiocratic concept of the State conclusively was connected with the creation of the Universe by God. Therefore, the "natural order" was qualified as the "best order," and the "positive order" was understood to adapt the legislation to the criteria of the "natural order" (Stavenhagen 1969, 36).

Romantic "Staatswissenschaft"

The term "Romantic Staatswissenschaft" focuses on the views and writings of authors of the German Romantic School on problems of social policy and political economy. According to a related article by Jakob Baxa, the time period of the Romantic Staatswissenschaft dated from 1794 to 1830 (Baxa 1926, 117–119). As younger persons, the concerned authors, like Fichte, Friedrich Schlegel, Ludwig Tieck, and Josef Görres, celebrated the French Revolution as great political action of liberalization. They were convinced that the new political movement would abolish the barriers of nations and realize eternal peace following the ideas of Jean Jacques Rousseau and Immanuel Kant. The German authors of Romanticism therefore were orientated politically to be strictly republican. In economic perspectives, they were adherents of Adam Smith and classic economics. But the underlying philosophy of natural rights of the individual and of the concept of individualism became object of their criticism, at first by the philosopher Fichte. In his work on the "Basics of Natural Rights according to the Principles of Science" (Wissenschaftslehre) (1796/97), he focused on the term "Gemeinschaft" as basic fact of life and culture. He concluded that natural rights were contradictory to reality. Instead of the theory of contracts, the "State" should be recognized as an a priori existing totality ("ein von vornherein gegebenes Ganzes"; Baxa 1926, 118). Fichte compared the "State" with an "organized natural product." This was called the period of "Pre-Romanticism" (Baxa 1926, 118). The later periods were described as "Early Romanticism" (Table 5) and "Late Romanticism." German philosophers tried to develop a "pantheistic" system based on the principle of unity, intellectuality and divinity of reality. Conclusively, they did no more follow the principles of enlightenment. Fichte and his disciple Schelling aimed at the resurrection of antique natural philosophy. Especially, Schelling strived for his "concept of organism": society, state, and economy should be conceptualized as one unity. Schelling's natural philosophy influenced the romanticism in literature (Friedrich Schlegel, August Wilhelm Schlegel, Novalis) and the romanticism in "Staatswissenschaft," to which mainly Adam Müller's book on "Elements of the arts to govern a State" ("Elemente der Staatskunst") contributed by publication in 1809. According to this German–Austrian author's concept, the state and the economy turned out as a vivid organism, structured by estates and guilds. The German author of literary romanticism Novalis Friedrich

Table 5 Romantic "Staatswissenschaft"

German Romantic School

in Literature — in academic disciplines and research

in Fine Arts — In Political Economy

Basic orientation: Opposition towards Enlightenment, individualism and classic economics (A. Smith)

Criticism of the philosophy of "natural rights" by German philosophers (Fichte);

The State as "organized natural product".

Three periods of Romanticism:

- Pre-Romanticism (Fichte a.o.)
- Early Romanticism (Pantheistic system)
- Late Romanticism (Theocracy)

In Staatswissenschaft: Adam Müller and Franz Baader (warning against poverty and social misery as effected by industrialism.

Opposition: Liberal authors took the warnings and recommendations (by Müller a.o.) as strange dreams of medieval ages.

Frhr. von Hardenberg (1772–1801) even projected a pattern of a political organism of Europe under the supremacy of hierarchy, but it was more of an idealistic imagination of the Middle Ages united by religion (Novalis: Die Christenheit oder Europa 1799). These authors, including the philosopher Fichte, poets like Friedrich Schlegel, and writers like Josef Görres, turned off the former identification with the French Revolution, and against liberalism and cosmopolism having been proclaimed by the German adherents of Adam Smith. The German authors instead aimed at proclaiming the "Nation" as basic unity and object of politics and political economy. This was the second period of "romantic Staatswissenschaft": the philosophical, pantheistic phase also designated as "Early Romanticism" (Baxa 1926, VI, 118).

After the wars against Napoleon in Europe, since 1815, political reforms, yet, were not oriented to the ideas of estates and guilds, but backwards to the principles of absolutism. The consequence was a diminishing influence of the German idealistic philosophy and increasing effects of catholic religion on culture and politics, also on German "Staatswissenschaft." The basic idea of estates and guilds as components of the organism "State" was kept up; society and economy were no more interpreted as "natural products"; instead, the religious ideas of the society, economy, and the "State" were taken as basic results of divine wisdom (Stiftungen der göttlichen Weisheit). Consequently, the whole pattern of "Staatswissenschaft" became based on theological dogma. The ideal of the "State" was exposed to be a system of theocracy. As for political economy, the former concept of balanced power of clerical and secular power – by the institutions of the "Pope" and the "Kaiser" – should be proclaimed. But in fact, a reduced influence of the church on politics was complained, and the increasing effects of capitalism and monetary affairs on the economy and society were heavily discussed and refused. Especially, authors like Adam Müller and Franz Baader warned against social misery and poverty affected by the industrial system. Liberal authors of political economy, yet, interpreted these warnings as reactionary tendencies, to which they were opposed. The political restauration of power in Europe, the "July-Revolution" of 1830, then decreased the influence of "Romanticism" in political economy. The "Spätromantik" as the third phase of romantic Staatswissenschaft came to its end. This last period was designated by catholic theological thinking. The main important effects of Romanticism in Staatswissenschaft may be recognized in emphasizing the idea of "Gemeinschaft" as basic social fact. Jakob Baxa put it in his informative article (Baxa 1926, VI, 117–119):

"Das Hauptverdienst der Romantik ruht in der Betonung des Gemeinschaftsgedankens als sozialer Grundtatsache; hiermit hat sie den Individualismus der Aufklärung überwunden und ist zum Ahnherrn einer deutschen Gesellschaftslehre (Soziologie) geworden. Wertvoll ist ferner ihre organische Staats- und Wirtschaftsauffassung und ihre Theorie des Volkstums" (Baxa 1926, 119)

Furthermore, Adam Müller's contributions to monetary policy and agricultural policy were evaluated as not to be disregarded, even in discussions on European political economy at the present time (Müller-Schmid 1987, Sp. 1235 f; Andreae 1961, 466).

The question for utopian elements in "Romantic Staatswissenschaft" may be answered by discussing the underlying concept of "organism" (Table 6). It covers the society, the economy, and the State. The logical deduction of the State apart from Enlightenment, but with reference to pantheistic ideas or – as during the phase of late romanticism, with reference to catholic religious thinking – remains open for interpretation and uncertain for future results. Therefore, the concept of "organism" turns out to contain basic utopian elements, and the romantic Staatswissenschaft to be of speculative character.

Even though, it should be acknowledged, that also authors of the late nineteenth and twentieth century referred to authors of "Romantic Staatswissenschaft." Bruno Hildebrand wrote a whole chapter on "Adam Müller and the national-economic romanticism" (1848, 1922), in which he pointed out "Müller's view of the State." Wilhelm Roscher published a study on "The romantic school in Germany" (1870). Othmar Spann in his works referred intensively to Adam Müller and to the romantic school of national economics, including forerunners and followers of Adam Müller: poets (f.e. Novalis), philosophers (f.e. Fichte), economists (f.e. Baader, and Bernhardi), and politicians (f.e. Bismarck).

Concerning the reasons for the State in Adam Müllers writings, Bruno Hildebrand pointed out that according to Adam Müller the "State" covered the "totality of human opportunities and finds its purpose in itself" (Hildebrand 1848, 36). Müller combined the antique structure of the State with German contents, as he

Table 6 Utopian elements in Romantic German "Staatswissenschaft"

- Idea of "Gemeinschaft" as basic social fact;
- Deficit of operational definition of "organism";
- Reference to pantheistic ideas or to religious thinking open for different interpretation;
- Speculative character of the doctrines;
- Critics of Romantic Staatswissenschaft:
  - Bruno Hildebrand's statements and evaluation of Adam Müller's works;
  - Wilhelm Roscher's comments on the "Romantic School";
  - Othmar Spann's interpretation of Adam Müller's works and of the "Romantic School" of national economics.
- Conclusion:
  Utopian elements of Staatswissenschaft can bring about positive and negative effects on the development of economic and social sciences and on political economy.

deducted the State from "freedom" according to principles of the former Germans: the permanent conflict of individual concerns of freedom carried out via the different levels of corporations and estates – as in the medieval feudal state – brought about the "organic nature product," the "State" realizing freedom and peace for all members. Hildebrand, yet, criticized Müller's view of the State, especially the assumed status of the individual, functioning only as part of the State, as a "vessel for general ideas," disregarding the fact that the individual simultaneously acts as a self-conscious person in an independent environment. Second, Hildebrand criticized Müller's deduction of the State combining the antique idea of the State with the structure of the former German states and with the medieval feudal states. The medieval state, which Müller described to have existed, did not exist, as Hildebrand emphasized. He pointed out, that Müller's deduction of the State was burdened with contradictions and was missing reliable historical knowledge and facts. Hildebrand concluded: Müller's approach to investigate the development of the State was a subjective and unhistorical idealization of a specific time period, being separated arbitrarily from the long-term history of states.

To summarize, Adam Müller's view of the State turns out to be based on utopian elements for two reasons: (1) a speculative definition and contradicting deduction of the State, and (2) an unhistorical and speculative idealization of the State as an "organic nature product" (Hildebrand 1848, 1922, 42 f)

Early Socialists and the State

The French Revolution of 1789 brought about social and political movements in France and in other European countries. In Germany the ideas of the French Revolution and of the philosophy of enlightenment accelerated the criticism of traditional political ideas and institutions. Freedom of the individual and effective measures against social poverty was demanded by political leaders representing the underprivileged classes of the population. Authors of early socialism sustained the demand for reforms of the political system. The demand for reforms included effective measures against poverty, the reduction of taxes to be paid by the lower classes, and measures in favour of the establishment of new firms, new workplaces, and higher incomes. Changes of the economic system, yet, were expressively demanded in France. Premarxist or early socialist authors demanded, mainly in France, to design new ideas and patterns of an intended ideal society. The authors aimed at the comparison of these patterns with the existing society, which they had criticized. But authors who were focused on changes of the economic system did not take the proposed patterns seriously. They even called the patterns "enjoyable fantasies," because the economic conditions for revolutionary actions were not exposed.

As for Germany, two authors may be emphasized as representatives of early socialism: Wilhelm Weitling (1808–1871) and Moses Hess (1812–1875). Their ideas were influenced by French authors of early socialism, f.e. by Fourier, Babeuf, Saint Simon, and Proudhon (Dobias 2002, 107). Marxist authors instead criticized these authors as writers on "utopian socialism" because they argued that the conditions for a change of the economic system were not yet fulfilled at that time. This argument is also valid for the evaluation of the State in the ideas of the early socialists. The crucial statement pointed out that the State in their view of "utopian socialism" will organize central planning and guidance (in France: Babeuf; in Germany: Weitling) or fade away (in France: Saint-Simon, Fourier; in Germany: Moses Hess). Conclusively, the remaining functions of the State differ in the patterns for "utopian socialism." The State as an institution of the society turns out to be utopian as far as the conditions of the change of the economic system are concerned.

Some other German authors, who considered the functions of the State in a new social and economic system, are registered also as authors of the transition from early to scientific socialism. This fact concerns von Rodbertus-Jagetzow (1805–1875) and Ferdinand Lassalle (1825–1864). Both authors are described to have prepared the ground for "State-Socialism."

"Scientific Socialists" and the State

The term "Scientific Socialism" should point out the impact of theoretical ideas and empirical analyses of the investigated economic system. But in history of economic thought the term covers on one hand, conservative authors like Johann Karl Rodbertus-Jagetzow (1805–1875) and on the other, socialist authors, mainly Karl Marx (1818–1883) and Friedrich Engels (1820–1895). Without considering the total concept of the related investigations of the capitalistic system and its social and economic development, the statements of these authors concerning the functions and long-term development of the State should be taken into account, to contribute to the discussion (again), if utopian elements are underlying their analyses of the State under the conditions of the capitalistic system.

Rodbertus may be considered as one of the early representatives of scientific socialism (Stavenhagen 4/1969, 138). He argued that the private property of land and capital should be transferred to the State. This change of the property rights should be realized in peaceful ways, not short term. During this long-term process, the State should carry out diverse measures to bring about an increasing rate of economic growth and an increasing share of labour at GNP. The needed measures should be: regulations of wages, working times (a regular workday), and of the volume of work to be carried out during the working time. The wage-rates should be increased according to the increase of labour productivity. Following this strategy, Rodbertus believed to overcome the instability of the capitalistic system and to realize the economy of the State without private property on land and capital. In the long run, "State Socialism" as the highest level of social development was foreseen by Rodbertus. He exposed his statements in writings on an organic theory of the society (Stavenhagen 4/1969, 141). Rodbertus has also been considered to have been one of the early theorists, who took into account the impact of social institutions on the economic development effecting from the legal framework and historical changes of institutions (Stavenhagen 4/1969, 142).

The statements of Karl Marx and Friedrich Engels concerned the long-term development of the society and economy towards a socialist society but with decreasing functions of the State. The socialist society will substitute the former capitalistic society. Yet, is it a utopian objective? It seems that the concept includes utopian elements as to the realization of the future society (political forces to introduce the new system). Moreover, the economic development of the existing system must have approached a phase near to breakdown, to ensure political actions to be carried out successfully. This idea was also a strong argument against Wilhelm Weitling during his discussion with Marx and Engels on the time schedule for the social revolution (Ramm 11/1961, 603 f).

"State-Socialism"

Contrasting to adherents of early and scientific socialism several German authors, who demanded effective measures "to solve the Social Question" not by social revolution, but by peaceful strategies of public policy, visualized the state "… as an engine of social progress" (Spiegel 1983, 453). Two politically orientated scholars should be exposed to show their different career and long-term aims, but similar concepts of practical policies against poverty and social instability: Karl Rodbertus-Jagetzow (1805–1875) and Adolph Wagner (1835–1917). Although they were of different origin and experienced a different professional career, they had some basic ideas about targets and needed political measures in common. Both persons have been designated as "State-Socialists," and both were authors of widely acknowledged publications on the role of the State in the capitalist system, given the constitution of a monarchy. Rodbertus was exposed also as "Scientific Socialist," but he is registered furthermore in history of economic thought and in Sciences of the State as "State Socialist" (Diehl 1926, 103 f). To point out utopian elements in their publications, the basic views of both authors will be considered.

Karl Rodbertus-Jagetzow grew up in a family of leading academics. He studied law in Göttingen and Berlin, was appointed in Prussian public administration, but retired after a few years as a young man, to turn to own studies of political economy. He became aware of increasing social conflicts, which in his view would necessarily come about by the development of the capitalistic system. Moreover, Rodbertus was afraid that the cultural level of Western mankind would be endangered to stagnate (Wendt 1956, 21). As a consequence, he decided to buy a larger farm (Jagetzow), where he settled and worked as a successful agricultural entrepreneur. But the agricultural colleagues soon motivated him to represent them as a member of the Prussian National Parliament (Gide, Ch. und Rist, Ch., 1923, 458 f). In his writings and publications, Rodbertus expressed his ideas about the role of the state concerning the solution of the social conflicts and the economic development (Diehl 1926, 597 f). To avoid poverty and economic crises, in his terms to compensate the negative effects of the "law of the decreasing share of wages" (in relation to GNP) (Wendt 1956, 22), the State should influence the wages on the grounds of exact calculations of the share of wages in every kind of product. The workers should receive the (increased) wages as "labor-money" to be paid in terms of paper-money ("Zettelgeld") instead of metal coins (Wendt 1956, 23). The payments of "labor-money" should be calculated according to the time–budget of a "normal workday" to be fixed by the State for every industry. The fixed wage-rates should be modified and changed according to the increase of labour productivity in the diverse industries (Gide, Ch. und Rist, Ch., 1923, 459 f). Rodbertus believed that the state could contribute to increase the share of wages and the share of labour in the property of land and capital with the consequence that poverty and economic crises of the capitalistic system would be decreased in the long run, and even avoided, when the steady change of property rights would transfer the capitalistic system into a "state economy without property of land and capital" (Stavenhagen 1969, 141 f; Diehl 1926, 578–612, esp. 598). The author believed that, in future, after about 500 years, a social order of communism may be realized. At his time and in the near future, only a compromise of the present and future socialistic order seemed to be possible. This long-term reorganization of the economic and social order would take time, but it could be carried out in shorter time than by the development of the capitalistic system without the strategy of "State Socialism." Rodbertus also had in mind to avoid the short-term breakdown of the capitalistic system by social revolution. He preferred the peaceful way of steady development towards the realization of the ideal of State Socialism (Stavenhagen 1969, 142 f).

The second considered author, Adolph Wagner (1835–1917), colleague of Gustav Schmoller as professor of the University in Berlin, entitled himself a "State-Socialist" in his publications on public finance and on "State Socialism" (Spiegel 1983, 426), especially when he answered the German Scholar Lorenz vom Stein by a special study (Wagner 1887, 3 f, 13 ff.). As an academic scholar, a Member of Parliament, and politician, he focused on the problems of social justice and stability of the economic system. He was known as a representative of Christian and social ideas, criticizing Capitalism and Marxism but demanding intensively a social performance of taxation and of political institutions (Heilmann 1980, 19 ff.; Stucken 1961, 471). Already in his textbook on general or theoretical economics (1879), Wagner had emphasized the economic potential of the State (Wagner 1879, 922, 94) and the long-term trend of the State to expand public activities, summarized as the "law of growing extension of the public and especially of the State-activities," also formulated as "law of growing public needs of the State and of the institutions of public administration" (Wagner 1879, 311). On the grounds of this former theoretical explanation of the long-term development of the State performance, Wagner exposed his version of a program of "State-Socialism" in his study on "Public finance and State Socialism," an answer to publications on public finance by Lorenz vom Stein und Wilhelm Roscher. Wagner's program (Heilmann 1980, 25–28) concerned several points which let conclude that Wagner intended to combine his ideal of a "social epoch" with advice to introduce measures of social policy and redistribution of incomes, to stabilize the existing Constitution of the State and the long-term economic and social development. The author mainly demanded: efficient allocation of economic resources; participation of the majority of the population, esp. the working classes, in the material results of the growth of resources; regulations focusing on the activities of public administration concerning the increase of mental, economic and social welfare of the population; transfer of an increased share of national income into the public budgets; transfer of private monopolies to public and social organization; furthermore, a concept of "social tax policy" (Wagner 1887, 4 f, 42–46).

The main important difference to Rodbertus' concept of "State-Socialism" is exposed by the statements focusing on the future structure of property rights and the long-term development of the State: Wagner wants to redistribute incomes but also to stabilize the monarchy based on the existing Constitution (Prisching 1997, 183 f). Rodbertus demands to change the distribution of incomes to reduce incomes in terms of interest, profit, and rent, focusing on the change of the economic and social order towards a socialist system. As mentioned above, he even was proclaimed to have been the first representative of the idea of State-Socialism and to have pointed out the alternatives of economic and social systems on behalf of the legal–historical character of social institutions (Stavenhagen 1969, 142).

Conclusively, both considered authors referred to utopian elements in their versions of State-Socialism, though Wagner's concept is orientated to the Constitution of the State, which existed in Germany at his time, whereas Robertus' concept in the long run was focused on the change of the economic and social system. Furthermore, the theoretical reasoning of Rodbertus' concept of income- (re-) distribution depends on the effects of measures to be introduced by the State on the incentives of capital owners and land owners to continue savings and investment. The related assumptions and statements are discussed continuously, if they are of utopian character.

Liberalism and the State

The basic idea of "Liberalism" came up during the Age of enlightenment. It was exposed as belief in the validity of human rationality and free, unrestricted actions (Boelcke 1988, 32–47). Three forms of freedom were based on the idea of "reasonable optimism": free individual thinking, free political actions and relation of the individual to the state and free economic activities (economic freedom). At the end of the eighteenth century, the writings of the French "Physiocrats" and Adam Smith's books on the "Theory of Moral Sentiments" (1759) and the "Wealth of Nations" (1776) explained the basic principles of a liberal economic, social, and political order. The essence of "Economic Liberalism" was proclaimed by demand for autonomy of the individual, free performance of individual decisions – corresponding to the idea of "prestable harmony" ("prästabilierte Harmonie"), and for institutions and legislation to guarantee an optimum of allocation of resources and social justice of the distribution of incomes and wealth. These principles were at first documented by the Constitution of the new republics after the "war of Independence" in North America 1776 and by the new Constitution after the French Revolution 1789. On the European Continent, the principles of Liberalism and the distinction between "Economic Liberalism" and "Political Liberalism" were proclaimed in the Netherlands, France, and Prussia. Although in France and Prussia a "neoabsolutistic system" was followed at the beginning of the nineteenth century, the practiced economic reform policy was orientated to "Economic Liberalism" (Gall 1987. 917 f). Both performances were also exposed by the movement of "National Liberalism." This concept, yet, brought about liberal nationalism and after the World War I the breakdown of "Liberalism" by the empowerment of "Nationalsocialism" (Gall 1987, 918).

Already since the late nineteenth century, attempts were made to develop and proclaim a concept of "New Liberalism," which should be distinguished from the former "Old Liberalism" (Hayek 1959, 591–595, esp. 594 f). But since the political breakdown after the World War II, the neoliberal movement brought about in Germany the concept of "Ordoliberalism," elaborated and proclaimed mainly by scholars of economics, law, history, and social sciences and by related politicians. Walter Eucken became the prominent leader of the "Freiburg School" (Boelcke 1988, 45 f). The concept of "Ordoliberalism" should be understood as a pattern of competitive economy in contrast to the centrally administered economy, especially of collectivist and state-monopolistic determination (Boelcke 1988, 45). Concerning the role of the state in the patterns of "Old" and "New" Liberalism, it is necessary to consider furthermore the distinction of "Economic" and "Political Liberalism." The pattern of "Ordoliberalism" then points out a form of "Economic Liberalism." Following "Old Economic Liberalism," the state should be restricted to legislation and public administration, as well as to financing specific public expenditures: education and schooling, infrastructure investment, and external security (military defence and warfare), as Adam Smith had demanded. The concept of "New Liberalism," even more strictly the pattern of German "Ordoliberalism," yet, foresaw that the state should be restricted to focus on constitutional principles (legislation and public administration) and regulating principles (Eucken 1952, 160 ff.). The power of the state was understood to be based on democracy, and the economy should be based on full competition. Permanent functions of the state were mainly to administer controls of monopolies and competition, interventions into the allocation of resources, especially for infrastructure investment, reduction of business cycles, redistribution of incomes, and organization of social security. Decisions on interventions by the state should be met according to the criteria of being conformable to the competitive market economy (Janssen 2009, 200).

Conclusively, the "State" according to "Ordoliberalism" is different from the "State" of former "Old" liberalism and from Anglosaxon "Neoliberalism" (Boelcke 1988, 45). The ordoliberal state shall be legitimated and empowered to determine, control, and invest in more sectors and processes of the economy than the former State of "Old" Liberalism and the coordinating and federalism – oriented state of "New" Liberalism. But historical experiences, theoretical criticism and the actual problems of economic and social policy strengthen the utopian character of "Ordoliberalism" more than the optimism to believe in the success of this concept.

Development Phases of the State

Three groups of authors of political economy in the nineteenth century were designated as "schools," though they also were summarized as the total "German Historical School" (GHS) in studies on the history of economic thought (Lifschitz 1914; Shionoya 2005, Introduction, IX f). The groups of authors, those "schools," were called "Old," "Younger," and "Youngest" German Historical School of Economics (GHS). The authors preferred inductive methods or combinations of inductive and deductive methods to investigate the long-term development of the economy and society on the national level or in specific regions (Shionoya 2005, 18). As the research concept of leading authors was opposed to classic economics, represented by Adam Smith a.o. authors, the studies of the GHS were focused on problems of empirical–historical research. They were based on specific collections of empirical data and historical studies on the long-term economic development. Herewith, the authors exposed their pattern of developmental stages of the economy and society, including the state and related institutions. Some examples may point out utopian elements of the underlying concept of research.

Referring to forerunners and to authors of the Old, Younger, and Youngest German Historical Schools (GHS), the patterns of stages of development can be investigated to point out utopia elements of the underlying concepts. For example, Friedrich List elaborated a series of stages of economic development from agricultural to manufacturing and further to commercial activities and culture. The author herewith intended to expose a general theory of economic development. The role of the state was orientated to specific measures of economic policy, to increase the productivity of economic resources and the growth rates of GNP. List mainly recommended external tariffs to be introduced during a distinct time period and to "educate" entrepreneurs to innovate and to invest at growing extent. The state instead was not expected to focus public policy on the redistribution of incomes and wealth. List's concept was based on the idea to increase the incomes of lower classes of the society by "educating tariffs," sustained by public investment in the infrastructure, especially in traffic systems, education, and schooling. In the long run, yet, the interventions by the state should be reduced in accordance with the vision of Liberalism (List 1841/1928, 271 f; Tribe 1987, 216–218). Utopian elements of List's concept of economic development instead are presumed in his belief in the long-term stabilization of economic growth and the reduction of unemployment and poverty in the market economy. List did not consider the need to redistribute incomes and wealth via taxation and social security.

In contrast to List, the authors of the "German Historical Schools" demanded, to a large extent, effective measures of redistribution policy to solve the "Social Question." They combined their pattern of stages of economic development with proposals to increase incomes of the lower social classes. Mainly, Gustav Schmoller's program of the stabilization of economic development combined the allocation of economic resources and stabilization of economic growth with the redistribution of incomes and wealth by a "strong State" and related institutions of social security (Schmoller 1919, 634 f). Other authors of the "Younger" Historical School instead emphasized the market mechanism and trusted the stabilizing effects of innovation and investment according to their schemes of development stages, to be found f. e. in Karl Bücher's writings on stages of economic development (Bücher 1914, 1–18, especially 10–14). Utopian elements are involved in this concept in the optimistic view of the long-term economic development and the presumption, that the "Social Question" of the market system can be solved without diversified interventions of the State.

Conclusions Demonstrating the Utopian Elements in the Concept of German "Staatswissenschaft"

To answer the question, how authors of different concepts of political economy, respectively of "Staatswissenschaft," exposed and evaluated the role of the "State" in different economic systems, the basic ideas of selected authors of the nineteenth century were considered. Although the focus of the article was to search for utopian elements of the concerned concepts, the visions of authors and the utopian character of their research could only be presumed or, in some cases, demonstrated for specific parts of their scientific <oeuvre>.

As Jürgen Backhaus had argued in his "Mansholdt Lecture" (2005): "The Sciences of State as a Research Paradigm," the important dates for the development of a specific academic discipline focused on the "State" were the years of mid-eighteenth century, when German authors Christian Wolff (1754) and von Justi (1750, 1751) (Becker 2009, 3, 6 ff.) on the grounds of von Seckendorff (1665) published basic books on cameralism, and after two academic chairs, cameralism had been established at the universities in Frankfurt/Oder and in Halle/Saale (1727) (Backhaus 2005, 5–7). As a further step in the development of the Sciences of State the intensive discussions on the Social Question at mid-nineteenth century and through its second half were pointed out, especially because the involved scholars either were members or opponents of the Verein für Socialpolitik, whereby the founders of this organization were trained in the Sciences of State (Backhaus 2005, 8).

The comparison of basic ideas of the considered authors, who investigated the role and impact of the State on the economic and social development, has pointed out that utopian elements can be recognized in the system of feudalism and mercantilism, but also in the concepts of political economy and German "Staatswissenschaft." The vision of a natural order, the setting of a positive order in the concept of cameralism, the belief in the long-term realization of social justice in socialist concepts and the vision of social harmony and efficient economic organization by markets, but also the idea of a "strong State" in the concepts of the German Historical Schools let conclude that the visions and concepts of German "Staatswissenschaft" throughout the nineteenth century and later were based on utopian elements: patterns of long-term tendencies of public expenditures and receipts (Wagner 1901, 947; Schmoller 1901, 552 f), economic stability and social harmony need fundamental ideas about the conditions and final objectives of political economy. That is also true for the Sciences of State.

References

Andreae, W.: Müller, Adam, in: HdSW, 7. Band, G. Fischer, Stuttgart u.a. 1961, 464–466.

Backhaus, J.: The Sciences of State as a Research Paradigm, Sixth Mansholt Lecture, 15 pages, Wageningen, August 25, 2005.

Becher, J. J.: Politische Discurs. Von den eigentlichen Ursachen des Auff- und Abnehmens der Städt, Länder und Republikken. 2. Auflage, Frankfurt 1673. See: Mann 1937, 7.

Baloglou, C. P.: Iambulus' "Sun State" and Campanella's "Civitas Solis": Some Comparative Parallels and Links. In: The State as Utopia, 22nd Heilbronn Symposium and Economics and the Social Sciences, Heilbronn, 2009, manuscript, 46 p.

Baxa, J.: Romantische Staatswissenschaft, in: HdSt, 7. Band, 4. Auflage, Verlag v. G. Fischer, Jena 1926, 117–119.

Becker, H.: Justis konkrete Utopie, 22. Heilbronn Symposium, 22nd June, 2009, manuscript, 24 pages, Heilbronn 2009.

Boelcke, W. A.: Liberalismus, in: HdWW, 5. Band, Gustav Fischer u.a., Stuttgart u.a., 1988, 32–47.

Bücher, K.: Volkswirtschaftliche Entwicklungsstufen, in: Grundriß der Sozialökonomik. 1. Abteilung, Tübingen 1914, 1–18.

Diehl, K.: Art. Sozialismus und Kommunismus, in: HdSt, 4. Auflage, 7. Band, Verlag v. G. Fischer, Jena 1926, 578–612.

Diehl, K.: Rodbertus, Johann Karl, in: HdSt, 7. Band, Verlag von G. Fischer, Jena 1926, 103–111.

Dobias, P.: Sozialismus, in: Issing, O. (Hrsg.): Geschichte der Nationalökonomie, 4. Auflage, Verlag Vahlen, München 2002, 93–110.

Dobias, P.: Sozialismus – Marxismus, in:: Issing, O. (Hrsg.), 2002, 111–130.

Engels, F.: See: Marx,K., Engels, F., 1961 ff.; Schmidt, K.-H.: Engels, in: Staatslexikon, 7. Auflage, 2. Band, 1986, 271 f.

Erzgräber, W.: Utopia und Anti-Utopia, München 1980.

Eucken, W.: Grundsätze der Wirtschaftspolitik, hrsg v. E. Eucken und K. P. Hensel, Tübingen 1952.
Gall, L.: Liberalismus, in. Staatslexikon, 3. Band, Verlag Herder, Freiburg u.a. 1987, Spalten 916–921.
Gide, Ch. und Rist, Ch.: Geschichte der volkswirtschaftlichen Lehrmeinungen, 3. Auflage, Verlag von Gustav Fischer, Jena 1923, 448–493, esp. 456–474.
Hayek, F. A.v.: Liberalismus (I) Politischer Liberalimus, in: HdSW, 6. Band, Gustav Fischer u.a., Stuttgart u.a., 1959, 591–596.
Heilmann, M.: Adolph Wagner – Ein deutscher Nationalökonom im Urteil der Zeit. Campus Verlag, Frankfurt 1980.
Hildebrand, B.: Nationalökonomie und andere Schriften, I, Verlag von G. Fischer, Jena 1922.
Hess, M.: Philosophische und sozialistische Schriften 1837–1850. Hrsg. von Auguste Cornu / Wolfgang Mönke, Berlin 1961.
Issing, O.(Hrsg.): Geschichte der Nationalökonomie, 4. Auflage, Verlag Vahlen, München 2002.
Janssen, H.: Walter Eucken (1891–1950), in: Kurz, H. D. (Hrsg.): Klassiker des ökonomischen Denkens, Band 2, Verlag C. H. Beck: München 2009, 187–204.
Justi, J.H.G.v.: Gutachten von dem vernünftigen Zusammenhange und praktischen Vortrage aller ökonomischen und Kameralwissenschaften, Leipzig 1754.
Justi, J.H.G. v.: Staatswirtschaft, oder systematische Abhandlung aller ökonomischen und Cameralwissenschaften, Leipzig 1755, 2. Auflage 1758.
Klock, C.: Tractatus de aerario, Norum bergae 1671. See: Mann 1937, 7, 24f.
Krabbe, J.J.: Roscher's organistic legacy, in: Journal of Economic Studies, Vol. 22, Nrs. 3/4/5, 1995, 159–170.
Lifschitz, F.: Die historische Schule der Wirtschaftswissenschaft, Bern 1914.
List, F.: Das nationale System der Politischen Oekonomie, Verlag v. G. Fischer, Jena 1928.
Lütge, F.: Morus, Thomas, in: HdSW, 7.Band,G. Fischer, Stuttgart u. a. 1961, 457 – 459.
Mann, F. K.: Steuerpolitische Ideale, Verlag G. Fischer, Jena 1937.
Manuel, F. E. und F. P.: Utopian Thought in the Western World. Press of Harvard University Press. Cambridge Mass.1979.
Marx, K., Engels, F.: Werke (MEW), Berlin 1961 ff.
Müller, A.: Elemente der Staatskunst, 3 Teile, Berlin 1809.
Müller-Schmid, P. P.: Müller, A. H., in: Staatslexikon, 3. Band, Verlag Herder, Freiburg u.a. 1987, Spalten 1235 f.
Novalis (F. Frhr.von Hardenberg): Die Christenheit oder Europa, 1799. See: Baxa 1926, 117 – 119.
Pieper, A.: Utopie, in: Staatslexikon, 5. Band, Verlag Herder, Freiburg u.a., 1989, Spalten 576–580.
Prisching, M.: The Preserving and Reforming State. Schmoller's and Wagner's Model of the State, in: Backhaus, J. G.: Essays on Social Security and Taxation. Gustav von Schmoller and Adolph Wagner Reconsidered. Metropolis-Verlag, Marburg 1997, 173–201.
Ramm, Th.: Weitling, Wilhelm, in: HdSW, 11. Band, Vandenhoeck & Ruprecht u.a., Göttingen u.a. 1961, 603 f.
Schäfer, H.: Kameralismus, in: Staatslexikon, 3. Band, Verlag Herder, Freiburg u.a. 1987, Spalten 276 f.
Schmoller, G.: Grundriß der allgemeinen Volkswirtschaftslehre, 2. Teil, Verlag von Duncker & Humblot, München, Leipzig, 1919.
Schmoller, G.: Volkswirtschaft, Volkswirtschaftslehre und –methode, in: HdSt, 2. Auflage, VII. Band, Verlag v. G. Fischer, Jena 1901, 543–580.
Spiegel, H. W.: The Growth of Economic Thought, revised and expanded edition, Duke University Press, Durham, North Carolina, 1983.
Stavenhagen, G.: Geschichte der Wirtschaftstheorie, 4. Auflage, Verlag Vandenhoeck & Ruprecht, Göttingen 1969.
Stucken, R.: Wagner, Adolph, in: HdSW, 11. Band, Verlag G. Fischer u.a., Stuttgart u.a., 1961, 470–472.

Tautscher, A.: Kameralismus, in: HdSW, 5. Band, G. Fischer, Stuttgart u.a. 1956, 463–467.
Tribe, K.: List, Friedrich (1789–1846), in: The New Palgrave, Vol. 3, London 1987, 216–218.
Wagner, A.: Lehrbuch der politischen Oekonomie, 1. Band, Allgemeine und theoretische Volkswirtschaftslehre, erster Teil, C. F. Winter'sche Verlagsbuchhandlung, Leipzig und Heidelberg 1879.
Wagner, A.: Finanzwissenschaft und Staatssozialimus, 1887, in: Sozialökono-mische Studientexte, hrsg. V. A. Skalweit, Verlag V. Klostermann, Frankfurt a.M. 1948.
Wagner, A.: Staat in nationalökonomischer Hinsicht, in:HdSt, 2. Auflage, VI. Band, Verlag v. G. Fischer, Jena 1901, 940–951.
Wendt, S.: Rodbertus, Karl, in: HdSW, 9. Band, Verlag G. Fischer u.a., Stuttgart u.a., 1956, 21–24.

Utopia: Johann Peter Süßmilch and the Divine Order

Gerhard Scheuerer

Introduction

Johann Peter Süßmilch lived in the 18th century in Germany. Süßmilch served as Prussian army priest and provost in the parish Berlin-Cölln. He is a representative of German cameralism, who cautioned about turning away from religion to listen to reason, and was engaged as a statistician and demographer concerning actual statistical data of the time. In this essay, Süßmilch Divine Order of population is shown as part of the intellectual and spiritual antagonism towards the upcoming importance of reason at the time. Finally, Süßmilch's awarenesses are compared with Multhus' later-published Principle of Population.

Süßmilch was born on 3 September 1707 in Zehlendorf, at that time a village two miles farther off from Berlin, and nowadays an urban district of the City of Berlin; he died on 22 March 1767 in Berlin, at the time the capital of Prussia. Süßmilch was a contemporary of well-known German philosopher and exponent of natural justice Christian Wolff (*1679, †1754) and cameralist Johann von Justi (*1717, †1771), both treated in former Heilbronn Symposia.[1] His main publication is a little cumbersome, named 'The Divine Order in the circumstances of the human sex, birth, death and reproduction'. (*Die göttliche Ordnung in den Veränderungen des menschlichen Geschlechts, aus der Geburt, dem Tod und der Fortpflanzung desselben erwiesen*); Berlin 1741 (first edition, including a preface of Christian Wolff), 1762 (authorised enlarged second edition), 1765 (third edition). He can be regarded as the pioneer of scientific statistics and demography. Süßmilch gathers and describes the existing statistical methods of his time and his analysis is based on empirical records, for example of the Breslau (today: Wroclaw) priest Kaspar Neumann, who administrated parish registers on births, marriage and deaths by age as well as death causes. Ahead of others, Süßmilch worked on life tables.

---

[1]20–21 Heilbronn Symposium. Backhaus, Jürgen (2009)

G. Scheuerer
University of Erfurt, Erfurt, Thüringen, Germany
e-mail: gerhard.scheuerer@uni-erfurt.de

J.G. Backhaus (ed.), *The State as Utopia: Continental Approaches*, The European Heritage in Economics and the Social Sciences 9, DOI 10.1007/978-1-4419-7500-3_14,

Curriculum Vitae of Süßmilch[2]

During his school days, Süßmilch wanted to become a physician. He attended lectures on medicine at Theatrum Anatomicum, Berlin, which had been reorganised in the year 1723, and took an exam in osteology. In his spare time, he prepared a pharmacological booklet on medical plants.

His parents wished that he should follow the family tradition and study law. Therefore, in the year 1724, he attended a grammar school (Lateinschule) in Glaucha (near Halle, a city in Saxony-Anhalt) to learn foreign languages and prepare for the study of law. The grammar school was part and parcel of the orphanage, which had been founded by the priest August Hermann Francke (*1663, †1727). Francke can be called a pathfinder of pietism, which is a reform movement of European Protestantism of those times.

Probably, Francke aroused Süßmilch's interest in Theology. In the year 1727, Süßmilch enrolled as a student of Medical Science and Theology at Friedrichs University, Halle. A year later, after Francke's death, Süßmilch moved to the University of Jena. During that time, Süßmilch maintained an offering, went back to Berlin and became educator (magister curiae – Hofmeister) in the house of General von Kalckstein, who was an important official in the Prussian kingdom then. From 1718, for nearly 11 years, von Kalckstein had been the educator of the crown prince, who was later, in 1740, crowned the Prussian King Frederick II (Friedrich II). At that time, Süßmilch hoped to return to the scientific world at the university together with the eldest son of the General. In the year 1731, Süßmilch defended his dissertation 'De Cohaesone et Attractione Corporum', a physical matter.

In the year 1734, Süßmilch started collecting facts and empirical data for his main publication 'The Divine Order…' of population and travelled together with his pupil to Holland. Two years later, Süßmilch became field preacher in the Kalkstein Regiment. Now it was possible for him to start a family.

On 27 June 1737, he married the 16-year-old Charlotte Dorothea Lieberkühn, the youngest daughter of the Royal goldsmith. He had 10 children with his wife, of which only one died, which was exceptional in those times. After the death of his child, Süßmilch proposed the composition of midwives' schools.

In the year 1741, Süßmilch quit the military service and took office as pastor of the parish county Etzin and Knoblauch, located in Havelland near Berlin and published his main publication 'The Divine Order …' in the same year. After 1742, Süßmilch served as Provost in the Sankt Petri Church in Berlin-Cölln, later as senior councillor of the consistory of the Prussian state Brandenburg. At the same time, he was appointed to different committees, especially those that concerned pauperism. Particularly honourable was the appointment to the Prussian Academy of Sciences in the year 1745. Süßmilch was in contact, and had discussions, with Gotthold Ephraim Lessing (German writer and philosopher) and Immanuel Kant (German philosopher).

---

[2]For detailed depiction see: (Elsner 1986).

From the résumé of Süßmilch, we observe that children often have other interests than their parents. At first, Süßmilch followed his parents' desire for a short time. But, influenced by other well-educated and well-known persons, the young man found his own occupational way, dissenting from his parents' opinion. This was possible owing to the status and the informal network of his family, which offered him excellent educational facilities and paved the way for top scientific efficiencies in due time. The complete work of Süßmilch demonstrates his excellent education and shows him to be a man of vast reading in actual English and French scientific literature of that time.

What is Utopia?

Sir Thomas Morus used the term Utopia for the first time in the year 1516 and titled his book 'Of the Best State of a Republic, and of the New Island Utopia'. He deduced the term from Old Greek 'eutopia', which means 'good place' and describes a vision of a seemingly perfect society. Universally valid, utopia can be defined as the preferable status of the world or a state. Unfortunately, there exists no common sense about the definition of utopia. Furthermore, the term utopia is defined differently in diverse science disciplines. The political science researcher Richard Saage differentiates four types of utopia.[3] In the following, I will act on the assumption of Saage's distincted type 'lived utopia', which means that alternatives are tested empirically against the existing reality. The following analyses suppose Christian ideals, which Süßmilch requires to follow, and empirical data as utupia, which are taken as the basis in Süßmilch's studies.

Cameralism in Germany

Some Foundations of German Cameralism

German cameralism is a subspecies of mercantilism and differs to a certain extent when compared with mercantilism. The foundation of German cameralism was a complete natural order. Promotion of trade came less to the fore than promotion of farming and population growth. The reason was that Germany had lost many people during the 30 Years' War from 1618 to 1648. Certain areas were depopulated, and Germany suffered from famine and epidemics. Therefore, in view of cameralists, population is an important production factor and prosperity of a

[3]Saage (1992), pp. IX.

nation depends on the highest possible number of subjects, which is correlated with quantity of achievable food. An active population policy by immigration prevailed in the seventeenth/eighteenth century; for example Prussia recruited French Huguenots to follow the aim of increasing the population.

Süßmilch's Foundation of Demography

Süßmilch continued along the mainstream of cameralism and rests on the natural order, which is given by the Lord to the soul of all humans, and the accurately defined Divine order. Additionally, he was affected by Francke's pietism. Süßmilch combined natural order and the Divine order with political economy and empirical data and above all, he included physico theology, which came up as a reaction to secularisation developments during the seventeenth century (William Derham, *1657, †1735). He pitted himself against the zeitgeist of the time, turning away from religion to reason. He wanted to show that 'The Divine order' protects from misuse of reason. In his outlook, reason leads necessarily to the Lord. Furthermore, Süßmilch summed up and pursued a concept of empirical scientific statistics in the tradition of political arithmeticians (for example, John Graunt, William Petty, and in Germany, Gottfried Achenwall,*1719, †1772, assistant professor since 1753 and professor since 1761 at the University of Göttingen). Achenwall was a doyen of political arithmetic, but deriders badmouthed him chart slave. He can be put down as one of the inventors of scientific statistics as well as a precursor of econometrics.

Süßmilch's Divine Order of Population

The starting point of Süßmilch's scientific considerations are the significant effects of the 30 Years' War from 1618 to 1648 on depopulation of urban and rural areas as well as change for the worse in human health. Most of the territorial states suffered from famine and epidemics from time to time and were underpopulated territories, 'for many of them, the villages cannot be named'.[4] Süßmilch bases on the words in the Bible 'be fruitful and multiply, and fill the Earth' (GENESIS 1:28)[5] and acts on six theses:

1. Existence and goodness of the Lord,
2. The Lord and nature are not splitted up,

---

[4]Süßmilch (1741), pp. 308.

[5]Süßmilch (1741), p. 183.

3. Evils – like war, bad living conditions, poverty, lack of hygiene, famine – are not the Lord's will,
4. Theology and science are combined,
5. Increasing population number and population density are the Lord's will
6. Population increase depends on the extent of urbanisation (which means that urbanisation is a variable of population development)

Süßmilch reflects on a social–cultural approach. He places a single person of a population in the centre of his thought and connects it with ideas of political economy and police science. This projection is contrary to cameralism, which treats demography as part of political economy and police science. Based on parish registers on births, marriage and deaths by age as well as death causes of the church of Breslau (today: Wroclaw) and other European cities, Süßmilch assessed the sex birth ratio of 100 girls to 105 boys and found out that the sex ratio is compensated for at the age of marriage. As he showed, the cause of this phenomenon originates from the higher mortality of younger boys. Süßmilch searched for the medical reasons of this higher mortality and reasoned that this is the visible expression of the Lord's will towards monogamy.

Süßmilch deduced from empirical data and numerical patterns different rules of population development. With a view to frame a population policy, he wanted prosperity and wealth of the community and population to be set as goals and as a necessary duty of sovereigns. Concerned about an underdeveloped and underpopulated country, Süßmilch considered how women could be encouraged to give birth to more children. He enunciated, among other things, that nuptial fertility can be supported when marriages happen at the right age and not at too late an age. As we can see nowadays in many highly developed countries, later age of first births reduces the number of children of women and diminishes population ceteris paribus. Furthermore, Süßmilch postulated – just as Thomas Morus did – that unequal marriage between old and young persons should be prohibited in order to prevent marriage for material reasons. He himself married a 16-year-old young lady and she gave birth to 10 children, of which only one died. Süßmilch stressed additionally the limitation of nurses, which had been widely established at the time.[6]

Another focal point of Süßmilch's exploration concerns the world population. He calculates on the basis of agricultural load capacity and predicts around four billion persons.[7] In his opinion, fertility increases to the balance point between food and population and decreases above this balance point. In this context, Süßmilch adverts to the fact that food is in stock, but that the distribution of food is insufficiently organised. Insofar, he neglects that scarcity of food needs consequent political measures in reality.

---

[6] Süßmilch (1741), pp. 285.

[7] Süßmilch (1741), p. 74.

Comparison of Süßmilch's Divine Order and Malthus' Principle of Population

Malthus (*1766, †1834) published his Essay on 'the Principle of Population'[8] for the first time in the year 1798. This pamphlet did not incorporate empirical data, which he added step by step in the following print runs by exploiting many empirical data composed by Süßmilch as a quarry. However, he uses these empirical data in several cases in wrong relationships. Malthus reflects biological facts and his entry incorporates considerations of marginal revenue, which had been discovered by Turgot (* 1727, †1781). He acts on two theses:

1. Population decreases when prosperity increases.

This pessimistic view is contrary to the thought of cameralism and Süßmilch's considerations, but equates to the modern finding of the Theory of The Family and is approved by current empirical data.

2. Population increases in geometrical ratio while food increases in arithmetical ratio.

Increasing utilisation of the land diminishes marginal revenue; agricultural per capita income from property diminishes when population increases. This approach is also contrary to Süßmilch's considerations, whose population prediction is based on agricultural load capacity.

Malthus insinuates that libido is a permanent steady impulse for multiplication of population. This is hampered by repressive obstructions, which he considers 'general checks to population'.[9] Malthus distinguishes[10]

(a) *Positive checks* such as misery, hunger, illness, war and
(b) *Preventive checks* such as sexual abstinence, late marriage age.

Population increases when general living conditions improve, and per-capita income has grown to a subsistence minimum. As soon as per-capita income exceeds the subsistence minimum, the population decreases. By his own admission, evolution theorist Charles Darwin (*1809, †1882) has been influenced by the biological facts of Malthus.

Malthus argues that improvement of life conditions of lower classes increases the birth rate. This induces wars and famine, which increases the death rate. Pauperism, misery, and scarcity of food for workers go along with overpopulation. Süßmilch argues first that fertility increases after repressive obstructions have passed. This means that – according to Süßmilch – repressive obstructions are determinants of fertility. Second, he argues that repressive obstructions produce the

[8]Malthus (1878).

[9]Malthus (1878), pp. 6.

[10]Malthus (1872); pp. 8.

positive checks – in Malthus' terms – which become necessary for the sovereign to avoid. Above all, in view of Süßmilch's moral restraints, which Malthus calls preventive checks, is the Lord's will.

Malthus concludes that social progress is not possible. In contrast, Süßmilch acted on the assumption that around 4 million persons can be fed all over the world, while actually only about one million persons lived at that time. Malthus postulates late marriage and sexual abstinence, while Süßmilch argued for chastity and prohibition of unequal marriage age.

It demonstrates the excellent education of Süßmilch and shows him as a man of vast reading in the actual English and French scientific literature of the time.

Final Remarks

Multhus' theory has been criticised from the very beginning, but it is relevant for developing countries till today, though the above-named theses are incorrect on a big scale. Many of Süßmilch's theses and suggestions have been forgotten for a long time. They have been rediscovered partially in modern demographic theories and in The Theory of The Family. Süßmilch is one of the pioneers of scientific statistics, demography as well as use of empirical statistical data and an early precursor of econometrics.

References

Achenwall, Gottfried: Abriss der neuesten Staatswissenschaft der vornehmsten Europäischen Reiche und Republicken; Schmidt, Göttingen 1749

Backhaus, Jürgen Georg (Ed.): The beginnings of political Economy: Johann Heinrich Gottlob von Justi: The European Heritage in Economics and the Social Sciences, Vol. 7; Springer Science + Business Media New York 2009

Elsner, Eckehardt: kurzer Überblick über das Leben und Wirken des Johann Peter Süßmilch (1707–1767), in: Birg, Herwig (Hg.): Ursprünge der Demographie in Deutschland. Leben und Werk Johann Peter Süßmilchs (1707–1767); Campus Verlag: Frankfurt 1986, pp. 143–151

Malthus, Thomas R.: An Essay on the Principle of Population, or, a View of Its Past and Present Effects on Human Happiness; with an Inquiry into Our Prospects Respecting the Future Removal or Mitigation of the Evils which It Occasions; Reeves and Turner: London, eighth edition 1878

Saage, Richard: Vorwort, in: Saage, Richard (Hrsg.): Hat die politische Utopie eine Zukunft?, Wissenschaftliche Buchgesellschaft Darmstadt 1992, pp. VII–XII

Süßmilch, Johann Peter: Die göttliche Ordnung in den Veränderungen des menschlichen Geschlechts, aus der Geburt, dem Tod und der Fortpflanzung desselben erwiesen; Nachdruck der Ausgabe Berlin 1741, Georg Olms Verlag Hildesheim, Zürich, New York 2008

Eugen Dühring and Post-Utopian Socialism

E. James Gay

Introduction

In keeping with the historical mission of the Heilbronn Symposium to draw attention to significant German thinkers in the field of political economy whose work has largely been inaccessible to the English speaking world, we once again turn to the today obscure, but in his day highly influential, political economist and philosopher Eugen Dühring. Dühring belonged to a generation of German thinkers who came to prominence in the 1860s and 1870s, denouncing not only the tradition of German idealism as represented by Hegel, but also distancing themselves from the Hegelian school, which had tried to revise and improve their master's work. Before Dühring, men such as Ruge, Feuerbach, and Marx had carried out a thorough critique of the theological aspects of Hegel's thinking but retained his dialectical method. Dühring was influenced by these "young" or "left" Hegelian thinkers but strongly rejected their dialectical approach to history. He attempted to develop what could be termed a type of idealistic materialism, i.e. a realistic and materialistic philosophy, which refrained from what he saw as mystical historical argumentation while espousing high ideals for individual conduct.[1]

Following (and simplifying) August Comte's three-stage philosophy of history, Dühring was convinced that the French Revolution had ushered in a new "positivist" era for western civilization where science would be able to do away with religious superstition and construct society rationally and justly. This philosophy of history, with its adherence to the leftist ideals of the Enlightenment, was optimistic, believing that society was growing up as it were and leaving behind an immature childhood, which was holding back human progress.[2]

---

[1] *The Ideals of Materialism* was used as a book title by Dühring's follower Heinrich von Stein.

[2] Cf. Dühring (1875a, p. 301).

E.J. Gay (✉)
University of Erfurt, Erfurt, Germany
e-mail: edwardjamesgay@gmail.com

J.G. Backhaus (ed.), *The State as Utopia: Continental Approaches*, The European Heritage in Economics and the Social Sciences 9, DOI 10.1007/978-1-4419-7500-3_15,

The vehicle through which society would be structured was to be what Dühring termed "societarianism," to his mind, a more progressive version of socialism, which went beyond and was to replace the utopian socialism of the past. The concept of "utopian Socialism" was used polemically by Dühring – as it had been by Marx and Engels – to find fault with the ideas of early French socialists such as Owen, Fourier and Blanc.[3] Without wanting to lose the main thrust of socialism, which Dühring saw as a movement to catalyze intellectual and political emancipation of society through a reshaping of material interests, he set out to reform its tenets replacing older doctrine with a more scientific model, as he saw it, free from fantastic suggestion. Whereas Marx and Engels had attempted to do much the same, Dühring's work had a more thorough philosophical approach, which gave greater value to the individual and focused on metaphysical, ontological, and epistemological concerns.[4]

To understand Dühring's attempt rise above utopian socialism, it will be necessary to look into the historical background of the concept of utopia as well as to consider the chief underpinning of utopia: the human faculty of reason (Vernunft). It will be shown that Dühring's social philosophy was based on a modern interpretation of reason and that this application of reason had consequences for his interpretation of socialism. We examine his philosophy including his metaphysics, which he labeled "world schematism," as well as his epistemology (or, as he defined it, conceptual critique), specifically the relationship between Vernunft (reason) and Verstand (understanding) in his thought. Next, we look into his concept of "rational imagination" (rationale Phantasie) and finally his design for a "free society" run by economic communes.

Dühring's belief in the progress of history and the dawning of a new scientific era brought about by scientific socialism lends itself to using the term "post-utopian socialism" for his efforts.[5] It will be asked to what degree Dühring's societarianism can be seen as post-utopian, i.e. as having overcome utopian socialism. Did it present a realistic alternative to the dreamy speculation of his predecessors, or to what degree if at all is Dühring to be seen as a utopian thinker himself?

Utopia and Reason in Modern History

Utopia was originally a vision created at a time when European men and women were severing their ties with their homelands and beginning to journey in great numbers to settle in the new world. During the early modern period as Europeans

---

[3]Cf. Dühring (Dühring 1875b, p. 273).

[4]August Bebel spoke of Dühring as a new type of communist. Bebel, 1874. Harold Höfding labeled Dühring's philosophy one of the "most interesting speculative attempts of our day," and emphasized the "close connection between the thought and the personality of the thinker." In Dühring's work. Cf. Höfding (1955), p. 561).

[5]Although I have never come across the term "post-utopian socialism," it is generally agreed that the early utopian socialist thought, which was inspired by the French Revolution, came to an end in the 1840s. Cf. Sombart (1908), pp. 34f).

branched out into all corners of the globe, the concept of a far off place, an attainable social paradise somewhere in the distant future had great appeal.[6] The term utopia, which was invented by Thomas More, became historically relevant in the seventeenth and eighteenth centuries as the strong absolutist state of this period, which was the result of the religious conflict following the Protestant Reformation, became the object of the social critique of a bourgeois class that was now establishing itself throughout the world. For the first time, an abstract "social question" was discovered and the concrete order was questioned.

The basis of Utopia and the critique of society involved a new application concept of reason and it is relevant to consider what we mean from an epistemological point of view when using the term. Reason, as a human faculty of the mind, involves the ability of abstraction, which is the starting point of any utopia, to contemplate better alternatives to the policies of the order of the here and now. As Fritz Mauthner has pointed out, the clearest distinction between reason and understanding was given by Arthur Schopenhauer 1969.[7] With reason, we are dealing with the advantage that man has compared to beasts. Whereas animals and men share the concrete burdens of life as represented in the actual moments, the here and now of life, struggling and suffering, ultimately dying, only man possesses the power of abstraction.[8] Man possesses a double life as it were: one as it appears to us at the moment before our eyes and one separated completely from immediacy and existing in the abstract. Reason is not to be confused with intellect or understanding (Verstand) as it is the source of abstract, discursive, reflective, indirect knowledge. It enables us to look into the past and into the future. Reason has the purely practical advantage of allowing us to look past trivial distractions of the moment and to consider future needs and plan for them.[9]

Reason has the "realistic" function of helping humans not only live but also lead their lives. It need not remain practical or concentrated on a task that is lying directly before us; it can also be applied through imagination, which allows us to "think away" a reality, which is not desired. In imagination, reason has the idealistic function of contemplating conditions or scenarios of how the world in which we live can be made a better place; here, ideas of morality and justice come into play.

It is probably not coincidental that the "physical abstraction" of the European emigrants who separated themselves from their countries' origin to live in the new world was accompanied by the "intellectual abstraction" of utopia. The faculty of reason gained, as it were, new historical significance. A better future for society was thought up and pursued. The new imagined ideas were soon followed by concrete actions to improve society and to create a just society. These ideals ultimately led to the French Revolution in 1789 becoming what has been termed "the age of enlightenment."

---

[6]Cf. Koselleck (1992), pp. 6–9).

[7]Cf. Mauthner (1912). Cf. Zweiter Band, XIV. Ursprung und Geschichte von Vernunft.

[8]Schopenhauer (1969), p. 35).

[9]Thomas Hobbes once wrote: human beings are animals who are famished by future hunger. Cf. Gehlen (1986), p. 50).

Nineteenth Century Change in Utopia

The French Revolution, which had achieved the unseating of the monarchy and the feudal order, was seen as the starting point towards a just social order and the abstract power of utopia did not lose strength. The visions sought by the revolutionaries were not fulfilled immediately and the forces of reason and utopianism now adjusted themselves to the impending industrial revolution. Rather than simply "thinking away" the unpleasant present social conditions with abstract plans and visions, utopian reason changed into a more realist theory of progress with emphasis towards creating "productivity" through work. Saint-Simon, who was perhaps the most important ideologue in this new vision, proclaimed that all men will be able to work in "the industrial workshop of the future."

As the nineteenth century progressed, much of the once seemingly endless space had been filled and social visionaries changed their way of looking into the future. As technology rapidly progressed, it became harder to envision just what the future would hold and one could say that in a sense, utopians became more myopic, that is to say, they no longer looked into the distant future but now turned to positive science to show that paradise was just around the corner if only certain obstacles were eradicated. What had once been a pure abstraction, now took on a more concrete form as a new "social question" was discovered.[10] Soon, science and philosophy were used to show how the best society could be achieved. The idea of servitude and domination (and the opposition to the existence of such a relationship) became a dynamic force in society.[11] The goal of "overcoming suppression" became a mighty instrument for the mobilization of the masses to change society. Specific "obstacles standing in the way of a better society" were shown to be unjustifiably standing in the way of moral progress; in the nineteenth century, these "hindrances" to a better humanity had many different names: the state, the bourgeoisie, capitalists, freemasons, Jesuits, Jews.[12]

The socialist movement, which clearly involved bourgeois utopianism, had many different focal points. "Work" was a common denominator, but the idea of "taking away" or confiscation to better society also became influential. Pierre Joseph Proudhon proclaimed "property is theft" and dispossession became a common cry among radicals. Saint-Simon's emphasis was not on "taking away" but rather on creating productivity. Half a century later in their Communist Manifesto, Marx and Engels introduced the term "utopian socialism," which for them signified

[10] Cf. Backhaus ed 2006).

[11] Kesting (1973).

[12] It should be noted that the emphasis on such "hindrances" to a better, just society is still a strong political factor in our day. The terminology for the groups to be fought has changed, however, to groups such as "radicals," "racists," "neo-nazis," and "islamo-fascists," etc.

unrealistic thinkers who simply conceived the best possible world but were unable to do what was necessary to have it happen. The Marxist alternative became known as "scientific socialism."

The newly founded emphasis on work and production, which had begun long before Marx and Engels, and the development of a scientific political economy curbed the utopian fantasies of the eighteenth century, but did not end them. The utopias of More and Harrington were discounted, but others based more on an appreciation of the reality of work as a social factor came into being, e.g. Fichte's Utopian book "Der geschlossene Handelsstaat," which bears a strong resemblance to Saint-Simon's ideas. Owen and Fourier also aimed for a scientific application of socialism, and in contrast to Marx and Engels, as neo-conservative author Joshua Muravachik has pointed out, tested it by attempting to form socialist communities.[13]

Marx and Engels wanted to rise above Utopia through science, but, as Muravchik has written, postulated theories, which could be neither proven nor disproved. Thus, particularly with their views of a classless society, the Marxists seemed to have remained captured in an unrealistic utopianism, the roots of which were in the Hegelian dialectic. The Hegelian philosophy, which highlighted the Social Question emphasizing the dynamics of domination and servitude, had given legitimacy to the dissolution of the old feudal and half-feudal society.[14] Marx was only one member (by no means the most prominent) of the young or left Hegelians, followers of Hegel who utilized the master's methods, but, opposed to the right Hegelians, rejected Hegel's more traditionalist views, particularly his view on Christianity and religion. Marx sought to legitimize Hegel's theories orientating them more towards the concrete, i.e. by integrating them into scientific political economy. The dialectic was to be complemented by economic realism and only then could society be revolutionized.

As Karl Löwith 1986 has pointed out, within a short time of their rise to fame, the Young Hegelians had "the rug pulled out from under their philosophy" and became overpowered by the political realities of the 1850s.[15] It had become apparent that the revolution that they desired would not happen and they sank into oblivion. The turn away, as it were, from the revolutionary spirit of the young Hegelians also largely involved a rejection of the Hegelian philosophy itself, which was now seen as being unscientific and reactionary.

Dühring Challenges Marxist Socialism

Eugen Dühring, 15 years junior to Marx, was to become Marx's greatest rival, vying for the intellectual leadership of the German worker's movement in the 1870s. Taking a cue from Arthur Schopenhauer whose independent spirit and indignant pessimism

[13] Muravchik (1999).

[14] Cf. Kesting (1959, p. 8).

[15] Cf. Löwith, (1964, p. 119).

he admired, Dühring became one of the loudest and most influential voices denouncing Hegel (as well as Fichte and Schelling) and labeling the early nineteenth century as a period of reactionary thought. Here was a young socialist thinker seemingly uninfluenced by the flawed Hegelian philosophy, who was completely independent of Marx and was now espousing his own concrete plans for changing society through science. For many a young socialist, Dühring's vivid demonstrative style of presenting his theories was a breath of fresh air from the abstract often clumsy dogmatism of Marx. The revolutionary Gustav Landauer pointed this out, proclaiming that Dühring's writings were in many ways superior to Marx's: more universal, more modern and scientific, less dogmatic, and more understandable.[16]

Dühring burst upon the scene and became one of the leading figures in the social democratic movement. With two books published in 1865, "Natürliche Dialectic" and "Der Werth des Lebens," he picked up the ball of two of the strongest currents developing in the aftermath of the collapse of the Hegelian movement, epistemology and the philosophy of life, and ran with it.[17] In the years that followed, Dühring would gravitate away from epistemology and more towards positivism, rejecting all religious metaphysical concepts, and thereby postulating a theory of reality that one would think would leave little room for utopia.

In his *Critical History of Political Economy and Socialism*, first published in 1871, Dühring reproached Marx not only for ignoring the factor of politics in the field of economics, but also for abusing healthy logic, for playing a metamorphosis game with concepts and history and for "siring a bastard of historical and logical imagination".[18] He found that the Marxist offered no realistic vision for the future and remained caught in an unproductive "logic of sorrow" (Elendslogik), which prevented true socialism, or using Dühring's terminology "sociatarianism" from advancing. Owing to their misunderstanding of the eminent political nature of modern society, the Marxists advocated, according to Dühring, an unphilosophical perspective. Dühring believed that a more individualistic and yet scientifically minded philosophy using the methods of positivism could advance the socialist cause beyond the utopian historical constructions that stemmed from Hegel's dialectic.

World Schematism

An important aspect of Dühring's attempt to overcome utopian socialism was a modern application of the faculty of reason. Dühring believed in the ability of consciousness to solve the greatest quandaries of existence; philosophy and science were not to

---

[16]Landauer (1892).

[17]This path was paved by Schopenhauer who combined epistemological expertise with inspired vitalism.

[18]Dühring (1875, p. 498).

be separated from one another. Whereas Marx and his followers had refrained from giving their work a fixed philosophical foundation from which to proceed, Dühring created his own philosophy as a basis from which his works in political economy could progress.[19] We have described his philosophy above as idealistic materialism: Dühring advocated a strict adherence to reality as the foundation for the conception of the world and life, and yet was not against metaphysics completely.

In his main philosophical work *Cursus der Philosphie*, he came up with a metaphysical concept by another name, which he called "world schematism." Here, he attempted to create a logical application of reason to the highest principles of being. The original and most elementary Schematism Dühring labeled "singleness". The all-encompassing being is single. Accordingly, the world is something in which everything is unified.[20] The ultimate being does not change, it is eternal and endless, but at some point and for some unknown reason it began to develop and this development cannot regress. The universal being creates from within, without changing on the whole; there are according to Dühring no recurring patterns, but rather persistent elements, which function amid change. In the concept of universal being, the philosopher is able to see everything in its context and dismantle the elements of being into its unchanging components. The most basic division is between the changing and stable components of universal being.

Dühring's basic point of departure was the field of mathematics and theoretical mechanics. His philosophy begins with the abstraction of the exact number, which for him was no abstraction at all but a mirror of reality. This he contrasts with continuous interconnection and uninterrupted continuance. Every real datum, every actual result is limited and represents a definite number. Infinity indicates a possibility of advance, but remains, according to Dühring, just that: a possibility and not a reality. If a quantity is advanced, then it does so by the gradual means of particular and definite elements. Here, we have before us the difference between "thought" and "reality." Exactly how the exact number changes its quantity is as unclear as how the primordial being originally began to evolve, but Dühring believes in the powers of reason to solve this dilemma some day.

The Concrete Intellect: Conflation of Understanding and Reason

The metaphysical thoughts just described show Dühring's proclivity for abstract thought. Houston Steward Chamberlain, a popular writer in the Germany of the early twentieth century, emphasized Dühring's command of the richness of the abstract

---

[19] Dühring did his doctorate and afterwards habilitated in Philosophy at the Friedrich-Wilhelms Universität in Berlin.

[20] Dühring had been inspired by Robert Mayer's theory of energy conservation, which postulated that energy was neither destroyed nor created, but simply changed its form.

world of thought and went as far as to say, in reference to Dühring's blindness, that Dühring was a thinker who possessed "gar keine Anschauung," i.e. no visual intuition at all.[21] This assessment is, I believe, misleading as a closer examination of Dühring's philosophy reveals that his thought is far more geared to the concrete than to the abstract. As Gustav Landauer's above-mentioned remarks show, Dühring's philosophy is presented in a clear understandable form that exhibits a strong sense of intuition (Anschauung).

Dühring's thought is driven far less from the power of abstraction than it is by original perceptive power and instinct. In catering to the more irrational force of intuition, Dühring's thought is based far more in the understanding (Verstand) than on reason (Vernunft). Reason, as stated above, involves the abstract, taking something that is given and forming words, concepts, and terms from them and thus questioning and examining it. The counterpart to reason is the understanding (Verstand, acumen, perspicacia, sagacitas) whose sole function is determining causality of reality as it is perceived by us through space and time.

This traditional distinction between reason and understanding (zwischen Vernunft and Verstand), which had been changed first by Kant and later even more by Hegel, was rejected altogether by Dühring.[22] There was no good reason, according to Dührin, to isolate two different faculties here. Departing from the Hegelian understanding of reason, which defined the concept as a speculative power from which human action stems, Dühring fused Verstand and Vernunft together choosing therefore, in most cases, to use the term Verstand. For him, the understanding encompassed reason and its deepest function was the recognition of cause as it appeared through perception. Although this may be characteristic of a deficit in conceptual precision, it is significant for Dühring's system as the intellectual, i.e. concrete and perceptive elements in his system dominate the pure rational ones. Dühring intentionally chooses to let the faculty of reason take a back seat to the faculty of understanding or the intellect. In choosing the "reality" of understanding above the abstract "truths" of reason, Dühring's approach is not only more practically directed and more focused on the here and now, but also more open to the risk of failure.[23]

Dühring's Concept of Rational Imagination

Dühring's thought was characterized by realism and pragmatism, but as already seen in his concept of a world schematism, he did not refrain from philosophical speculation. The intellect and science possessed for him a very powerful tool,

[21] Chamberlain (1905, pp. 23f).

[22] Dühring (1875a, pp. 179f).

[23] In his works on intellectual history, Dühring often emphasized the importance, if not the necessity, of "failure" (Scheitern) in paving the way for new ideas; this gave his perspective a touch of existantialism. Cf. Geldsetzer (1968, p. 161).

which he called "rational imagination." Rational imagination acts, according to Dühring, as a constructive force in the process of perception itself. It cannot create something from nothing and remains chained to the facts of experience, and yet it embodies human freedom at its best. This freedom comes from its ability to "compose" from what is given by experience. Dühring is convinced that the way that human imagination creates is to a certain degree on par with the inner workings of nature. If this were not the case, then there would never be the chance of gaining ideal insight into existence; we would be forced into a slavish reproduction of facts alone.[24]

According to Dühring, imagination's value in art, particularly poetry, was widely recognized, but its value for science had gone little noticed. Rational imagination remains fixed on an immediate or future reality and in this sense can perform scientific anticipation. It is a productive impulse and a key to the riddles of the history of science. Rational imagination is for Dühring a component of reality and while thought and reality were not the same, there was an inner connection between the two. There is a kinship between what works in things and that which works in the intellect. Dühring, who warns against the common realistic perspective, also sees a difference between "Wirklichkeit" and "Realität," both of which must be translated as "reality" in English and many other languages. Realism is for Dühring something that can be touched as opposed to something that is thought, something matter of fact as opposed to something ideal. Wirklichkeit for Dühring includes something higher and more powerful and this is the consciousness from which imagination stems. The power of imagination is not only a part of reality; it is also higher and superior to the rest of reality. Consciousness itself is based on something that does not exist in thought and that which enables us to think is what enables nature to work. We should not according to Dühring follow Schopenhauer's example in this case and see the unconscious factors as being higher than and superior to the conscious ones. Dühring was convinced that human consciousness was the highest reality and that society's problems could be solved through the valuable tool of rational imagination. He set out to move beyond the older utopian socialists and to outdo the Marxists as it were in creating a realistic feasible plan for a future society.

The Free Society and Economic Communes

At the 21st Heibronn Symposium, I spoke in depth about Dühring's concept of the tyrannical state, which he believed developed with increasing centralization. The counterpart of the historically inherited "Gewaltstaat" was for Dühring the "free society" ("freie Gesellschaft") of the future, based on the principle of "free association," just as Carey had used the term. Following Jean Jacques Rousseau, Dühring advocated a type of social contract that would respect the rights of the individual

[24]Dühring (1875a, 46).

while preserving a balance of power between the individual groups of society. In the "free society," individuals would stand on an equal basis and there would be no room for domination and subordination. Believing as did Henry C. Carey in the possibility of a harmony of interest, Dühring wrote that the highest principle of communal life is the exclusion of domination and servitude.[25] In a state based on justice, it was not a third force that would arbitrate between two conflicting parties, but rather the parties themselves who would work out their differences together. The state would apparently be there only to preserve the "natural justice," which involved balancing the given powers in the society.[26]

Dühring designed plans for a society of free association between individuals where tyrannical power was to be eliminated. No member of society should exploit another and the state should only have minimal influence over the citizens. His concept is strongly individualistic and rational in its nature. He believed that once all compulsion, be it human to human or group to group, was taken away, society could be structured in a way that would allow free economic competition to be attained in the way that Adam Smith had envisioned it. Competence, disposition, and energy vary among individuals and each person should have the ability to develop his or her talents.

The individual human being was seen as the starting point and purpose of all societal life. The sovereign individual will is the final instance of all societal development. The basic form of all socialization is the unification of two people through interests or through likeable feelings. This unification is only possible through an understanding of working together, i.e. through free volition.

Dühring's design for free society contained an elaborate scheme to restructure society through pedagogical reform, as the control of education of the youth was inevitably control of the future. In Dühring's society, poetry becomes an instrument of education (as it was in Plato's state).[27]

Private property, the basic element of society, was to be respected in the free society and was not to be based on work – as in Marxism – but on the right of use in the positive sense and the right of exclusion of others in the negative sense. When an unjust distribution of wealth came about, there were two ways of changing the disproportion: one, by making the right to property general and the same for everyone including those without property in an egalitarian sense, or second, by pooling those lacking property together to strengthen their position by increasing their earnings. Dühring chose the latter alternative. Property was to correspond to freedom of trade, which allowed humans to compete against each other. The role of the state was held to a minimum and had the primarily negative function of stepping in and settling grave violations.

---

[25] Dühring (1875a, p. 265).

[26] In the last part of the first edition to his book "Werth des Lebens," Dühring claimed that reactive feeling or resentment was the only recognizable principle of justice or injustice. Cf. Dühring (1865, pp. 219ff). This emotive element existed according to Dühring not only in individuals, but also in societal groups. Cf.Dühring (1875a, p. 224).

[27] Dühring (1875a, p. 423).

The free society in its original conception was borderless and was to ultimately encompass the entire world. Its construction was based on the connection of individuals and its dimensions fit the historical state areas of Europe.

In the second edition of his *Cursus der National- und Sozialökonomie* from 1876, Dühring specified a system of communes that would create an ancestral and linguistic community upon whose leadership the free society would be based.[28] The communes would function under the basic principle that work and not property ownership should be the basis of earnings.[29] Earnings were to be distributed according to performance and workers were to be given the political right to a position in the economic management. Thus, the organized forced management, which Marxist socialism advocated – and was later historically realized – would be replaced by cooperative leadership, which respected the rights of the individual. Property was not to be abolished, but rather belonged to each individual community. Dühring wished to negate the exclusive character of property by allowing free entry into the given communes. Free trade was to exist between the communes on the basis of the gold standard so that free association and competition between them could develop. Interest was to be used by the communes to maintain and improve the means of production, thus giving the value-added surplus to the community and not to individuals. Individuals would be able to collect wealth, not in the form of capital but rather in consumptive goods. A "societarian free association of movement" (socialitären Freizügigkeiten) would allow individuals to pursue activities that correspond to their given talents. As soon as a community had a particularly high profit to where its members attained a higher income than the average earnings of the individuals of the other communes, the working force of the financially more successful community was to be increased until a balance with the other communes was attained. In doing this, Dühring hoped to have the entire system benefit from the success of a particular industrial branch. An absolute equality of earnings was never to be reached, but this corresponded to economic justice according to Dühring as some performances were harder, less pleasant, or more dangerous than others. The workers entering and leaving the communes would allow the supply of the communes to adapt to the demand. If the demand for a product was higher than the supply, the prices would rise and thus the income of the members of the commune would increase; this would set off a migration of workers, which would enable an increase in production until a balance of earnings was created. With a balance of earnings as goal and not the increase of profit and rents, the emphasis of the economic commune plan was to increase the quality of life of the workers and create a harmonic society.

[28] Dühring's system of economic communes was analyzed by Chilosi in: Backhaus (2002, pp. 293–305).

[29] Dühring (1876, pp. 322).

Critique of Dühring's Vision of Socialism

It is not hard to find fault with Dühring's design for a free society of economic communes. How the free society will be initiated, how the workers will be emancipated from their current salary conditions to gain an independent economic existence is unclear. Dühring gives a plan for a society free from oppression and where the individual's rights are respected, but he fails to show exactly how this design is to be implemented. He correctly advocated the need for free competition between individuals to create necessary motivation and societal progress and suggested that different activities of the communes should be ranked, but the specifics of how the ranking of earnings is to be determined remains unmentioned. Dühring warns of the danger to individual interests when the majority rules and yet it in his free society it remains unclear how decisions to prevent infractions against particular interests are to be practically instituted if the will of the majority is not to be taken into consideration.[30] Indeed, there is no concrete plan for the inner workings of the economic communes. The problem of having income not based on work is likely to reappear: if individual members of the communes are thrifty, this will lead to the creation of private capital, which would presumably be lent to the more needy commune, creating what would be a capital rent, which the economic commune plan hopes to avoid. Beyond this, the creation of new communes is given little consideration. Dühring's free society seems to suffer from the same weakness of all utopias, namely that it does not show a practical path to its realization.

Despite these shortcomings, it would be a mistake however to lump Dühring into the category of the utopian socialists who preceded him. In drawing out his plan for a free society in keeping with the philosophical tenets of his perceptive or intuitive approach described above, he focused on real societal entities and institutions. The communes' activities were based on the existing political organization and not on abstract possibilities. Dühring foresaw the free interplay of real societal forces with the precondition of a price mechanism and the use of gold, as it existed in capitalism. Beyond this, he attempted to delineate the mechanisms of egalitarian arguments by suggesting that personal qualities, dispositions, and capabilities should be taken into consideration. He thus tries to give the free society room for developmental possibilities, which would prevent social congealment and stagnation. As Albrecht correctly points out, Dühring was far from simply pointing out societal injustice, the reasons thereof, and believing that change would come about by simply enacting what has been recognized as better.[31] He understood the phrase *natura non facit saltus*, a basic assumption of Greek philosophy and natural science and knew that world history moves extremely slowly; he had no illusions that some new power could come out of nowhere and change society and was intent on practical suggestions, e.g. the advocacy of worker's coalitions as a starting point for change.

---

[30]Cf. Albrecht (1927, p. 229).

[31]Cf. Ibid (p. 243).

Conclusion

Eugen Dühring was not a utopian thinker in the usual sense of the word, although his philosophy of reality contained certain utopian elements. Following the socialization theory of Marx and Engels, he went beyond pure utopian socialism by creating a vision of the future that was based on the development of the given modern capitalist system, rather than the construction of a rational "natural order." But whereas Marx and Engels advocated revolution as an answer to the social question, Dühring denounced *deus ex machine* solutions that would change society suddenly. Furthermore, his brand of socialism contrasted with the Marxism of his time in that it offered a clear philosophical foundation to his work, which included, as we have seen, an epistemological interpretation of reason.[32] In contrast to Schopenhauer's pessimism and belief in irrational factors governing man, Dühring espoused a naive optimism that believed in the power of reason to solve society's problems. Dühring viewed reason in concrete practical terms, however, and avoided the one-sided "cult of reason" (Sombart) inspired by the French Revolution.[33] Dühring understood reason to include concrete intuitive understanding and a will for pragmatic action. Reason as Dühring saw it was not merely an abstract reflective power, but an intuitive and creative device that could help humanity to progress and become emancipated. This focus on the concrete in Dühring's concept of reason caused him to go beyond his utopian predecessors.

Dühring visualized a better society free from suppression and compulsion by trying to neutralize the main dynamic of utopian philosophy of history, namely the concept of domination and subordination. His design for a free society was an attempt to rationally abolish compulsory subordination. It was not a call to revolution, but an attempt to limit the power of the state to an absolute minimum. Unlike the utopian socialists, and also Marx and Engels with their vision of a dictatorship of the proletariat, Dühring did not present a concrete finished order of things that was destined to be implemented through the course of world history. Speaking for this assertion and for labeling Dühring's socialism as post-utopian is additionally the fact that due he ultimately gave up his design for economic communes in the third edition of his Cursus der Nation-Sozialökonomie to concentrate more on helping the workers through organized coalitions.[34]

[32]Friedrich Engels' attack against Dühring in 1878 should be viewed in the background of the philosophical deficits of Marxism at the time which Engels was attempting to make up for.

[33]Sombart speaks of an "all powerful goddess of reason". Cf. Sombart (1908, p. 38).

[34]Dühring (1892, pp. 316) and also Dühring (1903, p. 270).

Bibliography

Albrecht, G., (1927), Eugen Dühring, Ein Beitrag zur Geschichte der Sozialwissenschaften, Gustav Fischer, Jena.
Backhaus, J., ed., (2002), Eugen Dühring (1833–1921) and the freedom of teaching and research. Journal of Economic Studies, 29(4/5) 255–363.
Backhaus, J., ed., (2006), The social question (part I and II). Journal of Economics, 33(3/4) 175–236, 239–316.
Bebel, A., (1874), Ein neuer "Communist", in: Der Volksstaat, Nr. 30, 33, März.
Chamberlain, H.S., (1905), Heinrich von Stein und seine Weltanschauung, George Müller, München und Leipzig.
Dühring, E. (1865), Der Werth des Lebens, Edward Trewendt, Breslau.
Dühring, E.(1875a), Cursus der Philosophie, Erich Koschny, L. Heimann's Verlag, Leipzig.
Dühring, E. (1875b), Kritische Geschichte der Nationalökonomie und des Sozialismus, Theobald Grieben, Berlin (1871).
Dühring, E. (1903), Sache, Leben und Feinde, C.G. Naumann, Leipzig (1882).
Dühring, E. (1892), Cursus der National- und Socialökonomie, O.R. Reisland, Leipzig.
Dühring, E. (1875a), Cursus der Philosophie, Erich Koschny, L. Heimann's Verlag Leipzig.
Dühring, E. (1875b), Kritische Geschichte der Nationalokonomic und des Sozialismus, Theobald, Berlin (1871)
Dühring, E. Critical History of Political Economy and Socialism, 1871
Dühring, E. (1876), Cursus der National and Sozialokonomie, Fues's Verlag (R. Reisland), Leipzig.
Gehlen, A. (1986), Urmensch und Spätkultur, Aula Verlag, Wiesbaden (1956).
Geldsetzer, L., (1968), Die Philosophie der Philosophiegeschichte im 19. Jahrhundert – Zur Wissenschaftstheorie der Philosophiegeschichtsschreibung und – betrachtung, Anton Hain, Meisenheim am Glan.
Höfding, H. (1955), A History of Modern Philosophy, Dover Publications Inc., New York (1921).
Kesting, H. (1973) Herrschaft und Knechtschaft.
Kesting, H. (1959), Geschichtsphilosophie und Weltburgerkrieg, Karl Winter Univiversitätsverlag Hiedelperg.
Koselleck, R. (1992), Kritik und Krise, Eine Studie zur Pathogenese der bürgerlichen Welt. 7 edn., Surkamp, Frankfurt am Main (1973).
Landauer, G. (1892), Referat über Dühring's Kursus der National- und Sozialökonomie, in: Der Sozialist, Aug. 1892.
Löwith, K.(1986), Von Hegel zu Nietzsche. Der revolutionäre Bruch im Denken des neuzehnten Jahrhundert, Fritz Meiner, Hamburg (1941).
Löwith, K. (1964), From Hegel to Nietzsche. The Revolution in Nineteenth-Century Thought, Holt, Rinehart and Winston, New York, Chocago, San Francisco.
Mauthner, F. (1912). Zur Sprachwissenschaft, Beiträge zur Kritik der Sprache, 2 edn., Cotta, Berlin.
Muravchik, J. (1999), The Rise and Fall of Socialism SPEECHES AEI Bradley Lecture Series, Date Feb. 8, 1999.
Schnädelbach, H. (1984), Philosophie in Deutschland 1831–1933. Surkamp, Cambridge.
Schopenhauer, A. (1969), The World as Will and Representation, Dover Publications, Inc., New York (1818).
Sombart, W. (1908), Sozialismus und Soziale Bewegung, Gustav Fischer, Jena (1897).

Index

A
Administration, 41, 47, 51–53, 63, 65, 66, 108, 132, 136, 138, 139, 141, 143, 166, 174–177
Agriculture, 60–61, 63, 82, 92, 110, 124, 125, 145, 164
Altruism, 21, 29, 129, 130, 142
Anarchism, 77, 85, 118

B
Banks, 50, 62, 64, 127, 131, 143, 145, 153
Becher, J.J., 63, 64, 164
Benthamism, 29
Blanc, L., 192

C
Cameralism, 42–44, 47, 50–53, 174, 175, 185–186, 188
Capitalism, 21, 22, 28–31, 33, 34, 86, 127, 134, 166, 170, 202
Carey, H.C., 199, 200
Carlyle, T., 21, 32
Chamberlain, H.S., 197
Character education, 22, 23, 25
Checks and balances, 25, 26
Christian utopianism, 27, 29, 35–39, 59, 195
Commercial council, 62, 64
Common good, 21, 41, 47, 48, 58
Communism, 78, 79, 85, 86, 97, 100, 107, 117, 170
Comte, A., 21, 191
Conditioning, 19, 23, 24, 27, 33, 82
Constitution, 1, 3, 8, 23, 26, 44, 48, 49, 59, 63, 77, 82, 96, 119, 136, 137, 140, 142, 145, 169, 171, 172
Constitutionalism,
Cooperative socialism, 77, 83–86
Cooperative(s), 30, 77, 83–86, 162, 201
Craft(s), 61–63, 75, 92, 116
Currency, 53, 62, 140, 143

D
David Hartley,
Democracy, 19, 24, 26, 27, 39, 48, 49, 117, 142, 143, 145, 172
Distribution of wealth, 80, 86, 172–174, 200
Division of labour, 166

E
Economic Man, 21
Economics, 1–4, 7–9, 11, 21, 22, 28, 31, 32, 38, 39, 47, 49–53, 57–66, 77, 79–87, 90, 94–98, 102, 104, 106–107, 109, 115–117, 119, 122, 123, 125–128, 130–136, 138–141, 143–146, 161–175, 192, 195, 196, 199–203
Education, 19, 20, 22–25, 28, 33, 51, 58, 59, 63, 65, 69, 75, 84, 90, 92, 97, 98, 105–107, 109, 110, 119, 121, 124, 125, 127, 134, 135, 137, 138, 139, 143, 146, 172, 173, 184, 188, 200
Egalitarianism, 95, 200, 202
Enlightenment philosophy, 57, 165, 167
Euhemerus, 98
Evolutionary socialism, 23, 29
Excise tax, 52, 61, 62, 63, 65

F
Felicity, 42, 45–48, 50

J.G. Backhaus (ed.), *The State as Utopia: Continental Approaches*, The European Heritage in Economics and the Social Sciences 9, DOI 10.1007/978-1-4419-7500-3,

H
Hellenistic economic thought, 90, 93–96, 98, 102
Hegel, 191, 195, 198
History of economic ideas,
History of economic thought, 168, 169, 173
History of political economy, 196
Humanitarianism, 36
Hume, D., 27

I
Interventionism, 77, 79–81, 86

K
Kant, 198

L
Labour, 2, 12, 23, 30, 31, 163, 164, 168, 170
Labouring classes, 30
Landauer, G., 196, 198
Löwith, K., 195
Luxury consumption, 50, 107

M
Malthus, T., 22, 187–188
Malthusianism, 22
Marx, K., 21, 77, 78, 162, 168, 169, 191, 192, 194–197, 203
Mauthner, F., 193
Mercantilism, 164, 174, 185
Mercantilist thought, 50, 57–66, 164
Mill, H.T., 31
Mill, J., 24
Mill, J.S., 19–43
Monarchy, 39, 46, 48, 49, 59, 108, 169, 171, 194
Moral education, 59, 65
More, Th., 193

O
Organization of labor, 78, 83, 84, 96, 107

P
Phalange, 84–86
Philosopher-king, 25, 27
Plato, 7, 9, 11, 20, 25, 27, 89, 90, 95–99, 106, 108, 126, 127, 144, 200
Politics, 39, 44, 47–49, 52, 53, 57–60, 96, 97, 108, 109, 143, 162, 165, 166, 196
Poor relief,
Price regulation, 61, 168
Proudhon, J., 194
Production, 31–33, 50, 51, 61, 63, 78, 80, 81, 83–85, 97, 98, 107, 110, 120, 129, 131, 132, 134, 135, 141, 164, 185, 195, 201
Property tax, 63, 65
Public magazines, 61, 64

R
Rational self-interest, 20, 22
Religion, 29, 37, 39, 46, 58–60, 63, 66, 70, 73, 98, 103, 127, 132, 137, 140, 143, 165, 186, 195, 443
Religious conflict, 39, 193
Rousseau, J.J., 199

S
Saint-Simonism, 77, 81–83, 86
Science of cameralism, 42–44, 47, 51–53
Science of police, 42–44, 47–53
Schopenhauer, 193, 195, 203
Seckendorff, 57, 63, 65, 174
Sectors of production, 83
Selfishness, 21, 22, 29, 31, 32, 34
Simon, S., 21, 81–83, 86, 168, 194, 195
Smith, A., 26–28, 79, 130, 165, 171–173, 200
Social equality, 60, 66
Social peace, 57, 60
Social reform, 79, 83, 86
Socialism, 2, 23, 28, 29, 30, 33, 34, 77–87, 100, 127, 128, 151, 167–172, 191–203
Standard of living, 31, 60, 65, 66
State authority, 78, 87, 136
Stationary state, 1, 31–33
Sumptuary laws, 60
Sustainable development, 33, 117

T
The Republic, 8, 9, 20, 39, 48, 103
Theory class, 25
Trading companies, 64
Tripartite division of population, 8
Two Mills hypothesis, 28

U
Utopia, 1–5, 20, 24–26, 29, 32, 35–39, 41–53, 57–68, 79, 89–110, 118, 123, 143, 161, 162, 173, 175–176, 183–189, 192–196, 202
Utopian socialism, 2, 77–87, 168, 191–203
Utopian thought, 19, 20, 23, 34

V
von Justi, J.H.G, 42, 178, 183
Voting systems, 25, 26

W
Welfare, 45, 53, 59, 65, 81, 82, 86, 109, 126, 171
Work, 2, 12–15, 19–22, 24, 26, 30, 31, 41–47, 50–53, 60–62, 67, 72, 74, 75, 78–87, 89, 90, 92–105, 107–110, 116, 118–125, 129–134, 137, 140, 144, 147, 155–159, 162, 165, 166, 168, 184, 191, 192, 194, 195, 197, 199–203

GPSR Compliance

The European Union's (EU) General Product Safety Regulation (GPSR) is a set of rules that requires consumer products to be safe and our obligations to ensure this.

If you have any concerns about our products, you can contact us on ProductSafety@springernature.com

In case Publisher is established outside the EU, the EU authorized representative is:

Springer Nature Customer Service Center GmbH
Europaplatz 3
69115 Heidelberg, Germany

Batch number: 10837190

Printed by Printforce, the Netherlands